WITH

Learning and Memory

33-41

Neural Organization and Behavior:
A Systems Analysis Approach to Brain Function

Learning and Memory

DONALD G. STEIN

CLARK UNIVERSITY
WORCESTER, MASSACHUSETTS

JEFFREY J. ROSEN

BOSTON UNIVERSITY
BOSTON, MASSACHUSETTS

Macmillan Publishing Co., Inc.
New York

Collier Macmillan Publishers
London

Macmillan Publishing Co., Inc.
866 Third Avenue, New York, New York 10022

Collier-Macmillan Canada, Ltd.

Library of Congress Cataloging in Publication Data

Stein, Donald G. comp.
  Learning and memory.

  (Neural organization and behavior)
  Includes bibliographies.
  1. Neuropsychology. 2. Brain. 3. Learning,
Psychology of. 4. Memory. I. Rosen, Jeffrey J.,
joint comp. II. Title. [DNLM: 1. Learning.
2. Memory. 3. Neurophysiology. 4. Psychophysiology.
WL102 S819L   1974]
QP360.S76   612'.825   73-3897
ISBN 0-02-416520-4

Printing: 1 2 3 4 5 6 7 8   Year: 4 5 6 7 8 9 80

Tell me, where is fancy bred,
Or in the heart, or in the head?
How begot, how nourished?
    Reply, reply.
It is engend'red in the eyes,
With gazing fed; and fancy dies
In the cradle where it lies,
    Let us all ring fancy's knell.
    I'll begin it—Ding, dong, bell.
    Ding, dong, bell.

Shakespeare
(*Merchant of Venice*, III, 2)

Preface

In general, a book of readings is constructed and used to acquaint the student with what the author considers to be exemplary work in a particular field of study. If the articles are well chosen, the student can often share in the flavor and excitement of the original research—a feeling not often conveyed in reviews of the literature, or as summarized in most textbooks. However, after looking over most of the anthologies available to students of physiological psychology, we have come away with the vague suspicion that these books may be written with a singular intent: to wit, keeping undergraduates out from underfoot in the periodical room of the university library. Rather than be associated with such a "conspiracy" we have attempted in this book to provide a conceptual and organizational framework within which all of the articles can be integrated. Thus, the reader will find that each section builds upon information presented in the preceding section, and that within a section each of the articles is similarly related. The same may be said for each of the volumes that make up this series.

Anyone who has devoted his time to the study of brain–behavior relationships is impressed and often awed by the complexity and magnitude of the problem. Although great strides have been made in the development of research techniques for studying brain function, less consistent progress has been shown in conceptualizing the nature of the problem. The difficulty in arriving at some unified view of brain function is perhaps best represented by the marked difference in thinking about brain processes as reflected in Sherrington's "switchboard" theory of neural circuits and the Gestalt theory of electromagnetic patterns of excitation.

Our particular bias has its roots, in part, in the concept of hierarchic integration as it was formulated by Heinz Werner.* This term implies that with

* Heinz Werner: *The Comparative Psychology of Mental Development*. International Universities Press, New York, 1957.

increasing differentiation of a structure into its constituent parts, there is a corresponding tendency for the parts to become, rather than autonomous, subordinated to the activity of the entire structure. For example, when one looks at the anatomy of the brain, he can discern a mosaic of different structures. However, according to the concept of hierarchic integration, it would be erroneous to assume that each structure, although anatomically differentiated, has an autonomous or unique behavioral function. In contrast to the view of functional localization, we are proposing that the brain must be viewed as a dynamic organization of differentiated, but highly interrelated, structures. A corollary of this position is that just as each subordinate structure or level can exert afferent control over each structure in the hierarchy, each higher level, in turn, exerts efferent control on subordinate structures. Within this view, no level or structure may operate independently of either subordinate or higher levels of activity; input into any one area of the CNS can affect activity in all areas of the brain. Thus, the concept of hierarchic integration provides an organization for the various structures which make up the brain.

This organization is amenable to an investigation of the functions of the CNS as well. One of the fundamental activities of the brain is information processing. This term refers to the ability of the CNS to transduce external energy forms into a neural "language" or "code." The generation, syntax, and utilization of this code by the brain are the focus of this collection of articles.

In a sense, each chapter of the volume on basic structure and function of the central nervous system represents a different level of analysis of neural organization and its relation to behavior. Part One studies activity and function of the single cell, Part Two deals with the way in which individual cells interact to produce complex patterns of activity capable of conveying information about various aspects of the environment, and in Part Three we study the ways in which the cortex discriminates and differentiates between incoming information.

In the volume on motivation and emotion we move to a structural level of analysis in which the brain is studied as a *system* of interrelated *parts,* each part contributing to the emerging pattern of activity that is represented as behavior.

The volume on learning and memory deals with these more complex processes and provides a multilevel analysis of the problem.

Each group of readings is preceded by a brief introductory statement that we hope will do the following: (a) relate the readings to one another; (b) relate them to the point of view established in the preceding chapters; and (c) relate them to a general systems analysis approach to brain function. To help the process of "integration" by the reader, we have provided some general thought questions that we feel will direct the student to the relevant issues in the field.

D. G. S.
J. J. R.

Acknowledgment

The authors would like to express their appreciation to Darel Stein, who carried out much of the library research, and to Alfhild Bassett, who patiently typed and revised the material for this book.

Contents

Part Three

Part I

Learning: Anatomical Aspects

For the most part, other volumes in this series concentrated on the theme that the central nervous system exists in a dynamic state, capable of modifying incoming sensory messages. In emphasizing this theme, we were only presented with half of the picture: how information is transduced and coded for future reference. To complete the picture, we also need to analyze how these incoming messages serve to *change* the state of CNS in such a way that the modification can alter subsequent information processing and behavior of the organism. We can call this change in activity "learning" if we use the term in a very general way. The problem with this general defin- tion of learning is that no one has yet been able to decipher how or why some alternations in CNS activity are associated with relatively permanent changes in behavior, whereas similar forms of activity seem to exert little, if any, observable effect.

Another problem of major concern is the kinds of behavior we are willing to subsume under the term "learned." For example, we know that repetitive stimuli will alter brain electrical activity, but can we call this learn- ing? Depending upon your point of view, you could say yes, for in order for an individual to detect that a stimulus or message is novel or redundant, he must compare that input with previously stored information. Even if the organism is unaware of the "matching process," something like this must go on in the CNS if selective response to the environment is to occur. For example, we constantly require feedback from our muscles, tendons, and points in order to guide precise motor behavior such as riding a bike. This control is provided by afferent and efferent loops from the brain to the spinal neural network, and typically, we become aware of this complex form of information processing only when some aspect of it is disordered or diseased.

Another very important question typically ignored by those doing research in learning and memory is: how do we get from input and decision-making processes, such as those we have discussed to the initiation and sequencing of an overt act? Must we leave our organism "buried in thought," as someone critical of cognitive psychology once said?

At the present time, we cannot offer an unequivocal answer to this critical question, but recent research in neuroanatomy provides us with some substantial clues as to how translation from thought to act may occur. It appears that there are a number of structures in the brain, such as the frontal granular cortex, hippocampus, temporal lobe, and other areas of the limbic system that receive and send fibers to and from many other areas of the brain. By using recently developed histological techniques, neuroanatomists have been able to demonstrate a great deal of overlap between sensory, association, and motor fields in the CNS. Thus, patterns of excitation generated in these "processing areas" of the CNS can affect subsequent sensory input as well as succeeding motor activity.

It would probably be conceptually easier to deal with learning and memory as a reflection of *only* the encoding and preserving of particular forms of information. However, conceptual "ease" is rarely the criterion for understanding. At this point, it becomes necessary to reintroduce the concept of hierarchic integration (a concept that served us well in the first two volumes in this series). According to this integrative model, the inclusion of new information into the system introduces a change in the organization of ongoing activity. In preceding volumes, we saw that the brain is capable of modifying and controlling sensory input, and now, if we are to complete the model, another important dimension must be considered: how particular kinds of input change the organization of CNS activity that mediates complex forms of behavior.

Several questions immediately arise when one tries to conceptualize the physiological bases of learning and memory. First, we must ask: what are the *specific* mechanisms responsible for acquisition? Second, how is information about the environment *stored* within the existing organization of the CNS? Third, how does preservation of input *change* the ongoing activity of the brain, and subsequently, the behavior of the organism? At the present time, no single approach to the study of brain mechanisms and learning has been judged to be most fruitful. Consequently, we have decided to present three separate sections on the physiological bases of learning and memory. Each of the sections represents, in part, a major approach to the analysis of the problem; the first deals with the effects of brain lesions on performance, the second with electrophysiological *correlates* of behavior change, the third with pharmacological and biochemical manipulation of the CNS. Actually, we could have used the same approach in the volume on motivation and emotion but we chose to organize the material on learning in this manner for several reasons.

First, we think that the research *techniques* one chooses will often shape the conceptual views and working hypotheses that a person has. For example, a biochemist interested in learning and memory is more likely to "search for the engram" among the proteins and enzymes floating about in the CNS rather than attempting to assess the function of a particular neural structure. In contrast, a skilled surgeon would probably assign memory to one of the anatomically differentiated areas of the CNS since his ability would permit him to manipulate parts of the brain rather than molecules within it.

Second, the methods and techniques used in research on learning and memory are quite paradigmatic of the whole field of physiological psychology. Third is the fact that all of the aspects of behavior that we have discussed so far really deal with the problem of the organism's ability to adapt to its environment, which is another way of saying that perception, emotion, and motivation cannot be separated from those processes involved in learning; thus, changes in any one of these spheres will have major influence on activity in all of the others. What is learned, stored, and eventually retrieved is very much dependent upon the activity of the total system and its stage of development at any given moment in time.

The most frequently used technique for analysis of brain function is the removal, or damage, of specific areas of the CNS. The lesion method is important in a historical sense in that it was the first experimental means of evaluating how the brain works; it was not necessary to be a scientist in order to observe that head trauma often produced severe disruptions of behavior.

By and large, the use of the lesion technique is based upon the assumption that the brain is organized into discrete units, with each unit, or system of units, playing a specific role in the determination of behavior. Following damage to a specific area, it is often possible to observe dramatic changes in behavior. If there is a constellation of behavior change such as inability to solve several tasks involving spatial coordination and altered eating or drinking behavior, the series of impairments is called a *syndrome*. Since the impairment *follows* the lesion, one often infers that the removed structure in some way mediates or controls the now absent form of response to the environment. However, in order to conclude that a particular area of the brain has a specific function, the investigator must demonstrate that only removal of area A produced syndrome A. In addition, one must show that removal of area B produces syndrome B and not A. This is called *double disassociation* and is considered by some investigators to be the necessary logic for inferring localization of function in the brain. We will discuss this problem further in the context of the specific articles presented in this section.

Attempts at localizing behavioral function in specific CNS structures have, in our opinion, met with limited success because the concept of localization presents a number of logical and methodological difficulties. First, with respect to learning, even seriously impaired animals (and humans) can eventually relearn in the absence of the tissue thought to be critical. Typically, the degree of impairment in different individuals following brain damage varies considerably. Some individuals show only slight deficits in learning ability following large lesions whereas others demonstrate drastic and debilitating effects.

On logical grounds, even if we are to accept the notion of double disassociation, it is not necessary to assume that a given lesion only produces changes
within a restricted area of the brain. Most likely, a lesion in the CNS will
exert anywhere from subtle to extremely marked changes of brain function at
all levels of organization; neuronal, biochemical, structural, and behavioral.
Indeed, histological examination of neural tissue has indicated that even
specific lesions in a single structure result in antero- and retrograde degeneration of cells in other areas of the brain. In other words, the entire system may
change, not just one small aspect of activity.

Another important point to consider is that the evaluation of brain
damage in both humans and animals is carried out in the laboratory using
what are, for the most part, relatively esoteric tests that may have little application to behavior in the home or field. For example, it may be that a monkey
with lesions of the frontal lobe is markedly impaired on a "delayed spatial
alternation task" when the delay is 12.6 seconds; however, the animal may
have a relatively normal "home life" or he may be impaired on forms of
activity that the investigator may not see, but that causes Mrs. Monkey a
great deal of aggravation. The issue here deals with the definition of the term
"impairment" or "deficit." Of course, one must also be concerned with the
general definition of learning before determining the nature of the deficit
produced by brain damage. The problem of what to study and how best to
measure behavior in an experimental situation is not just limited to brain
lesions research, but is an important point to consider for all laboratory investigation of brain-behavior relationships.

The articles in the present section will deal with each of the issues discussed briefly above.

Suppose that every time we surgically removed a particular structure
from the brain, we found that the lesioned subject had difficulty in performing only certain specific learning tasks. A sufficient number of replications
of this phenomenon would indeed make it very tempting to assume that the
destroyed tissue was critical for normal performance on these tasks. If we
follow the approach, two questions immediately arise. (1) Are there any
common factors that tie together these tasks that prove difficult for an animal
with damage to a specific area of the CNS? (2) Can we propose a meaningful relationship between the ablated structure and the behavioral impairment? The answer to this question may provide insights into the nature of
the behavioral deficit.

The authors of the first two papers working within this conceptual
framework attempt to provide answers to these two questions. The first article,
by Mishkin et al., provides an insightful analysis of the nature of the deficit
following frontal lobe lesions in the rhesus monkey. The authors first *disasso-
ciate* between the possible sensory and nonsensory nature of the deficit and
then go on to analyze various explanations of this syndrome.

The second paper, by Kimble, attempts to tap the nature of the impairment following bilateral hippocampal removal in the rat. To this end, the

author employed a variety of learning tasks, each of which was sensitive to a different aspect of learning and memory. His results suggest how difficult it is to place a singular function within a given structure.

Again, the above considerations are based on the assumption that the removal of a particular structure always produces a certain syndrome, but what happens to this assumption if it can be demonstrated that the observed syndrome may be more related to the *way* in which the structure is removed, rather than to the structure itself? The next two articles are relevant to this issue. The first of these, by Stein et al., examines the effects of simultaneous bilateral removal of a structure when compared to sequential removal of the same tissue. The authors compared the effects of these two techniques when applied to the removal of three different "associative" areas of the CNS. The evidence used to support current concepts of functional localization in the CNS is untenable.

The next paper, by Chow and Randall, suggests this serial lesion phenomenon is not just specific to "associative" areas in the rat. Their research also involved sequential ablation of the thalamic reticular formation in cats. As in the Stein et al. paper, the result of this procedure was to dramatically reduce or eliminate the syndrome generally associated with destruction of this tissue.

The two preceding papers suggested that the nature of the deficit following removal of a structure may not be directly related to the function of that tissue in the intact brain. If indeed this is the case, what can such deficits tell us about how the brain works? In the article by Gregory, metaphor suggests that the behavioral impairments one observes following ablation cannot, for many reasons, be taken as evidence for the function of that structure in the intact brain. The author concludes that it may be more conceptually profitable to envision the syndrome as a reflection of the capacity of the remaining system in the absence of a given component. Whether this reformulation of the issue is a study in semantics, or a distinct contribution to understanding CNS function, is something that we feel the student must decide for himself.

To reiterate, most proponents of the ablation technique have suggested that their task requires the localization of particular functions in anatomically defined areas of the brain. Their periodic successes and many failures are the subject of the last article in this part, by Lashley. The author reviews some 30 years of research dedicated to attempting to find the elusive engram, the encapsulated memory supposedly localized somewhere in the brain. In that this paper may represent one of the few *classics* in neuropsychological research, we shall not attempt to analyze it here. Just read it (draw your own conclusions).

A Re-examination of the Effects
of Frontal Lesions on Object Alternation

MORTIMER MISHKIN, BEVERLY VEST,
MORRIS WAXLER, AND H. ENGER ROSVOLD

Reprinted from *Neuropsychologia*, 1969, Vol. 7, pp. 357–363. Copyright 1969 by
Pergamon Press and reproduced by permission.

Several years ago, Pribram and the senior author reported that lateral prefrontal lesions in monkeys produce severe impairment not only in spatial
alternation but also in nonspatial, object alternation [6, 7]. This finding seemed
to dispose of their earlier hypothesis that a major source of the frontal animal's
difficulty on the classical version of the test was its spatial feature [2, 3]. Recently, however, evidence has been obtained which revives that earlier hypothesis by raising the possibility that the two delayed alternation deficits found
after frontal lesions do not, as had been tacitly assumed, arise from a single
disorder.

To review the new evidence briefly (see Mishkin [5]), one of the effects
of frontal damage in monkeys is a behavioral disturbance that seems to be
characterized by preseverative interfesence between competing central sets or
expectancies. This form of interference is reflected in a variety of simple learning situations including extinction, differentiation and discrimination reversal.
Perseverative tendencies in these situations were observed initially, in monkeys
with lesions of the lateral prefontal cortex, but it was discovered later that
even more pronounced perseveration could be produced by lesions of the
orbital cortex. The finding of greater interference after orbital than after lateral
ablations has been confirmed for the entire constellation of perseverative
deficits originally reported after the lateral removal, with one striking exception. On spatial discrimination reversal, although orbital lesions again produce
marked impairment, the effect of lateral lesions has been found to be equally
severe [5]. The data suggest that a spatial reversal problem such as classical
delayed alternation may be sensitive to two entirely different effects of frontal
damage: perseverative interference, which leads to difficulty with the reversal
element in the task; and a second, independent defect leading to difficulty with
the spatial element. A nonspatial reversal such as object alternation, on the
other hand, should be sensitive according to this analysis only to the frontal
animal's perseverative disorder.

As already indicated, perseverative interference is particularly pronounced after orbital lesions, but it is also present (and in fact was first
observed) after lateral lesions. A possible explanation for this pattern of
results is that while the frontal tissue which must be damaged to produce the

7

disorder is located mainly on the orbital surface, the critical area extends over the inferior lip of the frontal lobe to include the ventral portion of the lateral surface. It should be noted that the proposed extension on the lateral surface is considered to lie ventral to the sulcus principalis, damage to which consistently yields deficits on the classical spatial tests. The possibility that a lesion of the lateral surface produces two separately localized defects, each of which may interfere with spatial reversal for a different reason, suggests repeating the experiment on object alternation using animals with a slightly modified lesion. Thus, excluding the ventrolateral cortex from the lateral prefrontal removal might eliminate the perseverative disorder from the postoperative picture and consequently eliminate the impairment on object alternation without simultaneously eliminating the impairment on spatial alternation. The present experiment examined this possibility.

Methods

Subjects

The Ss were 13 monkeys (*Macaca mulatta*), ranging in weight from 3.5 to 5 kg. Six of the Ss were tested on object alternation, and 7 on spatial alternation.

Tests

Object alternation was presented in a Wisconsin General Testing Apparatus, using a tray with 10 foodwells arranged in 3 horizontal rows: a near and a far row of 3 wells each and a middle row of 4 wells (cf. Pribram [6]). Adjacent wells in each row were 15 cm apart. The two test objects, a grey funnel and a multicolored can, were positioned randomly over the 10 foodwells with the restriction that both objects were placed over wells within the same horizontal row (vertical and diagonal pairings were eliminated early in training when it was found that with such pairings the Ss tended to select whichever object was nearer). On the first trial of each daily session both objects were baited with peanut halves; on subsequent trials the object not chosen on the immediately preceding trial was baited. Thus, following the correct choice of one object the bait was placed under the other, but following an error, the bait remained with the same object as before until the error was corrected. Thirty trials (excluding the free trial but including the correction trials) were presented daily, and the intertrial delay interval was 5 sec. The six animals used in this experiment were the only ones out of an original group of 12 to attain the preoperative criterion of 90 object alternations in 100 consecutive trials. The six successful Ss achieved this score in an average of 1900 trials (range, 1200–3600), and were then given 500 trials of overtraining in an attempt to stabilize their preoperative performance at a high level. *Spatial alternation* was presented in the same apparatus and by the same procedures as described above except that the test tray contained two foodwells, one on the left and one on the right spaced 35 cm apart, and these were covered with identical, grey cardboard plaques. The criterion of 90 position alternations in 100 consecutive trials was achieved by the 7 *S*s in this experiment in an average of 480 trials (range, 350–550). They were then given 200 trials of overtraining.

Surgery

At the completion of preoperative training, three animals from each experiment received one-stage bilateral lesions of the lateral surface sparing the ventrolateral cortex. The lower boundary of the lesion was a line 3–5 mm below and roughly parallel to the sulcus principalis. The remaining animals received lesions of the entire orbital surface (except for the olfactory trigone) together with that part of the lateral surface which had been spared in the preceding animals. The two types of lesion will be referred to as dorsolateral and ventral, respectively, to distinguish them from the lateral and orbital lesions investigated previously [5]. Reconstructions, and cross sections through the lesions and through the retrograde degeneration in the thalamus, are illustrated in Figures 1–5. Ten days after surgery, the animals were tested for retention and relearning of their preoperatively acquired alternation habit.

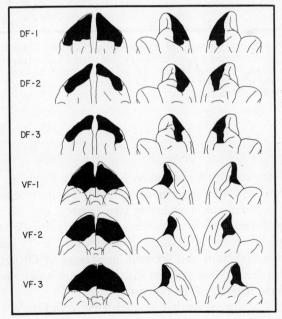

FIGURE 1. Reconstructions of lesions in the animals tested on object alternation. DF, dorsolateral frontal; VF, ventral frontal.

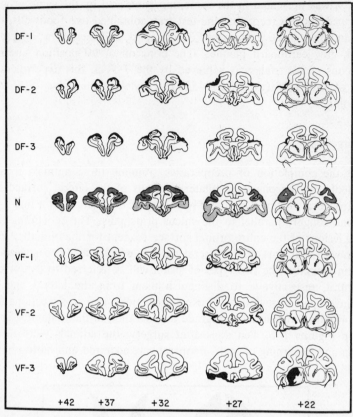

FIGURE 2. Cross sections through the lesions shown in Figure 1. Middle row (N) illustrates the standard dorsolateral lesion (hatching) and ventral lesion (stippling) transferred to cross sections through a normal brain at the indicated stereotactic levels. (Animal VF-3, with the infarct affecting the left basal ganglia, performed no more poorly on object alternation than the other VF animals.)

Results

Performance on object alternation is shown in Figure 6. From a final preoperative level of 85–90 per cent correct, both groups of operated animals fell to chance performance immediately after surgery, and the ventral group continued to perform at this level for the duration of testing (2000 trials). The dorsolateral group, on the other hand, rose to a level of 75 per cent correct responses within 600 trials and attained an average of 80 per cent correct by the end of training. After the first 400 trials there was no overlap among the scores for the animals of the two groups.

The results on spatial alternation are presented in Figure 7. As in object alternation, both groups fell to chance performance immediately after surgery. On this problem, however, neither group reattained a high level of per-

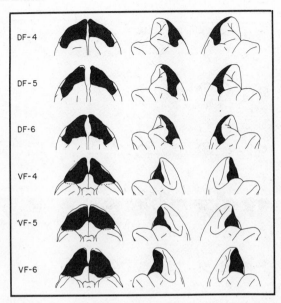

FIGURE 3. Reconstructions of lesions in the animals tested on spatial alternation. (VF-7 not shown.)

formance within the limits of testing (1000 trials). The ventral group scored an average of 64 per cent correct on the last 500 trials but, because of overlap, this level did not differ significantly from the 54 per cent correct scored by the dorsolateral group for the same period.

Discussion

Although excluding the ventrolateral cortex from the lateral prefrontal lesion did not completely eliminate the object alternation impairment found previously, it did serve to reduce the impairment considerably. It is therefore unlikely that the severe deficit produced by the same lesion on spatial alternation is related either to the reversal or to the delay feature in this test. Object alternation contains the same two features, and in addition, it is clearly the more difficult of the two delayed alternation problems for normal animals. The extreme difficulty of object alternation may account for the dorsolateral group's abrupt drop in performance immediately after surgery; a similar effect might have been obtained from any large cortical lesion. Alternatively, despite its difficulty, object alternation may indeed be sensitive only to perseverative interference, in which case the partial deficit shown by the dorsolateral animals could be accounted for by a failure to exclude completely the damage responsible for perseveration. Either of these possibilities is compatible with the view that the spatial alternation deficit resulting from a prefrontal lesion which spares the ventrolateral cortex is specifically related to the spatial aspects of the task.

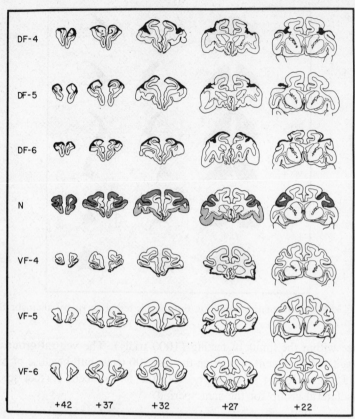

FIGURE 4. Cross sections through the lesions shown in Figure 3. For further explanation see legend to Figure 2.

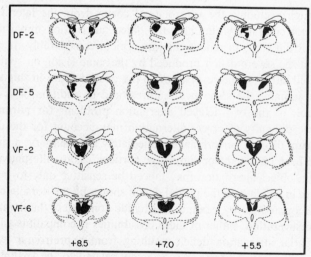

FIGURE 5. Retrograde thalamic degeneration in representative animals, one from each group, at the indicated stereotactic levels.

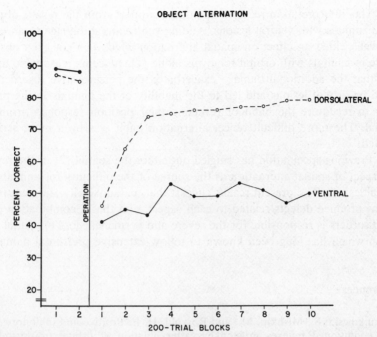

FIGURE 6. Performance on object alternation. Preoperative scores are for the last 400 trials of overtraining.

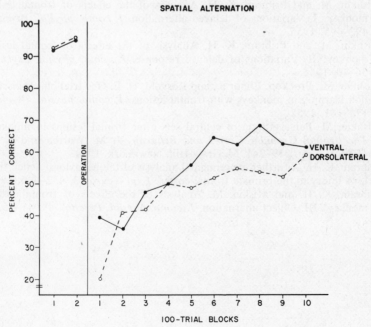

FIGURE 7. Performance on spatial alternation. Preoperative scores are for the 200 trials of overtraining.

This interpretation receives additional support from the results obtained in the animals with ventral lesions. Adding ventrolateral damage to an orbital removal yielded an effect on spatial alternation which has not been observed before in animals with orbital removals alone [1]. It seems reasonable to suppose that the additional damage exacerbated the perseverative disorder produced by orbital lesions and led to the inability of the animals in the present study to reacquire the habit of reversing their position responses from trial to trial. The more difficult object alternation habit was even more seriously affected.

Previous speculation has singled out either the spatial [2] or the reversal [4] aspect of spatial alternation as the source of the difficulty for animals with frontal lesions. The present results suggest that, paradoxically, different frontal lesions produce defects related to each aspect, and that a combination of the two disorders is responsible for the severe and permanent loss of spatial alternation which has long been known to follow extensive prefrontal damage.

References

1. Brutkowski, S., Mishkin, M., and Rosvold, H. E. Positive and inhibitory motor conditioned reflexes in monkeys after ablation of orbital or dorso-lateral surface of the frontal cortex. In *Central and Peripheral Mechanisms of Motor Functions,* E. Gutmann and P. Hnik (Editors), pp. 133–141. Czechoslovak Academy of Sciences, Prague, 1963.
2. Mishkin, M. and Pribram, K. H. Analysis of the effects of frontal lesions in monkey: I. Variations of delayed alternation. *J. comp, physiol. Psychol.* **48,** 492–495, 1955.
3. Mishkin, M. and Pribram, K. H. Analysis of the effects of frontal lesions in monkey: II. Variations of delayed response. *J. comp. physiol. Psychol.* **49,** 36–40, 1956.
4. Mishkin, M., Prockop, Elinor S., and Rosvold, H. E. One-trial object-discrimination learning in monkeys with frontal lesions. *J. comp. physiol. Psychol.* **55,** 178–181, 1952.
5. Mishkin, M. Perseveration of central sets after frontal lesions in monkeys. In *The Frontal Granular Cortex and Behavior,* J. M. Warren and K. Akert (Editors), pp. 219–241. McGraw-Hill, New York, 1964.
6. Pribram, K. H. A further experimental analysis of the behavioral deficit that follows injury to the primate frontal cortex. *Expl Neurol.* **3,** 432–466, 1961.
7. Pribram, K. H. and Miskin, M. Analysis of the effects of frontal lesions in monkey: III. Object alternation. *J. comp. physiol. Psychol.* **49,** 41–45, 1956.

The Effects of Bilateral
Hippocampal Lesions in Rats

DANIEL P. KIMBLE

Reprinted from *Journal of Comparative and Physiological Psychology*, 1963, Vol. 56, No. 2, pp. 273–283. Copyright 1963 by the American Psychological Association.

Behavioral effects of chronic lesions involving the hippocampus in various animals and man have been reported by several investigators. Such seemingly diverse findings as "short term" memory deficits (Milner and Penfield, 1955; Walker, 1957), increases in sexual activity (Kim, 1960), increases (Schreiner and Kling, 1953; Spiegel, Miller, and Oppenheimer, 1940) and decreases (Klüver and Bucy, 1937) in affective responses, and slower (Pribram and Weiskrantz, 1957) as well as faster (Isaacson, Douglas, and Moore, 1961) learning of an avoidance response have been noted. However, no clear-cut functional significance of the hippocampus has emerged from these studies.

The present experiments were designed to investigate the behavior of rats with bilateral hippocampal damage in a variety of behavioral situations. The experiments are reported in chronological order.

Method

Subjects

Thirty-three male hooded rats from the Long-Evans strain were gentled and acclimated to the laboratory environment for 2–3 weeks. Following pre-operative behavioral measures, 10 Ss received bilateral damage to the hippocampus and 11 Ss received only bilateral removal of cortex overlying the hippocampal formation. Twelve Ss served as unoperated controls.

Surgery

All operations were performed in one stage using clean surgical technique. The Ss were anesthetized with pentobarbital (40 mg/kg) and the lesions made while the Ss were held in a stereotaxic instrument. After suitable openings were made in the skull with trephine and rongeurs, the dura was opened and the cortex overlying the hippocampus aspirated, exposing the hippocampus in the ventral surface of the lateral ventricle. In the experimental group, the hippocampus was then removed by suction as completely as possible, both medially and ventrally, care being taken to spare the underlying thalamus. After all bleeding had ceased, gel-foam was inserted in the wound, the temporal muscles replaced over the opening in the skull, and the

15

scalp closed. In the operative control Ss the hippocampus was similarly exposed, but not damaged. The cortical lesion was enlarged before the wound was closed. The Ss received penicillin and terramycin for 3 days postoperatively.

Experiment 1: Open-Field Behavior

The hippocampal group, the cortically damaged group and the unoperated control group were compared pre- and postoperatively on open-field behavior. This experiment was designed to investigate exploratory behavior as well as "emotionality" among the three groups.

Procedure

The apparatus was an open-field maze, a square wooden enclosure, 30×30 in., with walls 5 in. high. The floor was divided into 36 5-in. squares marked off by black paint. The maze was placed on the floor of a windowless room, directly under a fluorescent light.

Three measures were used in the open field situation. (a) The number of squares S entered in a 10 min. test period. (b) The number of fecal boluses produced by each S during this same period. (c) The number of urinations produced by each S within this time period.

Preoperatively, all Ss were run consecutively during one evening. Each S was taken from its individual living cage, carried by hand into the experimental room and placed in the center of the open field. After the 10 min. observational period, it was removed and replaced in its living cage. Between observations of Ss, all feces and urinations were removed and the floor of the maze cleaned with a damp sponge and paper toweling.

Each of the operated Ss was retested on Day 8 following its operation, using an identical procedure. The unoperated control Ss, matched for elapsed time, were retested at the same time.

Results

The major result was that the hippocampal Ss entered over four times as many squares postoperatively as they had before operation. An analysis of variance (Lindquist, 1956) of the data presented in Table 1 revealed that no significant differences appeared among the three groups on the number of squares entered preoperatively. However, a significant difference was obtained on the *postoperative* data ($p < .01$).

Although both the unoperated and cortically damaged groups also increased slightly in the number of entries postoperatively, Scheffé contrast tests (Scheffé, 1959) showed that the cortical control-unoperated control mean difference did not reach statistical significance. However, the difference between the hippocampal Ss and each of the other two groups was significant ($p < .01$).

Table 1.

Comparison of preoperative and postoperative open-field behavior of hippocampal, cortical, and normal rats.

Experimental condition	Group					
	Hippocampal		Cortical		Normal	
	M	Range	M	Range	M	Range
NUMBER OF SQUARES ENTERED						
Preoperatively	118	21–218	126	35–213	144	75–224
Postoperatively	505	303–685	230	55–550	157	64–294
NUMBER OF URINATIONS						
Preoperatively	<1	0–1	1	0–2	<1	0–2
Postoperatively	<1	0–1	<1	0–1	1	0–2
NUMBER OF FECES						
Preoperatively	6	3–10	5	0–12	5	3–9
Postoperatively	4	0–8	3	0–6	5	0–9

Qualitative differences between the hippocampal Ss and the other two groups were also observed. The hippocampal Ss initially ran rapidly along the perimeter of the open field, stopping only rarely. They typically traversed the interior of the field only after 2–5 min. The most striking characteristic of their behavior was an extremely repetitive running pattern. The behavior of the other two groups differed radically from that of the hippocampal group. It consisted of "bursts" and "stops." A typical performance was to run to one wall, explore around the perimeter of the field once or twice, stop and groom, stand up on the hind legs and sniff, run out into the center of the field, explore in a seemingly random fashion, and return to a corner for more grooming and occasional crouching.

Two measures were taken to obtain gross estimates of "emotionality" in the field situation. No significant differences were obtained in the number of boluses dropped by Ss in the several groups. However, both the hippocampal and the cortically damaged groups urinated less in the maze postoperatively than did the unoperated controls ($p < .01$). No significant difference appeared between the two operated groups on this measure.

Experiment 2: Simultaneous-Successive Brightness Discrimination Learning

Previous reports have indicated that hippocampal damage in both monkeys (Stepien, Cordeau, and Rasmussen, 1960) and humans (Milner, and Penfield, 1955; Walker, 1957) results in a behavioral impairment which is interpreted as one of *recall* of recent events. However, when the relevant stimuli are presented simultaneously (Stepien et al., 1960) or when *recognition* of the appropriate stimulus is required (Walker, 1957), these Ss are less handicapped.

A behavioral test similar to that employed by Stepien et al., consists of simultaneous and successive discriminations. In a simultaneous discrimination, all the relevant stimuli are present on each trial, but the solution of a successive discrimination appears to depend upon the strengthening of an approach response to a compound stimulus, occurring across individual trials (Spence, 1960). If the behavioral deficit seen in animals with hippocampal damage indeed stems from their inability to perform adequately when all of the relevant stimuli are not immediately present, this deficit should appear selectively on the successive discrimination problem.

Procedure

The apparatus was a Y maze with removable walls and floors in the arms serving as the stimulus cues. In the simultaneous discrimination, one of the arms was always white, the other black. In the successive discrimination, both of the maze arms were either black or white on any given trial.

Seven days prior to testing (17–41 days postoperative), all Ss were placed on a 23 hr. food deprivation schedule. Water was available at all times. During this time, the Ss were handled for 10 min. each day. Each S was run five trials on the first experimental day, and 10 trials each following day until a criterion of 10 consecutive correct responses was reached. Gellerman orders were used to determine the reward pattern, and identical patterns were used for all Ss. A noncorrection procedure was used. The reinforcement consisted of several small Purina lab pellets. The intertrial interval was *8 min.* in all cases.

The simultaneous discrimination was a black-white discrimination. Seventeen Ss were trained to approach black (5 hippocampals, 6 cortical controls and 6 normals). The remaining Ss were trained to approach the white goal arm.

In the successive discrimination both arms were the same brightness for any given trial and the pattern was consistent for a given S. The right arm contained the food reward when both arms were white and the left arm contained the reward when both arms were black, for the 17 Ss trained on black-right, white-left. The remaining 16 Ss were trained to black-left, white-right.

The order of the discriminations was balanced. Seventeen Ss (5 hippocampals, 6 cortical controls, and 6 normals) were trained first on the successive discrimination. The other 16 Ss were trained first on the simultaneous discrimination. After reaching criterion on the first task, the S was started on the second discrimination the following day. The E recorded latencies for the elapsed time from the S's emergence from the start box until its entrance into the goal arm. Each S was tested 7 days a week continuously from the beginning of training.

Retention tests of 10 trials were made on the sixth and seventh day fol-

Table 2.

Trials to criterion, latencies, and 1-week retention scores on simultaneous and successive brightness discriminations by hippocampal, cortical, and normal rats.

Type of discrimination	Group					
	Hippocampal		Cortical		Normal	
	M	Range	M	Range	M	Range
	TRIALS TO CRITERION					
Simultaneous	29	10–44	33	12–57	31	10–61
Successive	120	53–164	76	37–108	55	18–105
	LATENCY (IN SEC.)					
Simultaneous	4.0	1.0–6.9	4.0	1.4–10.6	5.0	0.7–18.7
Successive	3.0	1.6–7.1	4.2	1.7–15.0	4.0	1.4–7.6
	1-WEEK RETENTION TEST: PERCENTAGE CORRECT					
Simultaneous	72	50–100	74	50–100	81	50–100
Successive	70	40–100	75	50–90	72	40–100

lowing completion of the two discrimination tasks. Seventeen Ss (5 hippo-campals, 6 cortical controls and 6 normals) were tested on Day 6 for retention of the first discrimination they had acquired. On Day 7 they were tested for retention of the other discrimination. This sequence was reversed for the remaining 16 Ss.

Results

The hippocampal Ss took significantly more trials to reach criterion on the successive discrimination, while no differences appeared on the simultaneous discrimination.

A Type I analysis of variance (Lindquist, 1956) yielded F ratios significant at < .001 for the between groups component, the between problems component, and the interaction ratio.

Scheffé contrast tests showed that on the successive discrimination, both the hippocampal-cortical control mean difference and the hippocampal-normal mean difference were significant at < .01.

No significant latency differences appeared among the groups for either problem. No differences occurred among the three groups on the retention tests given 1 week subsequently. All groups performed well, showing better than 70% correct responses on both problems during the retention trials.

Experiment 3: Hebb-Williams Maze Learning

Several studies (Heyman, 1951, Lawrence, 1949, 1950; Spence, 1960) have indicated that the successive problem is more difficult for normal rats.

Therefore, a possible explanation for the results of Experiment 2 could be that the hippocampal Ss are impaired on complex tasks, but relatively unimpaired on simpler discriminations. In order to investigate the behavior of hippocampal Ss on a "complexity of task" dimension, a relatively simple Maze 1 and a relatively complex Maze 6 were chosen from the 12 mazes of the Hebb-Williams series (Hebb and Williams, 1946). The hypothesis was that if hippocampal damage causes impairment in performance as a function of complexity of task, it should be more severe on Maze 6 than on Maze 1. In this experiment, the Ss were the same as in the first two experiments, with the exception that two of the cortically damaged rats were removed because of illness.

Procedure

The apparatus was a standard Hebb-Williams maze (Hebb and Williams, 1946) painted a medium gray. The floor plans of the two mazes used in the present experiment are shown in Figure 1.

Each S received 3 days of pretraining, with food in the goal box. The Ss were placed in the maze in groups of 4–6 on the first pretraining day, no inserts being present. On the next 2 days the Ss were run individually with inserts presented to form extremely simple mazes. By the third pretraining day, all Ss were running seven complete trials in a maximum of 5 min. On Test Days 4 and 5, the Ss were run individually. Each S was run until he had completed seven trials or until the maximum time limit had lapsed. This time limit was 10 min. for the "simple" maze, and 20 min. for the "complex" maze.

An S was considered to have made an error if its two forepaws crossed an error line (see Figure 1). Errors were recorded as the total number committed during seven complete turns to the goal box or for the maximal time of the test period if S did not complete seven trials. The Ss were run in two

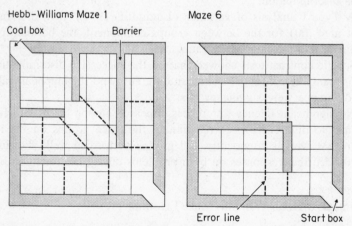

FIGURE 1. Floor plans of Hebb-Williams Mazes 1 (simple) and 6 (complex).

groups. One group (4 hippocampals, 4 cortical controls and 6 normals) was tested first on the "simpler" maze (1) and then on the "more complex" Maze 6. The order was reversed for the remaining Ss.

Results

The hippocampal Ss made significantly more errors on *both* maze problems, and were in fact *worse* on the simpler maze than on the more complex maze. The data are presented in Table 3.

Table 3.

Number of errors on two Hebb-Williams mazes made by hippocampal, cortical, and normal rats.

Maze	Group					
	Hippocampal		Cortical		Normal	
	M	Range	M	Range	M	Range
Simple	148	43–247	37	3–91	6	1–13
Complex	70	10–170	29	12–54	17	10–29

A Type I analysis of variance and Scheffé contrast tests revealed that the difference between the hippocampal group mean and each of the other group means was significant at $< .01$ for both maze problems. Although the cortically damaged Ss made more errors than the unoperated Ss on both problems, these differences did not reach statistical significance. The between-problem mean difference reached statistical significance only for the hippocampal Ss ($p < .01$).

Two factors are relevant in describing the behavioral differences among the three groups in the maze situation.

First, the simpler maze actually has more error lines (seven) than the more complex maze (four).

Second, the hippocampal Ss, when placed in the start box typically entered one of the two side alleys, progressed to the end and then turned and entered the other alley. These Ss, in sharp contrast to the other two groups, then re-entered the originally chosen alley, rather than moving into the center of the maze, as the typical control S did. This repetitive tracing of the two side alleys by the hippocampal Ss continued 50–75 times. Eventually, all the hippocampal Ss reached the goal box, yet the striking repetitive behavior was only slightly diminished on subsequent trials. This behavior was quite similar to that seen in the maze when it was used as the open field in Experiment 1.

Since the simpler maze contained almost twice as many error lines as the more complex maze, the repetitive tracing resulted in approximately twice as many errors on Maze 1.

Experiment 4: Passive Avoidance

The repetitive behavior displayed by the hippocampal Ss in both Experiments 1 and 3 suggested that these Ss may have been relatively unable to inhibit their motor responses. Kimura (1958) has reported that rats with small, posterior hippocampal lesions are less able to withhold an approach response which has been subsequently punished by electric shock. Experiment 4 was designed to investigate the ability of the Ss in the present study to inhibit an approach response.

Procedure

The apparatus consisted of a start box, straight runway, and goal box. The entire apparatus was 53 in. long, 4 in. wide and 4¼ in. deep. A guillotine door separated the start box from the runway. An aluminum food cup was attached to the rear wall of the goal box with a brass screw. This screw served as one of the terminals for the shock circuit. The other terminal was a copper wire soldered onto a metal plate which was fitted into the bottom of the goal box. This plate was wrapped in cloth and kept damp with dilute saline solution. The food provided was a wet mash. When S was eating the wet mash, his body completed the electrical circuit. The remainder of the circuit consisted of a variable rheostat and a telegraph key. The E controlled both the amount and timing of the shock.

The Ss were given 10 trials each day for 4 days. Each trial consisted of placing the S in the start box, lifting the guillotine door, and allowing the S to run down the runway and eat in the goal box for a period of 30 sec. It was then removed and replaced in the start box for the next trial. Latencies were recorded manually for the elapsed time from S's emergence from the start box until it began to eat in the goal box. No shock was administered until the fourth trial of Day 3. On that trial, S had approached the food cup and was eating the wet mash when E completed the shock circuit. The voltage was approximately 22 v. The appropriate voltage had been determined previously with pilot animals. The S was removed from the goal box (or runway) and replaced in the start box for the fifth trial of that day. No more shock was given.

Table 4.
Mean latencies during postshock trials in a passive avoidance situation by hippocampal, cortical, and normal rats.

Group	Latencies (in sec.)	
	M	Range
Hippocampal	25.0	3.2–52.2
Cortical	38.7	21.1–60.0
Normal	47.8	6.7–60.0

The latency of the *S*'s return was then measured. Each elapsed minute was considered a trial, even if *S* had not returned to the goal box. Six trials were run in this manner following the shock trial. If *S* did return to the goal box, it was allowed the usual 30 sec. to eat before being replaced in the start box. The criterion for a "return" was a complete four-footed entry and at least 5 sec. of consecutive eating. A two-footed entry or tentative sniffing at the food was not considered as a "return." The procedure for Day 4 was identical to that for Days 1 and 2.

Results

The hippocampal *S*s showed the *least* postshock avoidance, and the unoperated *S*s the most. The cortically damaged *S*s fell between these groups, but nearer to the hippocampal *S*s in their degree of avoidance. No differences had appeared among the three groups for the approach latencies of the two preshock days. An analysis of variance performed on the postshock latencies was significant for the between groups component ($p < .05$). Scheffé tests revealed that although the hippocampal-normal difference was significant ($p < .05$), the cortically damaged *S*s were not significantly different from *either* of the other two groups.

By combining the two operated groups, and comparing their group mean with the unoperated group, brain damage per se appeared as a significant factor in these results ($p < .05$) but the behavioral effects cannot be reliably accounted for by the locus of the lesion.

Anatomical Results

The brains of the two operated groups were fixed in 10% formalin, dehydrated, and embedded in paraffin. Sections were cut 20 μ thick. Every fifth section was mounted and stained with thionin.

An examination of the brains of the hippocampal *S*s showed that bilateral hippocampal lesions were produced in each *S* (see Figs. 2 and 3). These lesions included destruction of the fimbria. In no case was the hippocampus completely destroyed, but a complete transection of the hippocampus was effected bilaterally in every *S*. The lesions varied from about 60% to over 90% destruction. The portions generally escaping damage were the dorsal and rostral portions and the ventral tip of Ammon's horn. The middle aspect of the hippocampal formation was the most damaged. The overlying cortical lesions in the hippocampal group chiefly involved the projection areas of the auditory and visual systems. Slight damage to the optic radiations and lateral geniculate bodies was present in six of the hippocampal *S*s. In only two of these six was the thalamic involvement bilateral.

Damage among the cortical lesion group was largely restricted to lateral and dorsal neocortex (Fig. 4), although very shallow surface invasion of the dorsal hippocampus did occur in some of these *S*s. In two of these *S*s, the lesion

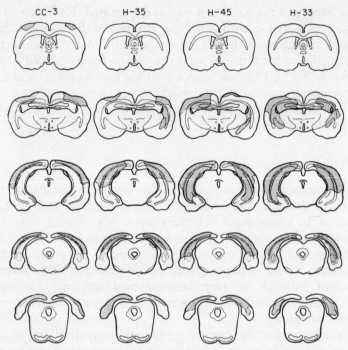

FIGURE 2. Lesion reconstructions. (CC–3 = representative cortical control lesion; H–35 = hippocampal *S* with minimal hippocampal damage; H–45 = hippocampal *S* with average hippocampal damage; H-33 = hippocampal *S* with maximal hippocampal damage.)

extended more deeply into the hippocampus. One of these two also suffered severe damage to the caudate nucleus and putamen, as well as the fornix and septal area. This lesion was presumably due to secondary bleeding subsequent to the operation. This *S* was the only one to show any apparent correlation between thalamic damage and subsequent behavior. While the other cortical *S*s entered an average of 125 more squares in the open field postoperatively, this *S* entered a total of 136 *less* squares than he had upon preoperative testing. Also, this *S* completed no runs on Maze 1 and only one run on Maze 6.

The extent of the cortical lesion among the cortical control group was consistently larger than the cortical damage incurred by the hippocampal *S*s. A planimetric analysis of the sections was carried out to determine the extent of *total* neural tissue removed. The extent of brain removed in the two groups proved not be significantly different ($t < 1$).

Discussion

The three results that separate the hippocampal *S*s from the other two groups are most likely to yield clues to hippocampal function. These results are:

1. The repetitive running behavior of the hippocampal *S*s in the open field situation which resulted in the greatly increased number of squares entered postoperatively.

2. The poorer performance of the hippocampal Ss on the successive brightness discrimination.

3. The greater number of errors committed in the Hebb-Williams mazes by the hippocampal Ss.

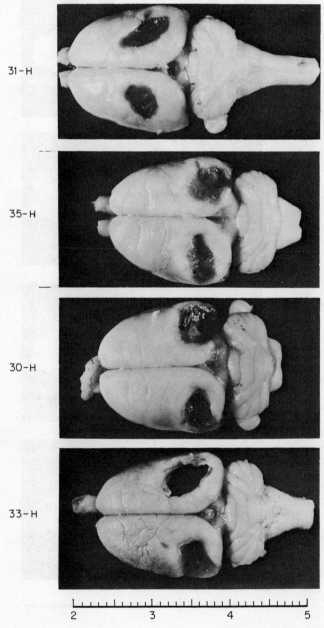

FIGURE 3. Dorsal view of four brains from hippocampal group.

One current idea is that the hippocampus is primarily concerned with motivational or emotional mechanisms. Another view holds that the hippocampus mediates "short-term memory." The present series of experiments do not lend support to either of these concepts.

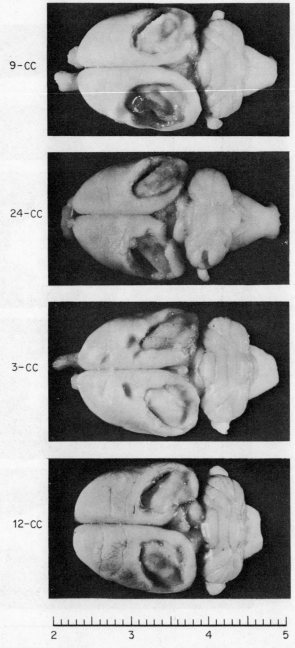

FIGURE 4. Dorsal view of four brains from cortical control group.

The emotional state of the hippocampal Ss did not appear to be changed by the operation. These Ss did not differ from either of the control groups in the amount of defecation in an open field, a standard measure of emotionality in the rat. Nor were any emotionality differences observed in handling the Ss. In the passive avoidance situation, analysis of the postshock latencies indicated that the shorter latencies observed in the operated Ss were most probably a result of brain damage per se, and not reliably related to the locus of the lesion.

Interpretation of the present results in terms of a simple short-term memory deficit is difficult because the hippocampal Ss were unimpaired in the simultaneous discrimination in which the intertrial interval was 8 min. Also, the experimental Ss showed good retention of both discrimination problems a week following acquisition.

One possible interpretation of these data is that the hippocampal Ss are "hyperactive." Hyperactivity might account for the increased square entries, and possibly for the greater number of errors in the mazes. It does not appear to explain the successive discrimination impairment. Several other facts diminish the explanatory value of the hyperactivity hypothesis. No differences appeared in the latencies in either of the discrimination problems. No latency differences occurred in the preshock trials of the avoidance situation. Also, Kim (1960) has reported hippocampal rats to be only slightly more active than normals, and then only when the ambient temperature is below normal.

The hippocampal Ss in the present study might be described in a general way as demonstrating an increased degree of perseverative behavior. This description seems particularly apt when applied to the open field and maze data. In the discrimination situations, however, a "perseveration" hypothesis would need qualification since a deficit was noted only during the successive discrimination. It might be postulated, for example, that perseverative behavior varies directly with the difficulty of the discrimination.

At the present stage of our knowledge of brain function in general and hippocampal function in particular, any monolithic interpretation of the behavior of hippocampectomized animals is likely to be an oversimplification. Although the present experiments have not fully clarified the role of the hippocampus in behavior, they do indicate that neither a motivational-emotional hypothesis nor a short-term memory concept is able to account for the behavior of the hippocampal Ss.

To determine whether variability in the behavioral data among the operated Ss might be related to the extent of either hippocampal or extrahippocampal damage, tau coefficients were calculated for the various behavioral measures. The coefficients between extent of hippocampal damage and behavioral impairment were low (none exceeding .37). However, with two exceptions, these correlations were in the direction expected from the data. The highest correlations were on the number of trials to criterion for the successive discrimination (tau = .37, $p < .06$), the number of squares entered postoperatively in the open field (tau = .33, $p < .10 > .06$), and the number of errors on the simpler maze in Experiment 3 (tau = .35, $p < .10 > .06$).

On the other hand, the correlations between the total amount of extrahippocampal loss and these behavioral measures either showed a smaller coefficient than those found in the hippocampal group, or were in the opposite direction. The only coefficient which reached a probability level of less than .10 was a negative relationship between the amount of extrahippocampal tissue loss and the number of squares entered postoperatively (tau $= -.33, p < .09$).

References

Hebb, D. O., and Williams, K. A method of rating animal intelligence. *J. genet. Psychol.*, 1946, **34**, 59–65.

Heyman, M. Transfer of discrimination learning following three conditions of initial training. Unpublished doctoral dissertation, State Uiversity of Iowa, 1951.

Isaacson, R. L., Douglass, R. J., and Moore, R. Y. The effect of radical hippocampal ablation on acquisition of avoidance responses. *J. comp. physiol. Psychol.*, 1961, **54**, 625–628.

Kim, D. Nest building, general activity and salt preference of rats following hippocampal ablation. *J. comp. physiol. Psychol.*, **53**, 11–16.

Kimura, D. Effects of selective hippocampal damage on avoidance behavior in the rat. *Canad. J. Psychol.*, 1958, **12**, 213–218.

Klüver, H., and Bucy, P. C. "Psychic blindness" and other symptoms following bilateral temporal lobectomy in rhesus monkey. *Amer. J. Physiol.*, 1937, **119**, 352–353.

Lawrence, D. H. Acquired distinctiveness of cues: I. Transfer between discriminations on the basis of familiarity with the stimulus. *J. exp. Psychol.*, 1949, **39**, 770–784.

Lawrence, D. H. Acquired distinctiveness of cues: II. Selective association in a constant stimulus situation. *J. exp. Psychol.*, 1950, **40**, 175–188.

Lindquist, E. F. *Design and analysis of experiments in psychology and education.* Boston: Houghton Mifflin, 1956.

Milner, B., and Penfield, W. The effect of hippocampal lesions on recent memory. *Trans. Amer. Neurol. Ass.*, 1955, **80**, 42–48.

Pribram, K. H., and Weiskrantz, L. A comparison of the effects of medial and lateral cerebral resections on conditioned avoidance behavior of monkeys. *J. comp. physiol. Psychol.*, 1957, **50**, 74–80.

Scheffé, H. *The analysis of variance.* New York: Wiley, 1959.

Schreiner, L., and Kling, A. Behavioral changes following rhinencephalic injury in the cat. *J. Neurophysiol.*, 1953, **16**, 643–659.

Spence, K. W. *Behavior theory and learning.* Englewood Cliffs, N. J.: Prentice-Hall, 1960.

Spiegel, E. A., Miller, H. R., and Oppenheimer, J. J. Forebrain and rage reactions. *J. Neurophysiol.*, 1940, **3**, 538–548.

Stepien, L. S., Cordeau, J. P., and Rasmussen, T. The effect of temporal lobe and hippocampal lesions on auditory and visual recent memory in monkeys. *Brain*, 1960, **83**, 470–489.

Walker, A. E. Recent memory impairment in unilateral temporal lesions. *AMA Arch. Neurol. Psychiat.*, 1957, **78**, 543–552.

Central Nervous System: Recovery of Function

DONALD G. STEIN, JEFFREY J. ROSEN, JOSEPH
GRAZIADEI, DAVID MISHKIN, AND JOHN J. BRINK

Reprinted from *Science*, Oct. 24, 1969, Vol. 166, pp. 528–530. Copyright 1969 by the
American Association for the Advancement of Science.

Although Lashley (*1*) considered the problem of equipotentiality of brain function 38 years ago, current research on brain-behavior relationships has tended to emphasize relatively strict localization of function. According to this later work, a particular area of the brain is necessary for the control of a behavior sequence, and its removal should impair or prevent the occurrence of that sequence. However, several studies have shown that successive two-stage cortical lesions have no effect upon retention of a learned discrimination under certain conditions, whereas bilateral, single-stage removal produced marked deficit in performance (*2*).

In view of the importance of these findings for general theories of brain function, we explored the possibility of obtaining similar results by testing acquisition as well as retention and by successively removing cortical as well as subcortical structures. Such data would indicate that, although a particular structure of the central nervous system may be involved in the mediation of certain behavior, its absence would not be a necessary condition for the elimination of that behavior. In addition, it would be difficult to claim that a specific behavioral function was localized in that structure. To test our hypothesis, we studied the effects of lesions in the frontal, hippocampal, and amygdaloid areas of the rat brain; it has been demonstrated that, in the rat, bilateral, single-stage damage in any of these zones produces a specific and highly replicable syndrome (*3*).

Our subjects were 72 male albino rats (approximately 275 to 300 g). Seven rats were randomly assigned to each of the following six groups, named for the treatment given: one-stage hippocampal lesions (1-HC), two-stage hippocampal lesions (2-HC), one-stage amygdaloid lesions (1-Am), two-stage amygdaloid lesions (2-Am), one-stage sham operation (1-S), or two-stage sham operation (2-S). Ten rats were assigned to each of the following three groups: one stage orbitofrontal lesions (1-OF), two-stage orbitofrontal lesions (2-OF), or unoperated control (UC). Surgery was performed under general anesthesia with a stereotaxic device for the placement of the stainless steel, epoxy-coated electrode. A Grass radio-frequency device (used for the radio-frequency subcortical lesions) was used to deliver a 65-ma current for 20 or 30 seconds to either the hippocampus or amygdala, respectively. The orbitofrontal lesions were produced by subpial aspiration.

In the groups receiving one-stage surgical lesions (called one-stage groups or animals), bilateral damage was effected in a single operation. In the groups receiving two-stage lesions (called two-stage groups or animals), lesions were first made in either the right or the left hemisphere and then, 30 days later, in the same structure on the contralateral side. Animals that underwent a sham operation were treated like either the one- or two-stage animals except that the electrode never penetrated the brain. To minimize age differences between groups, all one-stage surgery was completed within 4 days after the two-stage groups received their second lesion. All the rats were handled each day during the 30-day recovery period of the two-stage groups. Testing began 2 weeks after surgery on a given group. The animals were maintained on a 23-hour, 45-minute water-deprivation schedule during all test periods.

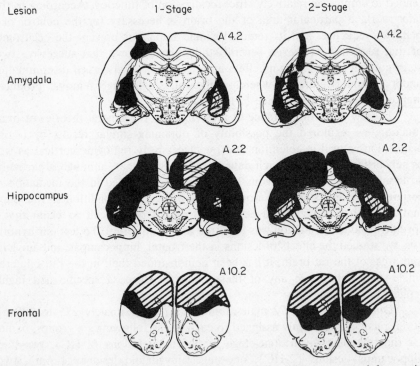

FIGURE 1. Representative sections of the maximum and minimum extent of damage in the three structures. The hatched portions of the sections represent the minimum amount of damage indicated, and the solid portions represent the maximum damage located by the coordinate shown.

Before discrimination training, rats with hippocampal or amygdaloid lesions and sham-operated rats were trained to run for water reward in an enclosed Y maze by being permitted a few sips of water upon entering either stem. Training on a light-dark discrimination problem began after each rat had learned to run regularly to water in the maze. Animals received a water reward in the left side of the maze when both arms of the Y were illuminated at the water spout and a reward in the right side of the maze when both arms were darkened. Testing was carried out under dim, red, room light. The intertrial interval was 30 seconds; during this period the rats were contained in the stem of the maze. Each animal received ten trials per day until it reached a criterion of nine correct responses in ten successive trials. The rats were then required to reverse their responses in the same apparatus to the same criterion used in the initial learning task.

Upon completion of reversal training, the rats were prepared for a passive-avoidance task; they received 100 water-reinforced trials (ten per day) in an enclosed straight alley marked off in squares. On day 11, the water spout was electrified, and the number of squares that the rats crossed and the number of shocks that they received were recorded. If an animal did not leave the starting area within 1 minute, trials for that day were terminated.

Because animals with frontal lesions are most impaired in spatial performance, we decided on a sequence of tasks sensitive to this deficit (3). Thus the rats with frontal lesions were tested for postoperative acquisition of (i) delayed spatial alternation, (ii) light-dark visual discrimination and reversal, and (iii) nonspatial, simultaneous visual discrimination. All these tasks involved water reward.

The first task was administered in a T maze with a 5-second intertrial interval. Subjects received 16 trials per day with either right or left response being rewarded on the first trial. On remaining trials, the rats were rewarded only when they switched from their last previously rewarded response. Training continued until the animals reached a criterion of 15 successive correct responses on a given day.

Upon completion of this task, the rats were trained on the same light-dark discrimination problem described earlier to a criterion of nine out of ten correct responses on a given day. This was followed by reversal training to the same criterion.

The final task required the animals to approach vertical and to avoid horizontal black-and-white stripes in a modified Grice-Thompson box (5). Animals received ten trials per day until they reached a criterion of nine correct responses on a given day.

We observed marked differences in performance among the groups (4). On acquisition of light-dark discrimination, 2-HC rats showed no deficit in comparison with the sham-operated groups, while 1-HC rats showed highly significant impairments in maze learning. Both 1-Am and 2-Am groups showed a deficit in acquisition; however, in neither case was it as severe as that observed in the 1-HC group. In reversal learning, the 1-HC and 1-Am groups still showed marked disruption of performance, whereas the 2-HC and 2-Am subjects did not differ from the sham-operated controls.

Similar results were obtained for passive avoidance; only the 1-HC and 1-Am animals were unable to avoid shock, and the 1-HC rats were even more disabled than the 1-Am rats. The impairment in light-dark discrimination appearing in the 2-Am animals was not observed in the performance of any subsequent task. (Table 1.)

Table 1.

Number of trials to criterion and number of shocks given in tasks performed by rats with lesions of the hippocampus and amygdala. Groups with one-stage lesions are labeled 1-S; groups with two-stage lesions are labeled 2-S; LDD, light-dark discriminations; PA, passive avoidance.

Group	LDD (mean)	LDD reversal (mean)	PA (mean)
HIPPOCAMPUS			
1-S	120.0	168.6	16.9
2-S	51.7	91.7	5.7
AMYGDALA			
1-S	94.3	120.0	11.3
2-S	84.3	92.9	5.7
SHAM-OPERATED			
1-S	50.0	71.7	7.7
2-S	55.0	106.7	7.2

We found that group 1-OF took significantly longer to reach criterion than either group 2-OF or the unoperated controls on each of the tasks. In marked contrast to group 1-OF, group 2-OF did not differ significantly from unoperated controls on any of the tasks used in this experiment. There was no overlap in performance of the subjects in groups 1-OF and 2-OF on the first three tasks (Table 2).

When the tests were completed, the animals were killed by intracardial perfusion, and the brains of rats with lesions were removed and prepared for histological examination (6). In all cases, there was extensive bilateral damage in the hippocampus or amygdala. Most animals with amygdaloid lesions also suffered damage to the ventral hippocampus and to the claustrum. The rats with lesions in the hippocampus also suffered damage to the overlying neocortex. In four cases there was slight, unilateral damage to the lateral geniculate body. In all cases, orbitofrontal damage was confined to the frontal lobes. There was only one instance of slight damage to the anterodorsal caudate nucleus and this was in an animal with two-stage lesions. The extent of damage in animals with one- or two-stage lesions was not significantly different (7).

Our data indicate that in adult rats successive removal of approximately

Table 2.

Number of trials to criterion in tasks performed by rats with lesions of the frontal cortex. Groups with one-stage lesions are labeled 1-S; groups with two-stage lesions are labeled 2-S; unoperated controls are labeled UC; DSA, delayed spatial alternation; LDD, light-dark discrimination; SD, simultaneous discrimination.

DSA	LDD (mean)	LDD reversal (mean)	SD (mean)
		GROUP 1-S	
300.0	278.5	313	120.0
		GROUP 2-S	
150.0	124.0	121	79.4
		GROUP UC	
104.6	148.0	132	73.0

equal amounts of brain does not produce the same deficits as single-stage removal. In our experiments sequential removal of cortical and subcortical associative areas of the brain did not render the animal different from normal and sham-operated controls with respect to performance on a variety of tasks. In contrast, rats with one-stage lesions at the same loci showed marked and long-standing deficits on these tests of learning and performance. Since no training intervened between first and second stages of the operations in the two-stage groups, and since all animals were handled in the same manner, the apparently normal behavior of the two-stage animals must be due to some naturally occurring reorganization of activity of the central nervous system.

Recovery of function in the absence of specific training has been observed in very young animals (8), but similar plasticity in the absence of prior learning or rehabilitative training has not been as clearly demonstrated in mature organisms. Several hypotheses have been presented in an attempt to account for reorganization, but they fail to specify the responsible mechanisms. Lashley thought that compensation or vicarious function might be due to overlapping neuronal fields such that specific memory traces are scattered over a large area of the brain (1). Kennard suggested that other structures take over the function of tissue that has been removed but was unable to specify the particular pathways or mechanisms involved (9).

Since we did not observe regeneration of neural tissue in any of our brain-damaged groups, it is likely that the remaining tissue, unaffected by surgery, must be involved in the recovery of function. If this is true, then it becomes somewhat difficult to infer that particular portions or areas of the central nervous system are necessary or critical for the mediation of complex behavioral responses; the behavior is apparently normal even though the tissue presumed to be essential has been removed. Luria suggested that complex adaptive activity is a function of the dynamic integration of the whole central nervous system and that functional systems mediating complex behavior are not fixed in any one area of the brain (*10*). His position is similar to Lashley's notion of overlapping zones, but it cannot explain why two-stage lesions permit rapid recovery, while the same damage, performed in one stage, does not. At present the physiological mechanisms which underlie this phenomenon are not well known, but there is recovery of function in the absence of retraining in mature rats subjected to lesions in a number of different brain areas.

References and Notes

1. K. S. Lashley, *Brain Mechanisms and Intelligence* (Dover, New York, 1963).
2. L. Petrinovich and D. Bliss, *J. Comp. Physiol. Psychol.* **61,** 136 (1966); J. W. Stewart and H. W. Ades, *ibid.* **44,** 479 (1951).
3. R. J. Douglas, *Psychol. Bull.* **67,** 416 (1967); G. Goddard, *ibid.* **62,** 89 (1964); J. M. Warren and K. Akert, *The Frontal Granular Cortex and Behavior* (McGraw-Hill, New York, 1964).
4. Analyses of variance and individual comparisons were used to evaluate the data. In all cases where differences are reported, $P < .01$ with α appropriate for a priori comparisons.
5. D. G. Stein and D. P. Kimble, *J. Comp. Physiol. Psychol.* **62,** 243 (1966).
6. Sections were cut at 40 μm, mounted in albumin, and stained with cresyl-echt violet. Every fifth section was saved and used to reconstruct the lesion.
7. Extent of damage was assessed by projecting sections of tissue onto a reduced page of the DeGroot atlas that most closely corresponded to the actual section. The perimeter of the lesion was then traced. In this way, the entire extent of damage could be mapped. A polar planimeter (Keuffel and Esser, No. 4236) was used to convert perimeter to area, and the values obtained were analyzed with a *t*-test.
8. A. Kling and T. J. Tucker, in *The Neuropsychology of Development*, R. L. Isaacson, Ed. (Wiley, New York, 1968).
9. M. A. Kennard, *J. Neurophysiol.* **1,** 477 (1938).
10. A. R. Luria, *Human Brain and Psychological Processes* (Harper & Row, New York, 1966), chaps. 1 and 2.
11. Partially supported by NIMH research grant MH-13705-01, general biomedical sciences grant SOS FR 07045-03 to D.G.S., and by NSF grant GB-7041 to D.G.S. and J.J.B.

Learning and Retention in Cats
with Lesions in Reticular Formation

KAO LIANG CHOW AND WALTER RANDALL

Reprinted from *Psychonomic Science*, 1964, Vol. 1, pp. 259–260.

Abstract

Cats with lesions in the reticular formation at the level of the superior colliculus and red nucleus learned conditioned avoidance responses and visual discriminations as well as normal cats. In cats with preoperative training, the midbrain surgery had little or no effect on postoperative performance. Cats with lesions in the midline nuclei of the dorsal thalamus exhibited a postoperative loss of a previously learned visual discrimination and required more trials to relearn. All cats had normal electrocorticogram (ECG) (awake and sleep), and exhibited normal conditioned ECG potentials.

Introduction

A large body of literature supports the generalization that the midbrain reticular formation participates critically as the anatomical substrate of consciousness, sleep, attention, and emotion (Magoun, 1963; Lindsley, 1960). Several authors also suggest that the reticular formation plays a central role in learning and memory (Gastaut, 1958; Hernandez-Peon and Brust-Carmona, 1961). Some of the evidence for considering the reticular formation as important in learning and memory are the progressive alterations in electropotentials obtained from the midbrain reticular formation during various conditioning procedures. However, such alterations have not been consistently found (Morrell, 1961). The present report is an attempt to assess the learning capability and the ECG of cats with lesions in the midbrain reticular formation and in the midline thalamus.

Method

Eleven cats were subjected to stereotaxic surgery, seven receiving lesions confined to the midbrain, two receiving lesions restricted to midline thalamus and two receiving both the thalamic and midbrain lesions. The stereotaxic lesions in the reticular formation were made in two to four stages, with 1–3 months recovery time between stages. After the surgery, as well as before in most cases, the cats learned conditioned avoidance responses and food-

rewarded visual discriminations. At the completion of these learning procedures, usually 3–4 months after the last surgery, epidural cortical electrodes
were implanted in various areas of the cerebrum for ECG recordings. The formation of conditioned ECG potentials, the surgical procedure, and the histological data will be reported elsewhere.

Nine of the eleven cats were trained both before and after the surgery;
the other two cats had only postoperative training. All cats learned two conditioned avoidance responses and two or three food-rewarded visual discriminations. For the conditioned avoidance responses the conditioned stimulus
for the first task was a buzzer and for the second flickering light (6–10 per
second), with the apparatus (shuttle box) and procedure the same as those
described by Chow, Dement and John (1937). For the visual discriminations,
a Y-shaped Yerkes box was used with the usual training procedure as previously described (Chow, Dement and Mitchell, 1959). A black vs. white
discrimination was used initially to familiarize the naive cats and to adapt the
operated cats to the learning situation. The main tasks in the Yerkes box
consisted of (1) a black circle vs. a black square on white backgrounds, and
(2) a black vertical bar vs. a black horizontal bar on white backgrounds. Ten
to 20 trials were given each day for both the conditioned avoidance response
and visual discrimination training, with criterion for learning selected as 90%
correct in 20 trials.

Results

The transection of the reticular formation was complete in seven cats,
including the two with additional thalamic lesions. The prefix of RF was used
to designate these animals in the tables. Cats RFA and RF11 had only partial
lesion of the reticular formation. The midline thalamus was completely destroyed in all four cats (T6, T7, RFC, RF6).

Table 1.

Learning scores of cats after midbrain and midline thalamic lesions (number of
trials to criterion, excluding criterion trials).

Cat	Conditioned avoidance		Visual discriminations	
	Buzzer	*Flicker*	*Square vs. circle*	*Vertical vs. horizontal*
RF3	60	60	120	60
RF5	60	60	30	50
RF12	—	—	—	60
RF14	—	—	—	100
T6	—	—	—	120
RFC	—	—	—	200
RFA	—	—	—	80

Table 2.

Pre- and postoperative learning scores of cats with midbrain and midline thalamic lesions (number of trials to criterion, excluding criterion trials).

Cat	Conditioned avoidance		Visual discriminations	
	Flicker (after buzzer training)		Square vs. circle (after brightness training)	
	Pre	Post	Pre	Post
RF12	80	0	180	0
RFH	20	10	200	0
RFA	100	20	140	40
RF13	140	100	220	120
RFC	40	0	120	140
RF6	60	20	160	300
T6	30	40	120	240
T7	30	50	120	430

Tables 1 and 2 present the learning scores for all cats. In Table 1 the learning scores for cats without preoperative training are presented; all these scores are within the normal range (c. f. Randall, 1964). Table 2 shows the results for the cats with both pre-and postoperative learning scores. On the conditioned avoidance problem, cats either retained or relearned rapidly. On the visual discrimination, the cats with only the midbrain lesion exhibited retention or rapid relearning. But the four cats with midline thalamic lesions required more trials than preoperatively to relearn the visual discrimination. These four cats with midline thalamic lesions (two of which also possessed the midbrain lesion) were not acquainted with the Yerkes-box problem after the surgery. They failed to follow the experimenter to the location and to operate the doors to the food as they did preoperatively.

Discussion

Our results show that cats with reticular formation lesions learn conditioned avoidance responses and visual discriminations as well as normal cats, thus confirming Adametz's informal observations (1959). Furthermore, no abnormalities in the ECG were present in any of these cats, which is consistent with a report on dogs without midbrains and caudal thalami (Batsel, 1960). It is apparent that there are two ways to prevent the acute effects (loss of consciousness and sleep-like ECG) of midbrain lesions: either do the lesion in stages (Adametz), or be thorough with the postoperative care (Batsel).

The failure of lesions of the midbrain reticular formation to disrupt learning does not imply that the reticular formation plays no roles in normal animals. The inherent limitations of the ablation method preclude any conclusions in this regard. The data on the midbrain-lesioned cats with both pre- and postoperative training indicate perfect retention or relearning in better or normal time for both the conditioned avoidance problems and the visual discrimination. Loss of a learned habit with relearning is the general finding after lesions in central nervous system. (See e.g. review by Morgan, 1951). Thus again no unique role may be attributed to the midbrain reticular formation.

In this study the first problem in both the shuttle box and the Yerkes box were not considered in the evaluation of the data. The buzzer-avoidance problem and black vs. white visual discrimination provided the essential controls for such non-specific influences on the learning scores as postural, motor or perceptual deficits, and motivational or emotional differences.

References

Adametz, John H. Rate of recovery of functioning in cats with rostral reticular lesions. *J. Neurosurg.,* 1959, **16,** 85–98.

Batsel, H. L. Electroencephalographic synchronization and desynchronization in the chronic "cerveau isole" of the dog. *EEG clin. Neurophysiol.,* 1960, **12,** 421–430.

Chow, K. L., Dement, W. C., and John, E. R. Conditioned electrographic potentials and behavioral avoidance response in cat. *J. Neurophysiol.,* 1957, **20,** 482–493.

Chow, K. L., Dement, W. C., and Mitchell, S. A. Jr. Effects of lesions of the rostral thalamus on brain waves and behavior in cats. *EEG clin. Neurophysiol.,* 1959, **11,** 107–120.

Gaustaut, H. The role of the reticular formation in establishing conditioned reactions. In H. H. Jasper, L. D. Proctor, R. S. Knighton, W. C. Noshay, and R. T. Costello (Eds.), *Reticular formation of the brain.* Boston: Little Brown & Co., 1958. Pp. 561–579.

Hernandez-Peon, R. and Brust-Carmona, H. Functional role of subcortical structures in habituation and conditioning. In J. F. Delafresnaye (Ed.), *Brain mechanisms and learning.* Oxford: Blackwell, 1961. Pp. 393–412.

Lindsley, D. B. Attention, consciousness, sleep and wakefulness. In J. Field (Ed.), *Handbook of physiology, neurophysiology.* Vol. III. Washington, D. C.: Am. Physiol. Soc., 1960. Pp. 1553–1593.

Magoun, H. W. The waking brain. (2nd ed.) Charles C. Thomas, 1963.

Morgan, C. T. The psychophysiology of learning. In S. S. Stevens (Ed.), *Handbook of experimental psychology.* New York: John Wiley & Sons, 1951. Pp. 758–788.

Morrell, F. Electrophysiological contributions to the neural basis of learning. *Physiol. Rev.,* 1961, **41,** 443–494.

Randall, W. Generalization after frequency discrimination in cats with central nervous system lesions. In D. Mostofsky (Ed.), *Stimulus generalization.* In press. Stanford University Press. 1964.

Note

1. The present study was supported in part by a Research Career Award (NB-K6-18, 512) to the first author, and Research Grant B-3816-03 from the NINDB. National Institutes of Health.

The Brain as an Engineering Problem

R. L. GREGORY

Reprinted from *Current Problems in Animal Behavior*, edited by Thorpe and Zangwill, 1961, pp. 307–330. Reproduced by permission of the publisher, Cambridge University Press, and abridged by permission of the author.

Introduction

Biologists generally refer to the activity of living organisms as "behaviour." When talking about machines, engineers tend to use the word "performance." To interchange these words is to raise a smile, perhaps an appreciative smile, but the speaker risks being labelled quixotic. It does appear, however, that the terms "behaviours" and "performance" are interchanged much more now than in the past, the reason almost certainly being the influence of cybernetic ideas, which have unified certain aspects of biology and engineering. Some biologists even go so far as to regard their subject as essentially a branch of engineering, and some engineers use examples from biology, such as living servo-systems, to illustrate their principles. The activity of organisms is most often referred to as "performance" when their efficiency is being considered. Thus play-activity is called "behaviour," while a skilled worker's activity may be called "performance." This change is interesting, for it brings out the influence of the engineering way of thinking upon even lay thought about human and animal activity.

It is worth stressing that physical principles have not always been accepted as appropriate to biology. Aristotle did not make any basic distinction between the living and the non-living, but a sharp distinction was drawn by Kant in the *Kritik der Urtheilskraft* (1790). Perhaps Kant was so influenced by the patent inadequacy of Descartes' attempts to describe organisms in terms of his Natural Philosophy that he was led to say that the behaviour of living systems cannot be governed by causal principles applicable to the physical world. To Kant, living systems are somehow outside the dictates of the laws of nature, and this has been held by some biologists since—certainly as recently as E. S. Russell (1946), who regards 'directiveness' as a special property of living organisms. The influence of Kant's teaching upon biology has been profound and (to the cybernetically inclined) disastrous. Historically, it has led to the creation of special entities to distinguish the living from the non-living, such as Dresch's Entelechy, Bergson's *élan vitale* and the Emergent Properties of the Gestalt school of psychology.*

* Köhler, in his book *Die physischen Gestalten* (1920), takes a different view from that of most Gestalt writers. He does not suppose that organisms are unique in this respect, but rather that Emergence is to be found in many physical systems. Some philosophers have also taken this view. It leads to the difficulty that "emergence" is used so generally that it points to nothing special. This point is well discussed by Madden (1957) and is also considered by Gregory (1953).

We do indeed think of inanimate matter as somehow different from animate matter. If we did not, these words have no special meaning, for no distinction would be implied. The point is this: is it useful to describe, or to explain, this difference by postulating some *special factor* which is held to be present in animate and absent in inanimate matter? To biologists looking for general explanatory concepts, after the manner of the physical sciences, such postulated special factors must appear harmful. These factors do not enable us to relate phenomena; they do not provide any sort of picture; they do not enable predictions to be made. The trouble with Entelechy, *élan vitale* and the rest is that they do not help us to understand. Such terms give a sacrosanct air to life, which may be pleasing, but which tends to warn off further enquiry. The Gestaltist's plea for the special nature of "organic unities" is effectively a warning against attempts at further analysis, the doctrine being that it is *in principle impossible* to analyse the whole in such a manner that its activity can be completely described by the causal relations between the parts. It is, however, just this sort of analysis which is the goal of exploration in the physical sciences. Further, it is important to note the *in principle impossible* here: it is not the complexity of the task which is held to make analysis impossible, but rather the claim that the organic world is such that analysis into parts is doomed to failure, however complete our knowledge of it may be. Curiously, this is regarded by some as an exciting and interesting discovery about living systems. This is an attitude puzzling to those who believe that useful explanations in science should take the form of analysis into simpler elements. Now it *could* be that there is something irreducible about living systems which defies such analysis, but surely we have no right to claim this until the traditional types of explanation have failed for a very long time, and certainly not now while exciting advances are being made in the biological sciences. If we seek the types of explanation found in the physical sciences, *élan vitale,* or the concept of Emergence, will appear as doctrines of despair. To postulate such special unanalysable factors is to make a philosophy of pessimism. To say that *x* is an Emergent Property is to put *x* into the limbo of the unknown and shut the door upon it, while warning others against peeping through the keyhole.

To regard the brain as a problem in engineering is to look for possible solutions in terms of engineering principles to the questions set by biological enquiry. This chapter is concerned not with answers to specific questions—such questions perhaps as: How are memories stored? How does the eye guide the hand? What are dreams made of? But rather will it attempt to discuss some of the difficulties in taking over engineering methods into biology, and some implications of this approach for the study of the central nervous system.

An alternative to the Kantian doctrine is to say that living systems are *machines.* The cybernetic view is often put in this way, but it has objections. If we use the term "machine" to include living organisms, it loses its major classificatory use. Further, the term "machine" is very difficult to define in general terms. We might call a given system a machine though it has no predictable output, displays goal-seeking behaviour, and is in fact indistinguishable in its behaviour from at least simple living systems. If we mean merely that it is man-made, then the distinction is trivial. We cannot get away with an extensive definition of 'machine' (pointing to all existing machines), for we must allow the possibility of future new kinds of machine, and these could not be included. If animate systems are called "machines," at least two important things might be meant: (1) that their functioning could be described in terms of known physical principles, or (2) that their functioning could be described, if not in terms of principles known at present, at least in terms of principles which *could* be known to us. This is to say that living organisms are in fact so constituted that we could in principle understand them as engineers or physicists understand their systems. It appears that to call an animal a machine is to indicate that its manner of functioning is not *essentially* different from machines which might be designed or made by men. To deny that animals are machines is, it would appear, to suppose that they *are* essentially different. Those who take the former view feel that existing or possible machines performing similar functions may provide clues as to how animals work, and in particular how their central nervous systems are organised. Those who hold that animals are not machines refuse to accept that this could ever give the whole story. Both types of biologist might well agree that we should go as far as we can in looking for analogies, while being careful not to oversimplify or to accept similarities in a naïve manner.

The Use of Engineering Criteria for Deciding
Between Models of Brain Function

When a biologist or engineer considers what sort of system might be responsible for producing a given function, he may run up against one of two difficulties: (1) that there does not seem to be *any* known type of system capable of just the observed functions under the given conditions, or (2) that there is a *large number* of possible mechanisms, any of which might provide the required functions. We cannot say anything here about the first contingency, except of course that further observation, experiment or thought might suggest possible mechanisms, but we can say something about the second. It is worth thinking about this, for the principles available for deciding which of various alternative types of mechanism are appropriate are just the principles we need for verifying cybernetic hypotheses. Without such principles we can do no more than guess.

Consider an engineer in a position of doubt about how an unfamiliar machine works. We may take an actual example of a dramatic kind: consider the problem of discovering the manner of function of the control mechanism of an enemy's secret weapon, such as the V1 rockets during the last war. The engineer could make use of the following considerations. First, it was clear that the rocket had been made recently by men in Germany. This knowledge that they were man-made was clearly enormously important, though probably never explicitly stated. Martian rockets would offer many more alternatives, including the high probability of principles quite unknown to us. As it was, new principles were unlikely, though possible. Secondly, examination of rockets which failed to explode revealed many already familiar components such as motors, condensers, valves etc., and a great deal was already known about these. Thirdly, it would seem certain that the rockets must have been designed as efficiently as possible. Now how far does the biologist examining brain function share these assets?

(i) Since living organisms are not designed and made by men, any number of new principles might be expected, as in the imaginary case of Martian rockets. As an example, it is now believed that feed-back loops are important in organisms, but these were not known to the engineer until Clerk Maxwell's work in the last century, and there could always be further more or less fundamental principles involved which are so far unknown to engineers.

(ii) Examination of the brain reveals many identifiable "components," such as Betz cells and amacrine cells, but the functional properties and circuit potentialities of cells are not as well understood as the functional properties of electronic or mechanical components—and even these have their surprises.

(iii) Efficiency is a difficult criterion to apply to biological systems for a logical reason: it cannot be assessed without some idea of purpose. It is, however, important to note that the notion of efficiency (and also that of purpose) does not imply specific design for a known end. Thus it might be said that a screw-driver makes a good paint scraper, though it was not designed for that purpose. For something to be said to be efficient, it must be efficient for a stated end though not necessarily for a designed end. Thus if it said that some postulated brain mechanism is more efficient than some other mechanism, we must know what end these mechanisms are supposed to serve, and we must know how to assess relative efficiency towards this end. We may ask, for example, "how efficient is the eye?" and its efficiency may be measured. Thus its acuity and its sensitivity may be measured and expressed in appropriate units. The difficulty arises when we do not know what to measure through not knowing the functional significance of the structure or system involved. Clearly we could not talk about the efficiency of the eye if we did not know that it subserved vision. If a system is found to be highly efficient, in general but few possibilities are left open when it comes to guessing how it works—not many engineering tricks would be good enough.

When an engineer talks about efficiency he may mean a number of things; he may simply mean that it works well, or that its fuel consumption is low, or that the capital or running cost is low, or a number of other things. If the biologist is to make a reasonable guess at which type of mechanism is responsible for a given type of function, and he wants to use efficiency criteria, he must be clear which criteria it is appropriate to take over, and this raises a number of difficulties.

Localisation of Cerebral Function *

What is meant by saying that some feature of behaviour is localised in a part of the brain? It cannot mean that the behaviour itself is to be found in the brain, or that a region of the brain can be sufficient for any behaviour. The intended meaning is that some necessary, though not sufficient, condition for this behaviour is localised in a specific region of the brain.

The evidence for localisation is mainly from studies of ablation and stimulation of regions of the brain. If, for example, when a point on the occipital cortex is stimulated, flashes of light are reported by the patient, it is generally held that this region of the cortex must be important for vision. If an area in the left frontal lobe is damaged and speech is found to be disturbed, it may seem that we have found something causally necessary for speech. But have we?

This area may be *necessary* for speech (i.e. if it is removed, speech may disappear) but so also are a number of other parts of the organism, for example the vocal cords, the lungs and the mouth. There is nothing special about the brain here. It may be that the "speech area" is concerned only with speech, but if so it is not unique in this respect either: if we except coughing, the vocal cords have no other function but to subserve vocalisation. Now we may say that the vocal cords are *causally necessary* for speech, and also that the "speech area" is somehow *causally necessary,* but it is not clear in the second case just what the causal functions are, though we do understand the causal role of the vocal cords. There is an important point here: we may say that A is the cause of B if A is found inductively to be a necessary condition for B, and the evidence may be purely inductive for this type of causal argument. No understanding of the mechanisms involved is required to assert the causal relation between A and B. But we may also say that A causes B on *deductive* grounds, when we understand (or think we understand) the mechanism by which A produces, or causes, B.

Once we distinguish these two types of argument from physical structure and function to causal relationship, we should ask which sort of causal argument is being used in discussions about brain function. Take the case of the speech area. It would appear that the reason why this region of the brain is held to be associated with speech is that speech is found to be defective or absent when the region is damaged. This is clearly an inductive argument, and it does not presuppose or imply any knowledge of how the speech area works, or what causal part it plays in the production of speech. Again, we know fairly clearly the causal role of the vocal cords, but not that of the "speech area."

Consider now the word "function." We may say that it is the *function* of the vocal cords to vibrate in certain ways, producing pulses of air which resonate in cavities . . . we see the causal role of the vocal cords and we

* I would like to express my gratitude to Mr. A. J. Watson and Professor O. L. Zangwill for their help in discussion of this section.

come to understand the mechanism of speech production. And now what about the word "localisation"? What is it to say that a *function is localised*? The question is: How can we say that a function is localised until we know what the function (of a given bit of brain tissue) is? To say this we need to know in some detail how the system works. It seems that before we can talk usefully about localisation of function we must have some idea of *how* the system works.

Ablation and Stimulation as Techniques for Discovering Functional Regions of the Brain

Suppose we ablated or stimulated various parts of a complex man-made device, say a television receiving set. And suppose we had no prior knowledge of the manner of function of the type of device or machine involved. Could we by these means discover its manner of working?

In the first place, and most important, to remove a part of a machine, even a discrete component, is not in general to remove a necessary condition for some feature of the output. If a part is removed from a complex machine, we do not in general find that simple elements or units are now missing from the output. It should be noted here that the functional processes taking place in the components, or groups of components, of a machine are generally quite different from anything in the output. Thus we do not see the spark in a car engine represented in its output—we see wheels turning and the car moving: no spark. If a component is removed almost anything may happen: a radio set may emit piercing whistles or deep growls, a television set may produce curious patterns, a car engine may back-fire, or blow up or simply stop. To understand the *reason* for these "behavioural" changes we must know at least the basic principles of radio, or television, or car engines, or whatever it is, and also some of the details of the particular design. Of course, if we already know about radio, or engines, then these abnormal manifestations may well lead to correct diagnosis of a fault: the difficulty is to reverse the procedure.

Consider a television set which has, of course, two quite distinct outputs—sound and vision. Some "ablations," or "extirpations," may quickly reveal which parts are *necessary* for each output, and also which parts are *common* to the two outputs. In the case of the brain, there is a large number of inputs and outputs: the limb movements, the face with its various expressions, the voice, and so on. It may be a fairly simple matter to discover regions of the brain which are necessary for these various outputs, and in general they will lie near the peripheral output of the system. The inputs, the senses and their projection areas, we might also expect to locate in this way without undue difficulty. What I suspect *is* difficult, indeed impossible, is to locate functional regions of the system. It seems to me that this conclusion is forced upon us by considering the possibility of isolating elements of a complex output in a single channel in the case of man-made machines. In a serial system the various identifiable elements of the output are not separately represented by discrete parts of the system. Damage to a part may indeed introduce quite new factors into the situation, and these could only be comprehensible when we are provided with a model indicating the function of the parts. If the brain consisted of a series of independent parallel elements with separate output terminals for each, like a piano, it might be possible to identify behavioural elements with particular parts of the system, as the various notes of the piano might be regarded as being "localised" in the piano; but where output is the result of a number of causally necessary operations taking place in a series, then this is not possible. The removal, or the activation, of a single stage in a series might have almost any effect on the output of a machine, and so presumably also for the brain. To deduce the function of a part from the effect upon the output of removing or stimulating this part we must know at least in general terms how the machine works. The point here, perhaps, is not so much that the piano is a parallel rather than a serial system, but that it is a set of largely independent machines in one box. Where they do interact, as in the pedal systems, then one "ablation" may affect all the notes. Parts of the brain could be independent.

The effects of removing or modifying, say, the line scan time-base of a television receiver would be incomprehensible if we did not know the engineering principles involved. Further, it seems unlikely that we should discover the necessary principles from scratch simply by pulling bits out of television sets, or stimulating bits with various voltages and wave forms. The data derived in this way might well lead to hypotheses once we knew something of the problem in engineering terms.

But we should, in some systems, be able to map projection areas and delimit pathways, and this is a good deal. Analogy with familiar physical systems strongly suggests that to go further these studies should be used to test rival hypotheses of brain function, rather than to attempt to isolate functional regions. This brings us back to the idea of physical model explanations, with ablation and stimulation studies as one way of trying to decide between rival models. We are left with the difficulties besetting this approach: in particular, the brain might work on some novel principle, and then its true manner of function would never come up for testing by any experimental technique. It would clearly require a most highly sophisticated set of techniques to discover a quite new principle in the living brain, but this is conceivable. Perhaps the principle of scanning, or heterodyning, could be discovered by these techniques, even in a jelly.

It is a common finding that with electronic equipment several very different faults may produce much the same "symptom." For example, anything which produces a change in the supply voltage will first affect the part of the system most susceptible to supply changes, and so anything affecting the supply will tend to produce the same fault. To aggravate the position, faults affecting the supply voltage are not limited to the power pack supplying the voltage to the various parts of the system, but may be in any of these parts, increasing or decreasing the load and so affecting all the other parts in greater or lesser degree. Thus the removal of any several widely spaced resistors may cause a radio set to emit howls, but it does not follow that howls are immediately associated with these resistors, or indeed that the causal relation is anything but the most indirect. In particular, we should not say that the function of the resistors in the normal circuit is to inhibit howling. Neurophysiologists, when faced with a comparable situation, have postulated "suppressor regions."

Although the effect of a particular type of ablation may be specific and repeatable, it does not follow that the causal connection is simple, or even that the region of the brain affected would, if we knew more, be regarded as functionally important for the output—such as memory or speech—which is observed to be upset. It could be the case that some important part of the mechanism subserving the behaviour is upset by the damage although it is most indirectly related, and it is just this which makes the discovery of a fault in a complex machine so difficult.

We may consider one or two further points. Since learning is important in at least the mammalian nervous system, it is clear that where animals and men have had different past experiences their brains are likely to be in some ways different. What is "stored" must at any rate vary between individuals of the same species. It is known that for man surgical removal of some areas of the brain, e.g. the frontal lobe, may pass almost unnoticed in some individuals, while in others it produces serious defect of function. This might perhaps be due to the different importance of specific causal mechanisms in individuals employing different "strategies," or possibly to the unequal importance of various pieces of stored information. In any case we should expect, and do in fact find, individual differences. This is a complicating factor in interpreting ablation studies which would hardly concern an engineer using man-made machines, except indeed for certain electronic computers.

A further point that might be made is this: Suppose we ablate or stimulate some part of the brain, and lose or evoke something in behaviour, then it is not clear—even quite apart from previous considerations—that this region is the seat of the behaviour in question. Might it not lie along a "trunk line" or "association pathway"? A cut telephone line might affect communication over a wide area, principally behind the region of damage. This has at least two important implications: first, unless the region is known not to lie on a "cable" the region cannot be identified with a brain "centre" responsible for some aspect of behaviour, since the "centre" responsible but cut off might lie anywhere from this region along the trunk line. This is further complicated by the consideration that it might be cut off in some conditions but not in others: it might conceivably depend upon whether the animal is motivated in a particular way, receiving information from a particular "store," or countless other possibilities, whether this block will matter; and the same is true of damage to, or stimulation of, a "centre," even if this word is taken as meaningful. In many machines it might be possible to remove large parts without any effect except under certain working conditions.

There are two points here: (1) damage might produce, so to say, a shadow within which brain function is lost to regions of the brain on the "other side" of the damage. If the better analogy is a short-circuited power line, the effect may extend both ways along the cable. (2) The damage may be important only under certain critical circumstances. It does not matter that a car's trafficators are not functional until the driver wishes to turn a corner in traffic—or that his brakes do not work until he tries to stop.

This view of what we mean by "function" is important in considering brain "centres." These are supposed loci for particular types of behaviour: thus Hess has a "sleep centre" for the cat, in the hypothalamus. This idea of "centres" has been taken over by Ethology and is particularly important in Timbergen's writings. But we may well feel worried about the concept of functional centres when we do not know what is going on, in functional terms, in the region concerned. The above considerations apply here *mutatis mutandis*. Why, if stimulation of a given region produces sleep, should this region be regarded as a "sleep centre"? To take a facetious example: if a bang on the back of the head produces stars and a headache, is this a "centre" for stars and headaches?

In summary: (1) it might be argued that "localisation of function" means that some feature of behaviour has certain vital (but not sufficient) causal mechanisms located in a given region of the brain. But before we know how, in general terms, the brain works we cannot say what these supposed causal mechanisms are, and thus it is very difficult to say what we mean by "localisation of function."

(2) Stimulation and ablation experiments may give direct information about pathways and projection areas, but their interpretation would seem to be extremely difficult, on logical grounds, where a mechanism is one of many inter-related systems, for then changes in the output will not in general be simply the loss of the contribution normally made by the extirpated area. The system may now show quite different properties.

(3) It would seem that ablation and stimulation data can only be interpreted given a model, or a "block diagram," showing the functional organisation of the brain in causal, or engineering, terms. Such data may be useful in suggesting or testing possible theoretical models.

(4) These models are explanations in the engineering sense of "explanation."

Conclusion

It would be nice to say something more constructive about the use of engineering thinking in biology. Given that there are certain difficulties in taking over engineering ideas of design into biology, can we not still use engineering techniques and devices to make some better-than-random guesses about how the brain works?

We have throughout looked at the brain as an engineering problem in a general way: we have not considered any particular engineering techniques, or mechanisms, or machines which might throw light on biological function. We have mentioned radio sets and car engines when thinking about localisation of brain function, yet it is at least clear that brains are very different from these. We could certainly think of machines more like brains—and this might be worth doing. What about computers? Obviously we should expect more similarities between computers and brains than between car engines and brains, for the inputs and outputs are similar for the one though not for the other. Now we might go further and ask: what *sort* of computer is most like the brain? There are many different types of practical computer. As is well known, they are divided into two main classes: analogue and digital. Each has certain advantages. The former are usually simpler in construction, they are fast, and are generally subject to rather large random errors. The best-known example is the slide rule. Their inputs and outputs are usually continuously variable, though this is not always so: a slide rule might be made with click stops and still be called analogue. The essential point is that the input variables are represented by the magnitude of some physical variable, such as a length or a voltage. Digital computers, on the other hand, are generally slower, and their answers tend to be either correct or wildly wrong. They work in discrete steps, and according to some fixed rules or calculus. The functional units (essentially switches) of a digital computer take up certain discrete semi-stable states according to a code. For some purposes the analogue type would be chosen by the engineer, and for others the digital type. Thus we may now ask: which would be the most suitable type of computer for a brain, an analogue or a digital computer? Or perhaps a mixture? To answer this question we may make a list of the relevant properties of the brain and try to decide which type of computer fits best (Gregory, 1953). Some of the difficulties we anticipated at the beginning: we found that engineering criteria are not easy to apply, and that some are indeed inappropriate. The basic efficiency criteria evidently may be applied, but they have their difficulties unless we know a good deal about the functional properties and efficiencies of the components of the brain. Thus it is not possible, for example, to say whether the brain works too fast to be a digital computer unless we know the rate at which the components can change their states, or count. If we also knew the minimum number of steps logically required to reach a given solution with the available data it would be possible to say whether the brain *could* work digitally.

Similar considerations apply to testing the hypothesis that the brain is an analogue machine. We may ask: is the brain too accurate for an analogue machine? We cannot answer this until we know how the "templates" representing the variables work; we need to know more about the actual ironmongery available; "ideal" considerations are not adequate here, we must know the properties of the components. If we invoke feed-back principles the brain might be an analogue device given rather variable templates—there are many such "saving" possibilities. In fact this view that the brain is in essential respects analogue is perhaps borne out by the type of errors observed in control situations. The point is that engineering here supplies the hypotheses for testing, and also (up to a point) the manner of testing them, but to make these decisions it is important to know in detail the functional limitations of the components of the brain. It is also important to have "engineering" performance data. Much experimental work in psychology is in fact undertaken for this purpose. It may well be vital for linking psychology with neurology, and we should use engineering concepts both to suggest appropriate experiments and to integrate and interpret the available data. For example, studies on tremor take on a new significance within the context of servo-theory, for all error-correcting servos are subject to "hunting."

A rather different approach, which we might do well to adopt, is the following: We might look for what we are virtually certain to find and then measure it. Two, rather different, examples must suffice. First, we believe that a system cannot itself gain knowledge without inductive generalisation, and we know that this is impossible without probability estimates. This involves some form of counting, and some form of store for count rates or relative count rates. This at once suggests that the brain should be looked at as in part an inductive machine e.g. (Gregory, 1952). It is probable that no one had actually built an inductive machine until Uttley (1954a and b) built his, specifically as a possible model of brain function, but the man-made induction machine follows standard engineering principles. To go to the next stage and ask whether the brain is the *same sort* of induction machine as Uttley's raises all sorts of difficulties, some of which we have already discussed. The point here is that we believe on *very general grounds* that probabilities must be important to achieve adapted behaviour, and so induction and probability mechanisms really must be found if we look for them.

The second example of this approach is the interesting though more specific problem of "noise" in the nervous system. It is well known that all communication systems are ultimately limited by random noise, which tends to cause confusion between signals. It seems impossible that the nervous system can be an exception, and so it is hardly a discovery that there is "noise" in nerve fibres, and in the brain. The assessment of the actual "noise" level in the various parts of the nervous system (Gregory and Cane, 1955; Gregory, 1956; Barlow, 1956, 1957) and of changes in "noise" level due to ageing or brain damage (Gregory, 1958) may throw some light on neural function, if only by helping us to apply efficiency criteria to test between rival explanatory models. It is interesting in this connection that Granit (1955) has recently summarized the evidence for random firing of the optic nerve but has not interpreted this as a background "noise" level against which visual signals must be discriminated, but rather regards it as necessary for keeping the higher centres active. Thus the same observation might be regarded as a necessary evil or a special and useful part of the mechanism. Here the very general properties of communication systems would lead us to the former interpretation, but without these general considerations there would have been no reason to suppose that random firing is not useful to the organism and, so to speak, part of the design. Given the engineering viewpoint, we should ask how the system is designed to *minimise* the effect of the background noise, and this is quite a different sort of question, leading to quite different experiments.

Information rates and noise levels will not in themselves tell us how the ear or the eye gives us useful information—how they work—but such measures are in conformity with the engineer's insistence upon knowing the performance limits, and the reasons for the limits, of his systems. Experimental psychology is currently, and for practical reasons, concerned with the limits of human ability in many directions, e.g. in steering and guiding. These measures may be vital in deciding how the guiding or steering is done. In many cases it is only limits, such as sensory thresholds, which can be used to provide "engineering" data from complex organisms. Now this idea of looking for properties which are found in all, or at least in most, engineering control systems, and then obtaining quantitative measurements of them under various operating conditions is rather different from the idea of thinking of a physical model as a possible "analogy" to a behavior mechanism and then testing this model with observation or experiment. Before we attempt seriously to test specific models of brain function—types of memory store and the like—we might do well to make careful estimates of such things as neural "noise" levels which we are virtually certain must be there to be found. Having done this, we may be in a stronger position to test specific hypotheses, for we should be able to apply engineering criteria with sufficient rigour to make some hypotheses highly improbable, while others might be shown to be quite possibly true.

These considerations have some relevance to the progress of experimental psychology. If we have no idea of the sort of system we are dealing with, controlled experiment becomes impossible, for we cannot know what to control. On the other hand, a too fixed and particular model tends to blinker the mental eye, making us blind to surprising results and ideas without which advance is impossible.

References

1. Kant (1790). *Kritik der Urtheilskraft.*
2. E. S. Russell (1946). *The Directiveness of Organic Activities* (Cambridge).
3. W. Köhler (1920). Physical Gestalten in *Source Book of Gestalt Psychology* (ed., London, W. E. Ellis, 1938) translation of Die physischen Gestalten in *Ruhe und im stationaren Zustand, Eine naturphilosophische Untersuchung,* Erlangen).
4. E. H. Madden (1957). A logical analysis of "Psychological Isomorphism." *Brit. J. Philo. Sci.,* **8,** 177–91.

5. R. L. Gregory (1953). Physical model explanations in psychology. *Brit. J. Philo. Sci.,* **4,** 192–97.
6. D. M. Mackay and W. S. McCullock (1952). The limiting capacity of a neuronal link. *Bull. Math. Biophysics,* **14,** 127–35.
7. R. Gregory and V. Cane (1955). Noise and the visual threshold. *Nature,* **176,** 1272.
8. R. L. Gregory (1956). An experimental treatment of vision as an information and noisy channel. *Third Lond. Information Symposium.* Ed. Cherry, London.
9. H. B. Barlow (1956). Retinal noise and absolute threshold. *J. Opt. Soc. Amer.,* **46,** 634–39.
10. H. B. Barlow (1957). Increment thresholds at low intensities considered as signal/noise discrimination. *J. Physiol.,* **136,** 469–88.
11. R. L. Gregory (1958). Increase in neurological noise as a factor in ageing. In *Proceedings of Fourth International Gerontological Congress.*
12. R. Granit (1955). *Receptors and Sensory Perception.* New Haven.

In Search of the Engram

K. S. LASHLEY

Reprinted from *Society of Experimental Biology Symposium No. 4: Physiological Mechanisms in Animal Behaviour* (Cambridge University Press), 1950, pp. 454–482. By permission of The Company and Biologists Limited. From Harvard University and the Yerkes Laboratories of Primate Biology.

When the mind wills to recall something, this volition causes the little [pineal] gland, by inclining successively to different sides, to impel the animal spirits toward different parts of the brain, until they come upon that part where the traces are left of the thing which it wishes to remember; for these traces are nothing else than the circumstance that the pores of the brain through which the spirits have already taken their course on presentation of the object, have thereby acquired a greater facility than the rest to be opened again the same way by the spirits which come to them; so that these spirits coming upon the pores enter therein more readily than into the others.

So wrote Descartes just three hundred years ago in perhaps the earliest attempt to explain memory in terms of the action of the brain. In the intervening centuries much has been learned concerning the nature of the impulses transmitted by nerves. Innumerable studies have defined conditions under which learning is facilitated or retarded, but, in spite of such progress, we seem little nearer to an understanding of the nature of the memory trace than was Descartes. His theory has in fact a remarkably modern sound. Substitute nerve impulse for animal spirits, synapse for pore and the result is the doctrine of learning as change in resistance of synapses. There is even a theory of scanning which is at least more definite as to the scanning agent and the source of the scanning beam than is its modern counterpart.

As interest developed in the functions of the brain the doctrine of the separate localization of mental functions gradually took form, even while the ventricles of the brain were still regarded as the active part. From Prochaska and Gall through the nineteenth century, students of clinical neurology sought the localization of specific memories. Flechsig defined the association areas as distinct from the sensory and motor. Aphasia, agnosia, and apraxia were interpreted as the result of the loss of memory images, either of objects or of kinesthetic sensations of movements to be made. The theory that memory traces are stored in association areas adjacent to the corresponding primary sensory areas seemed reasonable and was supported by some clinical evidence. The extreme position was that of Henschen, who speculated concerning the location of single ideas or memories in single cells. In spite of the fact that more critical analytic studies of clinical symptoms, such as those of Henry Head and of Kurt Goldstein, have shown that aphasia and agnosia are primarily defects in the organization of ideas rather than the result of amnesia, the conception of the localized storing of memories is still widely prevalent (52).

While clinical students were developing theories of localization, physiologists were analysing the reflex arc and extending the concept of the reflex to include all activity. Bechterew, Pavlov and the behaviourist school in America attempted to reduce all psychological activity to simple associations or chains of conditioned reflexes. The path of these conditioned reflex circuits was described as from sense organ to cerebral sensory area, thence through associative areas to the motor cortex and by way of the pyramidal paths to the final motor cells of the medulla and cord. The discussions of this path were entirely theoretical, and no evidence on the actual course of the conditioned reflex arc was presented.

In experiments extending over the past 30 years I have been trying to trace conditioned reflex paths through the brain or to find the locus of specific memory traces. The results for different types of learning have been inconsistent and often mutually contradictory, in spite of confirmation by repeated tests. I shall summarize today a number of experimental findings. Perhaps they obscure rather than illuminate the nature of the engram, but they may serve at least to illustrate the complexity of the problem and to reveal the superficial nature of many of the physiological theories of memory that have been proposed.

I shall have occasion to refer to training of animals in a variety of tasks, so shall give a very brief description of the methods used. The animals studied have been rats and monkeys with, recently, a few chimpanzees. Two lines of approach to the problem have been followed. One is purely behavioural and consists in the analysis of the sensory excitations which are actually associated with reactions in learning and which are effective in eliciting the learned reactions. The associated reactions are similarly analysed. These studies define the patterns of nervous activity at receptor and effector levels and specify certain characteristics which the memory trace must have. The second approach is by surgical destruction of parts of the brain. Animals are trained in various tasks ranging from direct sensory-motor associations to the solution of difficult problems. Before or after training, associative tracts are cut or portions of the brain removed and effects of these operations on initial learning or postoperative retention are measured. At the termination of the experiments the brains are sectioned and the extent of damage reconstructed from serial sections. The brains are also analysed for secondary degeneration, so far as available histological methods permit.

Elimination of the Motor Cortex

I first became sceptical of the supposed path of the conditioned reflex when I found that rats, trained in a differential reaction to light, showed no reduction in accuracy of performance when almost the entire motor cortex, along with the frontal poles of the brain, was removed. This observation led to a series of experiments designed to test the part played by the motor cortex or Betz cell area in the retention of various habits. The matter can be tested either by removing the motor cortex or by severing its connexions with the sensory areas of the brain. Both methods have been used with the rat and the monkey.

The sensory and motor areas of the brains of these animals have been mapped by anatomic methods and by electric stimulation. Figure 1 shows the principal areas of the rat's brain, the separate auditory and visual areas and the overlapping sensory and motor areas. Figure 2 is a composite from several sources of the chief sensory and motor areas of the brain of the macaque monkey.

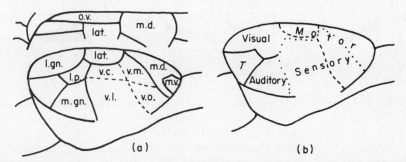

(a)   (b)

FIGURE 1. Functional divisions of the rat's brain. (*a*) The projection fields of the principal thalamic nuclei: av., anteroventral; lat., lateral; l.gn., lateral geniculate; l.p., lateral, pars posterior; m.d., median dorsal; m.gn., median geniculate; m.v., median ventral; v., the various divisions of the central nucleus. The projection fields of the median nuclei (m.d., m.v.) correspond to the prefrontal areas of primates. (*b*) Location of visual, auditory, and overlapping sensory-motor areas. (*After Lashley,* (44).) The region marked *T* is probably homologous with the temporal association area of primates.

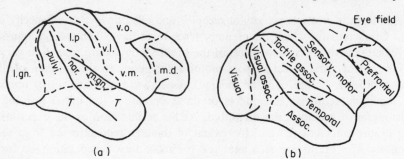

FIGURE 2. Functional divisions of the monkey's brain. (a) The projection of the principal thalamic nuclei. Abbreviations as in Figure 1. The homologies between the divisions of the central and lateral nuclei are uncertain. (b) Location of functional areas.

Incisions were made through the cortex and underlying fibres of the rat's brain such as to sever the visual areas more or less completely from the motor regions of the brain. The rats were then trained in what I have called the conditional reaction. They are taught to jump to a white triangle and to avoid a white $\times$ when both figures are on a black background, but to choose the $\times$ and avoid the triangle if the background is striped; the direction of choice is conditional upon the character of the background. This is the most difficult visual generalization that we have been able to teach the rat. Animals with incisions like those shown in Figure 3, which practically separate the motor regions from the visual, were able to learn this reaction as quickly as did normal controls (42).

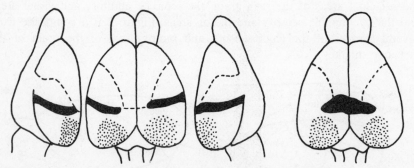

FIGURE 3. Lesions partially separating the visual area (stippled) from the motor areas (outlined by dashes) of the rat's brain without disturbing visual learning.

Monkeys were trained to open various latch boxes. The motor areas were then removed, as shown in Figure 4. Note that these lesions involved both the Betz cell area and the premotor area, including parts of the eye fields around the arcuate sulcus. This operation produces a temporary paralysis, but after 8 to 12 weeks this paralysis recovers to such an extent that the animals are capable of the movements required to open the boxes. During this recovery period they did not have access to the training boxes. When

FIGURE 4. Extent of cortical lesion which did not abolish latchbox habits. The lesion is bounded caudally by the central fissure and extends forward to include the arcuate sulcus.

sufficiently recovered, they were tested and opened the boxes promptly without random exploratory movements. The tasks require both visual recognition of the latches and semiskilled movements, such as turning a crank. Removal of the motor areas did not produce a loss of memory for the movements (33). Jacobsen has since confirmed these observations with a chimpanzee from which the motor cortex was removed (24).

These experiments seem to rule out the motor cortex or Betz cell area as containing any part of the conditioned-reflex arc. The traditional view of the function of this area regards it as the region of final integration of skilled voluntary movements. My own interpretation, to which few neurologists would subscribe, is that it has no direct concern with voluntary movement, but is a part of the vast reflex postural system which includes the basal nuclei, cerebellar and vestibular systems. Certainly there is no evidence that it forms a part of the conditioned reflex circuit.

For the rat the experiments rule out the whole frontal region of the brain from participation in visual habits. In the monkey there remains another possibility. The so-called visual associative area (area 18) has direct connexion with the cortex of the arcuate sulcus (area 8), and this in turn with the premotor cortex (area 6). This last area is also motor and perhaps equivalent in function with the Betz cell area (5). The cortex of the arcuate sulcus and of a considerable surrounding area was removed from five monkeys that had been trained in a variety of visual discriminative reactions. After the operations they showed perfect retention of all their visual habits (45). Jacobsen (24) has reported loss of certain latch-box habits in monkeys after removal of area 6, but there are indications that this may be a kinesthetic-sensory area (17, 57), and the loss cannot be ascribed to disturbance of its function as a final common motor path. I have removed it in combination with area 4 without disrupting motor habits (33).

I have occasionally seen the type of defect reported by Jacobsen after prefrontal lobe lesions, as also reported by Kennard (27), but it has not occurred consistently and its occurrence remains unexplained. I did not find it after removal of area 6 in conjunction with the Betz cell area.

Transcortical Conduction

There is evidence, not only that the motor cortex does not participate in the transmission of the conditioned-reflex pattern, but also that the transmission of impulses over well-defined, isolated paths from one part of the cortex to another is inessential for performance of complicated habits. The maze habit of the rat almost certainly involves the utilization of several sensory modalities, visual, tactile and kinesthetic. In a rather complicated set of experiments I attempted to test the importance of connexions across the cortex for maze performance. Rats were trained on the maze, then knife cuts were made through the cortex and underlying fibres, separating different functional areas or cutting through functional areas. The incisions were long, averaging half of the entire length of the cerebral hemispheres. After recovery the animals were tested in retention of the maze habit. In other experiments the incisions were made before training and their effect upon the rate of initial learning was tested. In neither initial learning nor in retention could any certain effect of separating the various parts of the cortex be demonstrated. If the incisions interrupted sensory tracts to the cortex, there was loss of the habit, but uncomplicated separation of cortical areas produced no effect on performance.

Both the anatomic evidence of Le Gros Clark (7) and the physiological evidence from strychninization of the cortex (4) shows that the primary visual area has direct axon connexions only with the immediately adjacent cortex. In experiments which I shall report in more detail in considering the function of associative areas, I removed the greater part of this band of cortex surrounding the visual areas from five monkeys that had been trained in a variety of visual habits (Fig. 5). This operation almost certainly destroyed all the relay connexions across the cortex from the macular fields. It produced no loss of visual habits based on discrimination of the colour, brightness, or form of objects (45).

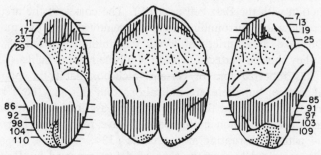

FIGURE 5. Lesions, marked by hatching, which destroyed the greater part of the so-called visual associative areas in a monkey without affecting visual functions.

Miss Wade trained monkeys in habits which are abolished by destruction of the frontal lobes and which require visual, tactile and kinesthetic adjustments. I cut the transcortical fibres of the frontal lobes in these animals, leaving only the projection fibres for the area. There was no disturbance of performance after the operations (unpublished experiments).

Such results are certainly puzzling. They leave us with almost no understanding of the function of the associative fibres which extend across from one part of the cortex to another. The results are difficult to accept, yet they are supported by various other lines of evidence. Smith (54) and Akelaitis (1) have reported careful studies of human patients in whom the corpus callosum (the great commissure of fibres connecting the two hemispheres) had been severed in an effort to stop the spread of Jacksonian epilepsy. These investigators were not able to demonstrate any effects of the operation except a slight slowing of reaction time, which was equally great, whether the reaction was on the same or opposite side of the body to that stimulated. Sperry (55) has divided the arm motor and sensory areas of the monkey's brain into a number of small square divisions (Fig. 6) by careful subpial section. Although the operations were intended to sever only the intrinsic fibres of the cortex, they actually destroyed most of the longer loop fibres as well. Such animals do not show any postoperative incoordination of the movements of the different segments of the arm and use the arm efficiently in the performance of habitual movements.

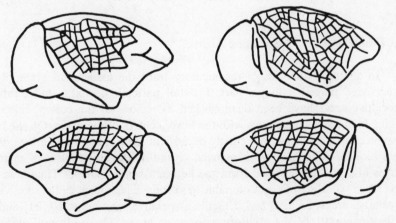

FIGURE 6. Pattern of incisions in the motor and sensory areas of two monkeys which did not produce incoordination movements. (*After Sperry* (55).)

It is difficult to interpret such findings, but I think that they point to the conclusion that the associative connexions or memory traces of the conditioned reflex do not extend across the cortex as well-defined arcs or paths. Such arcs are either diffused through all parts of the cortex, pass by relay through lower centres, or do not exist.

There is the possibility that the chief associative connexions between functional areas of the cortex are by connexions through the thalamus. I doubt this for two reasons. The techniques that have been used to demonstrate cortical efferents to the thalamus, the Marchi stain and strychninization of the cortex, are unreliable indices of the direction of fibres. The supposed cortico-thalamic fibres follow the paths of the afferent fibres and may not be efferent. Secondly, in the rat at least there is little evidence of an elaborate system of intrathalamic association fibres. After a cortical injury thalamic nuclei degenerate completely without leaving a residue of internuncial cells. The question of the importance of intrathalamic association is not settled, and none of the available anatomic or physiological techniques is capable of giving conclusive evidence.

A few experiments by Ingebritsen (23) on the spinal cord suggest that the essential pattern of a learned reaction can be transmitted by a diffuse nervous network. Ingebritsen made double hemisections of the spinal cord of rats, severing one half at the second, the other at the fifth cervical level. These lesions cut all long fibres connecting the brain with the spinal motor centres of the limbs. Nevertheless, such rats retained maze habits and were able to learn to operate latch boxes requiring that they rise on the hindfeet and depress a lever with the forepaws. . . . There are no long fibres, either sensory or motor, crossing over between the two levels of these sections. Habit patterns cannot be acquired by the isolated spinal cord (26). Somehow, the control of the motor pattern essential for the performance of the complex acts traverses the network of short internuncial cells of the spinal cord.

The Problem of the "Association Areas"

In anatomic theories of the memory trace the association areas of the cortex have played a major part. Frontal, parietal, occipital and temporal associative areas have been distinguished as regions of the cortex, relatively lacking in massive connexions with the lower centres of the brain. On the basis of some clinical evidence, but chiefly because of their anatomic relations, these areas have been considered as associative and as the storehouses of memory images of sensations derived from the adjacent sensory areas. Thus areas 18 and 19 of Brodmann's questionable divisions have been called the visual associative areas, areas 5 and 7 tactile associative, and areas 20, 21, and 22 of the temporal lobe the auditory association areas. The prefrontal area was considered by Hitzig to be a higher integrative region because he believed that it showed the greatest evolutionary growth in the primate brain. Special memory functions were also ascribed to it, however.

S. I. Franz reported that the removal of the frontal association areas of cats destroyed recently formed habits but left old, well-established habits unaffected (15). The actual observation was that the cats lost their habits of opening latch boxes but would still come when called. His operations destroyed much of the motor areas as well as the prefrontal cortex. I later trained monkeys on latch boxes and removed the prefrontal cortex, in an experiment designed to test the influence of the operation on learning ability. During the period allowed for recovery one of the animals found the experimental boxes piled in the corner of the room and promptly opened them. Test of the other animals showed perfect retention of the manipulative habits. There was no indication that the recently acquired habits had been lost. Jacobsen took up the problem at this point and carried it further. He found that visual discriminative habits and simple habits of latch-box manipulation are unaffected by loss of the prefrontal association areas. Habits requiring a series of acts, such as opening a box with several independent latches, may be lost. This is not, however, a simple removal of memory traces. The animals are incapable of relearning the functions which they have lost. They fail because of a difficulty in going on from one task to the next, not from loss of memory of the individual items of the task (25).

Loss of the delayed reaction after removal of the prefrontal lobes of the monkey has been interpreted as a loss of immediate memory. However, this task and others, which are affected by prefrontal injury, all involve a series of conflicting actions. Difficulty in maintaining a constant set or attitude is the real basis of the loss. Such an interpretation fits better with clinical findings than does the hypothesis of memory defect.

We have recently been testing the relation of other associative areas to memory functions in the monkey. Five spider monkeys were trained on a variety of visual tasks. A band of cortex surrounding the primary visual areas and including the visual associative areas of Campbell and Brodmann was then removed (Fig. 6), and the animals were tested for retention of habits based on discrimination of colours, of geometric forms, and of a number of familiar objects, such as visual recognition of their home cages, of the caretaker, and the like. No loss of any visual memories could be demonstrated (45).

Similar experiments with habits of tactile discrimination are now being completed. The monkeys are required to reach through a hole in a partition and to distinguish variously shaped covers of food dishes by touch alone. They learn readily such tasks as to choose a cylinder and reject a prism, if both are smooth, but to choose the prism, if both are coated with sandpaper. When they had reached a standard criterion of accuracy, the parietal associative areas (Brodmann's areas 5 and 7) were removed. No animal has shown significant loss of the habits based on tactile discrimination after removal of these areas alone (Dr. Josephine Blum).

Removal of the lateral surfaces of the temporal lobes alone has also not affected visual or tactile habits.

A number of experiments with the rat have shown that habits of visual discrimination survive the destruction of any part of the cerebral cortex except the primary visual projection area. Similarly for auditory habits and the auditory cortex. There is no indication of specialized memory areas outside the primary sensory fields. Although there are not clearly distinguished associative areas in the rat's cortex, I have become somewhat sceptical of the existence of any great difference in the extent of associative areas, as between the rat and monkey. The best anatomic index that we have of the functional differentiation of a cortical area is its connexions with the thalamus. The prefrontal cortex of man is the projection field of the dorsomedial and ventromedial nuclei. The corresponding nuclei in the rat's thalamus project to a large frontal region, perhaps proportionately as large as the prefrontal lobes of man (40). This region also includes the electrically excitable points for the head and part of that for the forelegs. It has therefore been classed as motor, but it is equally justifiable to class it as corresponding to the human prefrontal cortex.

It has been claimed that the differentiation of a number of cerebral areas contributes to man's superior intelligence by avoiding confusion of functions, but, if the anatomic relations in man and the rat were reversed, it would be concluded with equal assurance that, because intellectual activity requires close integration of different functions, the advantage lies with the brain in which functional areas are not sharply set off. Such *post hoc* arguments based on anatomic grounds alone have little value for functional interpretations. Many current conceptions of cerebral physiology are based upon just such dubious inferences from anatomic data.

The outcome of the experiments involving removal of the associative areas of the monkey was unexpected, in spite of the fact that it confirms the earlier results with the rat. The conclusion, which seems to be forced by the accumulated data, runs counter to the accepted tradition concerning the organization of the cerebral cortex. Memory traces, at least of simple sensory-motor associations, are not laid down and stored within the associative areas; at least not within the restricted associative area supposedly concerned with each sense modality. Memory disturbances of simple sensory habits follow only upon very extensive experimental destruction, including almost the entire associative cortex. Even combined destruction of the prefrontal, parietal, occipital and temporal areas, exclusive of the primary sensory cortex, does not prevent the animal from forming such habits, although preexisting habits are lost and their re-formation is greatly retarded.

These results, showing that the so-called associative areas are not essential to preservation of memory traces, have been obtained with rats and monkeys. Is there a greater cortical differentiation in anthropoid apes and man? We have experimental data only on the prefrontal associative cortex of the chimpanzee and of man. Bilateral removal of the entire prefrontal granular cortex in five chimpanzees in our laboratory has not resulted in any memory defect. One two-year-old animal, lacking prefrontal and parietal areas, removed in early infancy, falls well within the normal range in all aspects of development. Adult chimpanzees, trained in such complicated habits as choosing an object, like a model shown, retain the habits after removal of the entire prefrontal cortex. We have not been able to demonstrate loss of any memory or, in fact, of any function after such operations.

Clinical data, with amnesias following apparently small lesions, seem to contradict such experimental findings. However, lesions in the human brain are mostly the result either of tumor growth or of severe traumatism, both of which probably produce widespread changes in addition to the local injury. The surgical removal of parts of the frontal lobes in the recent topectomy studies has not produced such severe defects as usually result from traumatic destruction of the lobes (51).

The Role of Subcortical Structures

Perhaps we have been looking in the wrong place for the conditioned-reflex arcs or memory traces. Are they formed somewhere else than in the cortex? Experiments on the thalamus and other subcortical structures are technically difficult, and there is little direct evidence on this question. Since the classical experiments of Goltz a number of investigators have studied the capacity of the totally decorticate animal to learn. The outcome of these experiments is that such animals can form simple sensory-motor associations, although with extreme slowness in comparison with the rate of the normal animal (18, 53). We must ask, however, whether such learning occurs when the cortex is intact.

When the sensory or associative areas of the cerebral cortex are destroyed, the corresponding nuclei of the neo-thalamus degenerate, so this portion of the subcortex is eliminated from consideration by the same experiments which rule out the cortical association areas. The only experiments bearing upon the participation of other subcortical centres suggest that subcortical learning does not occur when the cortex is functioning.

Fischel (14) has maintained, solely from comparative psychological studies, that the basal ganglia are the seat of the space-coordinate elements of motor habits. I have destroyed the greater part of these structures in rats, trained in the discrimination box, without producing loss of orientation. The animals may perform forced circus movements but, in spite of this, they maintain their orientation in the problem box (31). The basal ganglia in man are subject to various degenerative diseases. The symptoms of such diseases are, in general, tremors and other disturbances of coordination at a primitive level, but without evidence of apraxia or other disorder of the learned patterns of motor coordination. The evidence seems conclusive that in mammals the basal nuclei are not an essential link in the patterning of learned activities.

It has been widely held that although memory traces are at first formed in the cerebral cortex, they are finally reduced or transferred by long practice to subcortical levels. The evidence for this has been the apparently greater fragility of recently formed habits than of old habits; the supposedly greater resistance of the latter to brain injuries. The amnesias following electroshock therapy indicate that it is the age of the trace and not the amount of practice that has built it up which determines its survival, and a difference of a few minutes in the age of memories may suffice to determine their loss or survival. This is scarcely evidence for reduction to lower levels of the nervous system.

The chief argument for the dropping out of memory traces from the cortex has seemingly run somewhat as follows: Consciousness is a function of the cerebral cortex; long-practised habits become automatic and are performed without conscious control; therefore they are no longer mediated by the cerebral cortex. Both premises of this syllogism are probably false, and the conclusion would not follow if they were true.

When rats are trained in a habit based upon the discrimination of intensities of light, to choose a brightly lighted alley and avoid a dimly lighted one, the removal of the striate cortex completely abolishes the habit. The animals are able to relearn the reaction and require as much practice as they did for initial learning. One group of animals was trained in this habit and given 1,200 trials of overtraining, daily practice for a period of 3 months. Their behaviour strongly suggested automatization of the habit. The striate areas were then removed. The habit was lost, just as in the case of animals which are operated as soon as they give evidence of the presence of the habit. The long overtraining did not eliminate the participation of the cortex (30).

This visual habit can be formed in the absence of the visual cortex, and the rates of learning with and without the visual area are exactly the same. The average for 100 normal animals is 125 trials; for nearly 100 without the visual areas it is 123 trials. After such animals, lacking the visual cortex, have learned the brightness reaction, any other part of the cerebral cortex may be destroyed without disturbing the habit. Apparently no other part of the cortex takes over the learning function (32). If, in addition to removal of the striate areas, the pretactile region of the thalamus and the optic tectum are destroyed, the animals cannot learn the discrimination reaction (37). These facts indicate that, in the absence of the visual cortex, the learning of the brightness reaction is carried out by the optic tectum. However, so long as the visual cortex is intact, removal of the tectum has no effect whatever upon the performance of visual habits. The tectum apparently does not participate in visual learning so long as the cortex is intact (37).

Dunlap (8) has advanced the hypothesis that complex serial habits, such as those of maze running, playing a musical passage, or speaking a sentence, are at first chains of sensory-motor reactions in which excitations from muscular contractions in one movement of the series serve as stimuli to elicit the next. He holds that, with continued practice, there is a short-circuiting of these conditioned reflex pathways through the cerebellum and that the peripheral elements drop out. McCarthy and I (47) attempted to test this hypothesis by training rats in the maze, removing the cerebellum, and testing for retention. The operations greatly disturbed the motor coordination of these animals. Some of them practically rolled through the maze, but they rolled without entering the blind alleys. There was no loss of memory of the sequence of turns in the maze.

These few experiments are, of course, by no means conclusive. They constitute, however, the only direct evidence available, and they definitely point to the conclusion that, if the cerebral cortex is intact, the associative connexions of simple conditioned reflexes are not formed in the subcortical structures of the brain.

The studies which I have reported thus far point to the conclusion that habits based upon visual discrimination are mediated by the striate areas, by the primary visual cortex, and do not involve the activity of any other part of the cerebral cortex. The conduction of impulses is from the retina to the lateral geniculate nuclei, thence to the striate areas, and from them down to some subcortical nervous mechanism. The path beyond the striate cortex is unknown. It may be direct to the spinal cord. There is some evidence that the pyramidal paths contain many fibres from all parts of the cerebral cortex, not from the Betz cell area only.

It seems probable that the same restriction of simple discriminative habits to the primary sensory areas holds also for other sensory modalities. The evidence is less complete, but what there is is consistent with the data on the visual system.

The evidence thus indicates that in sensory-motor habits of the conditioned reflex type no part of the cerebral cortex is essential except the primary sensory area. There is no transcortical conduction from the sensory areas to the motor cortex, and the major subcortical nuclear masses, thalamus, striatum, colliculi and cerebellum, do not play a part in the recognition of sensory stimuli or in the habit patterning of motor reactions.

The Engram Within Sensory Areas
(Equipotential Regions)

The experiments reported indicate that performance of habits of the conditioned reflex type is dependent upon the sensory areas and upon no other part of the cerebral cortex. What of localization within the sensory areas? Direct data upon this question are limited, but point to the conclusion that so long as some part of the sensory field remains intact and there is not a total loss of primary sensitivity, the habit mechanism can still function. Thus, in a series of experiments attempting to locate accurately the visual cortex of the rat, parts of the occipital lobes were destroyed in a variety of combinations. In these experiments it appeared that, so long as some part of the anterolateral surface of the striate cortex (the projection field of the temporal retina corresponding to the macula of primates) remained intact, there was no loss of habit. Any small part of the region was capable of maintaining the habits based on discrimination of intensities of light (37).

In a later experiment an attempt was made to determine the smallest amount of visual cortex which is capable of mediating habits based upon detail vision. The extent of visual cortex remaining after operation was determined by counting undegenerated cells in the lateral geniculate nucleus. Discrimination of visual figures could be learned when only one-sixtieth of the visual cortex remained (39). No comparable data are available on postoperative retention, but from incidental observations in other experiments I am confident that retention would be possible with the same amount of tissue.

In an early study by Franz (16) the lateral surfaces of the occipital lobes of the monkey were destroyed after the animals had been trained in pattern and colour discrimination. These operations involved the greater part of what is now known to be the projection field of the macula. There was no loss of the habits. I have destroyed the cortex of the retrocalcarine fissure (the perimacular field) without destroying visual memories. The results with monkeys thus support the more ample data for the rat; the visual memory traces survive any cortical lesion, provided some portion of the field of acute vision remains intact.

This lack of definite habit localization might really have been predicted from psychological data alone. Analysis of the effective stimuli in discriminative learning reveals that the association is independent of particular sensory nerve fibres. It is a response to a pattern of excitation which may vary widely in position on the sensory surface and consequently in cortical projection. The reactions involved in motor habits show the same sort of functional equivalence; a motor habit is not a predetermined set of muscular contractions but is a series of movements in relation to bodily posture and to the complex pattern of the environment. The writing of one's name, for example, is not a stereotyped series of contractions of particular muscles but is a series of movements in relation to the body planes which can be performed with any motor organ and with any degree of amplitude.

I have not time here to report in detail the experiments which justify the conclusion that neither the afferent path nor the efferent is fixed by habit. The mass of evidence accumulated by Gestalt psychologists shows conclusively that it is the pattern and not the localization of energy on the sense organ that determines its functional effect. Similar motor equivalence is demonstrated by a variety of less systematic evidence. The psychological studies, like the more limited direct experiments on the brain, point to the conclusion that the memory trace is located in all parts of the functional area; that various parts are equipotential for its maintenance and activation.

Facilitative Functions in Learning and Retention (Mass Action)

The experiments thus far reported have been concerned almost entirely with discriminative habits requiring only an association between a single sensory stimulus and a motor response. A very different picture develops in experiments with other types of learning. If rats are trained in the maze and then have portions of the cortex removed, they show more or less loss of the habit. If a small amount of cortex is destroyed, 5 to 10 per cent, the loss may be scarcely detectable. If large amounts, say 50 per cent or more, are destroyed, the habit is completely lost, and relearning may require many times as much practice as did initial learning. The amount of loss, measured in terms of the practice required for relearning, is, on the average, closely proportional to the amount of cortex destroyed. Figure 7 shows the relation for one group of rats on a relatively difficult maze with eight culs de sac. There is some evidence that the more difficult the task, the greater the relative effect of the larger lesions (34, 48). Similar results have been obtained with latch-box learning and retention (36). So far as it is possible to analyse the data from more than 200 diverse operations, the amount of loss from a given extent of cortical destruction is about the same, no matter what part of the cerebral hemispheres is destroyed, provided that the destruction is roughly similar in both hemispheres.

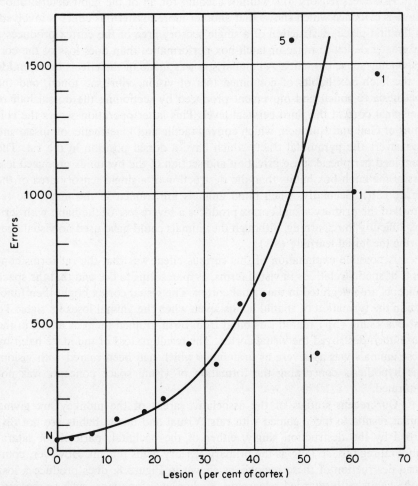

FIGURE 7. The relation of errors in maze learning to extent of cerebral damage in the rat. The extent of brain injury is expressed as the percentage of the surface area of the isocortex destroyed. Data from 60 normal and 127 brain-operated animals are averaged by class intervals of 5 per cent destruction. The curve is the best fitting one of logarithmic form. For lesions above 45 per cent the number of cases (indicated by numerals on the graph) is too small for reliability. (*After Lashley and Wiley* (48).)

The explanation of this quantitative relationship is difficult. In learning the maze the rat certainly employs a variety of sensory cues, visual, tactile, kinesthetic, olfactory, possibly auditory. Brain injuries destroy various sensory fields and the larger the lesion the greater the reduction in available sense data. The production of different amounts of sensory deficit would thus appear to be the most reasonable explanation of the quantitative relation between habit loss and extent of lesion (13, 22). Sensory deficit certainly plays a role in it. In the experiment on effects of incisions through the cortex, which was described earlier, the severity of loss of the maze habit correlated highly with the interruption of sensory pathways, as determined from degeneration of the thalamus.

However, sensory loss will not account for all of the habit deterioration. There is evidence which shows that another more mysterious effect is involved. In the first place, destruction of a single sensory area of the cortex produces a far greater deficit in maze or latch-box performance than does loss of the corresponding sense modality. A comparison was made of the effects on retention of the latch-box habits of combined loss of vision, vibrissae touch, and the anesthesia to touch and movement produced by sectioning the dorsal half of the spinal cord at the third cervical level. This latter operation severs the columns of Gall and Burdach, which convey tactile and kinesthetic impulses, and also severs the pyramidal tracts which have a dorsal position in the rat. The combined peripheral sense privation and section of the pyramids produced less loss of the latch-box habits than did destruction of a single sensory area of the cortex (36). Secondly, when blind animals are trained in the maze, the removal of the primary visual cortex produces a severe loss of the habit with serious difficulty in relearning, although the animals could have used no visual cues during the initial learning (43).

A possible explanation of this curious effect was that the rat forms concepts of spatial relations in visual terms, as man seems to do, and that the space concepts are integrated in the visual cortex. The visual cortex might then function in the formation of spatial habits, even when the animal loses its sight. To test this Tsang (56) reared rats blind from birth, trained them as adults in the maze, then destroyed the visual cortex. The resultant loss of the maze habit by these animals was as severe as in animals which had been reared with vision. The hypothesis concerning the formation of visual space concepts was not confirmed.

Our recent studies of the associative areas of the monkey are giving similar results to those gained with rats. Visual and tactile habits are not disturbed by the destruction singly, either of the occipital, parietal, or lateral temporal regions, so long as the primary sensory fields remain. However, combined destruction of these regions, as shown in Figure 8, does produce a loss of the habits with retarded relearning. Higher level functions, such as the conditional reaction, delayed reaction, or solution of the multiple stick problem, show deterioration after extensive damage in any part of the cortex. The capacity for delayed reaction in monkeys, for example (to remember in which of two boxes food was placed), may be seriously reduced or abolished by removal either of the prefrontal lobes or of the occipital associative cortex or of the temporal lobes. That is, small lesions, embracing no more than a single associative area, do not produce loss of any habit; large lesions produce a deterioration which affects a variety of habits, irrespective of the sensory-motor elements involved.

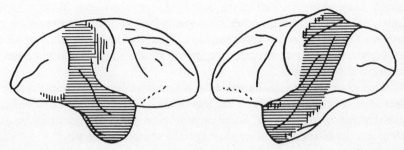

FIGURE 8. Minimal lesion which produces disturbances in tactile or visual memory in the monkey.

Results such as these have led me to formulate a theory of mass action or mass facilitation. It is, essentially, that performance of any function depends upon two variables in nervous activity. The reaction mechanism, whether of instinctive or of learned activity, is a definite pattern of integrated neurons with a variable threshold of excitability. The availability of such patterns, the ease with which they can be activated, is dependent upon less specific facilitative effects. This facilitation can come from a variety of sources. Some instinctive behaviour seems to require hormonal activation, probably a direct chemical effect upon specific nervous elements. Emotional facilitation may produce a temporary activation. Continued activity of related mechanisms may facilitate the whole group of associated reactions; a sort of warming-up effect.

There are indications (28), although little systematic evidence, that the severity of postoperative amnesia varies with the intensity of motivation. Rats trained in a discrimination without punishment with electric shock for errors may show loss of the habit after lesions which do not produce loss in animals which were trained with punishment. The greater effects of cortical lesions in monkeys than in rats may be in part a result of the greater difficulty in getting consistent motivation in the higher animals. In man an amnesia often seems to be a difficulty rather than impossibility of recall; recall may be possible but only with extreme effort and fatigue. I believe that the evidence strongly favours the view that amnesia from brain injury rarely, if ever, is due to the destruction of specific memory traces. Rather, the amnesias represent a lowered level of vigilance, a greater difficulty in activating the organized patterns of traces, or a disturbance of some broader system of organized functions.

In interpreting apparent loss of memory after cerebral damage, extreme caution is necessary. The poor performance in tasks may be due to the destruction of specific associative connexions, but is instead generally, I believe always, the result rather of interference with a higher level functional pattern-ing. Some experiments of Dr. Klüver's (personal communication) illustrate this point. Monkeys were trained in a variety of discriminative reactions calling for use of different sense modalities by a method that required them to pull in the stimulus objects by attached strings. Extensive lesions in different cortical areas all caused loss of these habits. The monkeys simply pulled the strings at random. They were retrained in the discrimination of weights. When this was learned, the habits based on other sense modalities (reactions to intensities of light, for example) returned spontaneously. What had been disturbed by all the operations was the set or attitude to compare stimuli, not the specific memory of which one was correct.

This example perhaps illustrates at a primitive level the characteristic of amnesias as seen clinically. Apparent loss of memory is secondary to a disorder in the structuring of concepts. Some physiological mode of organizing or inte-grating activity is affected rather than specific associative bonds.

The Complexity of the Memory Trace

The experiments that I have reviewed deal with only a small part of the whole problem of the memory trace; with those aspects which can most readily be studied in experiments with animals. Immediate memory presents a different type of problem. It is highly probable that immediate memory is maintained by some sort of after-discharge of the originally excited neurons. Such per-sistent activity can scarcely be the basis of more permanent memory, although Ebbecke (10) and Edgell (11) have formulated theories of memory in terms of persistent states of excitation. It is by no means certain that all memory is mediated by a single type of mechanism; that motor skills and eidetic images, for example, have any physiological properties in common. The attempt to account for all memory by any single theory involves assumptions which are not supported by any evidence now available.

Much of learning theory has been based upon supposedly isolated and simple instances of association, on the assumption that these represent a primi-tive prototype of all memory. However, an analysis of even the conditioned reflex indicates that it is not the simple, direct association of stimulus and response that it has been thought to be. I served as experimenter and subject for several years in experiments employing both the salivary method of Pavlov and the motor reactions of Bechterew. The experience convinced me that, far from being a simple sensory-motor reaction, the conditioned reflex is very complicated (29). The *S-R* diagram is misleadingly schematic. The effective stimulus is not only the object which the experimenter designates as *S,* but a whole background of other objects constituting the situation in which the experiment is conducted. Every stimulus has a space setting. When, for exam-ple, the rat is trained to react to a triangle, he fails to respond if the figure is rotated through more than 10 to 15 degrees (12). This means that the memory trace of the figure is tied in with the space coordinates of the animal's postural system. This system of space coordinates is a part of the postural reflex system which pervades every aspect of behaviour. There is scarcely a memory which does not have spatial orientation, either with reference to the planes of the body or to external space in addition.

Most skilled acts, from running a maze to playing a musical phrase or speaking a sentence, involve a timed series of actions which cannot be accounted for as a simple chain of conditioned reflexes (46). The serial timing of actions is among the most important and least studied of behavioural problems. Almost all memories except those of automatized motor habits are dated, as Bergson (3) has emphasized; that is, they have a temporal position in the series of memories which constitutes the individual's past. The memory trace is associated with this series as well as with the particular objects which make up its central core.

The conditioned reflex also includes an element of affective reinforcement. Corresponding to the nature of the conditioning stimulus, there is fear of electric shock, objectively demonstrable by cardiac and respiratory changes, anticipation of acid in the mouth with slight nausea, or expectation of food (29). Unless this affective element is aroused, the conditioned reflex does not occur. So-called extinction of the conditioned reflex is not a weakening of the specific association, but a waning of this affective reinforcement. Other types of association also have dynamic aspects. The amnesic aphasias seem to be due less to a weakening of specific associations than to a reduction in some general form of facilitation. Henry Head has expressed this as a reduction of "vigilance," without attempting to define further the nature of the function which is disturbed.

A variety of evidence (50) shows that, in a memorized series of nonsense syllables, associations are formed, not only between adjacent words but also between words remote from each other in the series. This, I believe, is an illustration at a primitive level of the fact that every memory becomes part of a more or less extensive organization. When I read a scientific paper, the new facts presented become associated with the field of knowledge of which it is a part. Later availability of the specific items of the paper depends upon a partial ·activation of the whole body of associations. If one has not thought of a topic for some time, it is difficult to recall details. With review or discussion of the subject, however, names, dates, references which seemed to be forgotten rapidly become available to memory. Head (20) has given instances of such recall by multiple reinforcement in his studies of aphasia. Although there are no systematic experiments upon this "warming-up" effect, it is a matter of common experience and is evidence, I believe, that recall involves the subthreshold activation of a whole system of associations which exert some sort of mutual facilitation.

All this is by way of indicating the probable complexity of the memory trace of even the simplest associations. The engram of a new association, far from consisting of a single bond or neuron connexion, is probably a reorganization of a vast system of associations involving the interrelations of hundreds of thousands or millions of neurons.

Some Quantitative Considerations

It has been customary to assume that, since the nervous system contains so many millions of neurons, there must be a large reservoir of cells or of synaptic connexions which can be modified and reserved for specific memory functions. Dunlap (9) has expressed the view that every individual has far more brain cells than he is ever called upon to use, and has urged this as an argument against any congenital restriction of ability. A similar view has been implied in the identification of intelligence as the individual's number of unpre-empted and available memory bonds. However, only the vaguest sort of ana-tomic data have been available to support such theories. Analysis of actual cell numbers involved in a reaction system gives little indication of a reserve of unused connexions and raises a very difficult question as to the way in which the same system can mediate different functions.

I have counted or estimated the number of cells at different levels in the visual system of the rat. The numbers, which I believe are correct within approximately 10 per cent, are given in Table 1. You will note that there is a marked concentration of paths from the retinal myoids to the lateral genicu-late nucleus, such that an average of nearly 300 myoids feed into each thalamo-cortical path. At the cortical level there is some dispersion, but it is not great. In the receptive layer (lamina iv) there are fewer than four neurons for each

Table 1.

The number of neurons at each level in the visual system of the rat (unilateral).

Level	Total no. of neurons	Ratio to fibres in radiation
Retinal cells		
Rods	9,180,000	273·0
Cones	120,000	
Bipolar	3,530,000	104·0
Ganglion	260,000	13·1
Lateral geniculate	34,000	1·0
Cortical cells		
Lamina vii	68,800	2·0
Lamina vi	135,400	4·0
Lamina v	147,700	4·3
Lamina iv (granular)	127,000	3·7
Laminae ii–iii	176,000	5·2
Total cortical	654,900	19·2

afferent fibre, and in the whole visual cortex there are only nineteen neurons for each afferent fibre.

The rat's maximal visual acuity is about 30 min. of arc, as determined by behavioural tests and from the resolving power of the lens system. Because of the extreme curvature of the cornea and lens the visual field of one eye subtends about 210 degrees. If acuity were uniform throughout the retina, it would require more than 80,000 fibres to represent each acuity unit of the retina by one central fibre. The concentration of ganglion cells falls off from 130 per hundredth square millimetre at the fixation point to 65 at the ora serrata (35). Assuming that acuity decreases proportionately, some 40,000 separate paths are required to represent each acuity unit at the cortex by a single afferent fibre. This corresponds fairly well to the 34,000 geniculo-striate paths actually counted. Since acute vision is continuous under light stimulation, it follows that all of the geniculo-striate cells must be firing constantly when the eye is stimulated by the usual lighted environment. Further, since there are not more than nineteen neurons in the visual area for each afferent fibre, it is almost certain that every cell in the striate cortex is firing during light stimulation. Certainly there is no large reserve of cells which can be set aside for excitation only in specific habits.

Corresponding counts of cells in the visual system of the monkey have recently been made by Chow and Blum (personal communication). The number of neurons in the lateral geniculate nucleus and visual cortex is enormously greater than in the rat, about 1 and 140 millions respectively, but the ratio of cortical cells to central pathways is only 140 to 1, so again there is no great reserve of cells for mnemonic purposes.

The rat is capable of retaining scores, probably hundreds, of visual habits involving discrimination of complex figures (38), and retention may sometimes be demonstrated a year after training. As I reported earlier, there is good evidence that visual habits are dependent upon the striate cortex and upon no other part of the cerebral cortex. The efferent path from the striate cortex is not known. It is not via cortico-tactile fibres. If by cortico-thalamic fibres, there are far fewer neurons within the thalamic nuclei than in corresponding cortical areas, and there is certainly no reserve of cells there for the storing of memories. There seems to be no justification for assuming that the specific shunting of nervous impulses constituting various memories occurs at some level beyond the visual cortex or that memory traces are stored elsewhere than in the cortex.

If the data on the restriction of visual memory to the striate cortex are correct, and they are supported by a variety of experiments, the conclusion seems inevitable that the same cells which bear the memory traces are also excited and play a part in every other visual reaction of the animal. In all probability, the same sort of quantitative relations holds for the other sense modalities.

Even if the associative areas are functional in memory, they do not provide the supposed excess of cells. The visual cortex is directly connected only to a band of cortex directly adjacent, the visuopsychic area of Campbell. The boundaries of this are indeterminate, but it certainly contains no more cells than does the striate area, probably fewer. There is no geometrical multiplication of cells and pathways. Many millions of cells of the striate cortex must be firing constantly into the adjacent area, so that its cells also must be constantly bombarded with nervous impulses and constantly firing. The conclusion is justified, I believe, by such considerations and is supported by electrical studies, that all of the cells of the brain are constantly active and are participating, by a sort of algebraic summation, in every activity. There are no special cells reserved for special memories.

Lorente (49) has shown that each neuron may bear a hundred or more end-feet or separate synapses. However, considering the enormous complexity of the nervous activity involved in performance of even the simplest habit, it is doubtful that even the multiplication of cell number by a hundredfold will provide separate connexions that function only for single specific memories.

The alternative to the theory of preservation of memories by some local synaptic change is the postulate that the neurons are somehow sensitized to react to patterns or combinations of excitation. It is only by such permutations that the limited number of neurons can produce the variety of functions that they carry out. Local changes in the cell membrane, such that combined excitation by several synapses excite the cell, would provide a possible mechanism for such response to patterns, but speculation about this mechanism without direct evidence is likely to be as futile as speculation concerning changes in resistance in the synapse has been.

Summary

This series of experiments has yielded a good bit of information about what and where the memory trace is not. It has discovered nothing directly of the real nature of the engram. I sometimes feel, in reviewing the evidence on the localization of the memory trace, that the necessary conclusion is that learning just is not possible. It is difficult to conceive of a mechanism which can satisfy the conditions set for it. Nevertheless, in spite of such evidence against it, learning does sometimes occur. Although the negative data do not provide a clear picture of the nature of the engram, they do establish limits within which concepts of its nature must be confined, and thus indirectly define somewhat more clearly the nature of the nervous mechanisms which must be responsible for learning and retention. Some general conclusions are, I believe, justified by the evidence.

1. It seems certain that the theory of well-defined conditioned reflex paths from sense organ via association areas to the motor cortex is false. The motor areas are not necessary for the retention of sensory-motor habits or even of skilled manipulative patterns.

2. It is not possible to demonstrate the isolated localization of a memory trace anywhere within the nervous system. Limited regions may be essential

for learning or retention of a particular activity, but within such regions the parts are functionally equivalent. The engram is represented throughout the region.

3. The so-called associative areas are not storehouses for specific memories. They seem to be concerned with modes of organization and with general facilitation or maintenance of the level of vigilance. The defects which occur after their destruction are not amnesias but difficulties in the performance of tasks which involve abstraction and generalization, or conflict of purposes. It is not possible as yet to describe these defects in the present psychological terminology. Goldstein (19) has expressed them in part as a shift from the abstract to the concrete attitude, but this characterization is too vague and general to give a picture of the functional disturbance. For our present purpose the important point is that the defects are not fundamentally those of memory.

4. The trace of any activity is not an isolated connexion between sensory and motor elements. It is tied in with the whole complex of spatial and temporal axes of nervous activity which forms a constant substratum of behaviour. Each association is oriented with respect to space and time. Only by long practice under varying conditions does it become generalized or dissociated from these specific coordinates. The space and time coordinates in orientation can, I believe, only be maintained by some sort of polarization of activity and by rhythmic discharges which pervade the entire brain, influencing the organization of activity everywhere. The position and direction of motion in the visual field, for example, continuously modify the spinal postural adjustments, but, a fact which is more frequently overlooked, the postural adjustments also determine the orientation of the visual field, so that upright objects continue to appear upright, in spite of changes in the inclination of the head. This substratum of postural and tonic activity is constantly present and is integrated with the memory trace (46).

I have mentioned briefly evidence that new associations are tied in spontaneously with a great mass of related associations. This conception is fundamental to the problems of attention and interest. There are no neurological data bearing directly upon these problems, but a good guess is that the phenomena which we designate as attention and interest are the result of partial, subthreshold activation of systems of related associations which have a mutual facilitative action. It seems impossible to account for many of the characters of organic amnesias except in such general terms as reduced vigilance or reduced facilitation.

5. The equivalence of different regions of the cortex for retention of memories points to multiple representation. Somehow, equivalent traces are established throughout the functional area. Analysis of the sensory and motor aspects of habits shows that they are reducible only to relations among components which have no constant position with respect to structural elements. This means, I believe, that within a functional area the cells throughout the area acquire the capacity to react in certain definite patterns, which may have any distribution within the area. I have elsewhere proposed a possible mecha-

nism to account for this multiple representation. Briefly, the characteristics of the nervous network are such that, when it is subject to any pattern of excitation, it may develop a pattern of activity, reduplicated throughout an entire functional area by spread of excitations, much as the surface of a liquid develops an interference pattern of spreading waves when it is disturbed at several points (41). This means that, within a functional area, the neurons must be sensitized to react in certain combinations, perhaps in complex patterns of reverberatory circuits, reduplicated throughout the area.

6. Consideration of the numerical relations of sensory and other cells in the brain makes it certain, I believe, that all of the cells of the brain must be in almost constant activity, either firing or actively inhibited. There is no great excess of cells which can be reserved as the seat of special memories. The complexity of the functions involved in reproductive memory implies that every instance of recall requires the activity of literally millions of neurons. The same neurons which retain the memory traces of one experience must also participate in countless other activities.

Recall involves the synergic action or some sort of resonance among a very large number of neurons. The learning process must consist of the attunement of the elements of a complex system in such a way that a particular combination or pattern of cells responds more readily than before the experience. The particular mechanism by which this is brought about remains unknown. From the numerical relations involved, I believe that even the reservation of individual synapses for special associative reactions is impossible. The alternative is, perhaps, that the dendrites and cell body may be locally modified in such a manner that the cell responds differentially, at least in the timing of its firing, according to the pattern of combination of axon feet through which excitation is received.

References

1. Akelaitis, A. J. A study of gnosis, praxis and language following section of the corpus callosum and anterior commissure, *J. Neurosurgery*, 1944, **1**, 94–102.
2. Bailey, P., Bonin, G. V., Davis, F. W., Garol, H. W., and McCulloch, W. S. *J. Neuropath. exp. Neurol.*, 1944, **3**, 413–415.
3. Bergson, H. *Matière et mémoire*. Paris: 1896.
4. Bonin, G. V., Garol, H. W., and McCulloch, W. S. The functional organization of the occipital lobe, *Biol. Symp.*, 1942, **7**, 165–192.
5. Bucy, P. C. The relation of the premotor cortex to motor activity, *J. nerv. ment. Dis.*, 1934, **79**, 621–630.
6. Bucy, P. C., and Fulton, T. F. Ipsilateral representation in the motor and premotor cortex of monkeys, *Brain*, 1933, **56**, 318–342.
7. Clark, W. E. L. Observations on the associative fibre system of the visual cortex and the central representation of the retina, *J. Anat., Lond.*, 1941, **75**, 225–236.
8. Dunlap, K. The short-circuiting of conscious responses, *J. Phil. Psychol. sci. Meth.*, 1927, **24**, 253–267.

9. Dunlap, K. Psychological hypotheses concerning the functions of the brain, *Sci. Mon., N.Y.*, 1930, **31**, 97–112.
10. Ebbecke, U. *Die kortikalen psychophysischen Erregungen.* Leipzig: Barth, 1919.
11. Edgell, B. *Theories of memory.* Oxford: Clarendon Press, 1924.
12. Fields, P. E. Studies in concept formation: I. The development of the concept of triangularity by the white rat, *Comp. Psychol. Monogr.*, 1932, **9** (2).
13. Finley, C. B. Equivalent losses in accuracy of response after central and after peripheral sense deprivation, *J. comp. Neurol.*, 1941, **74**, 203–237.
14. Fischel, W. *Die höheren Leistungen der Wirbeltiergehirne*, Leipzig: Barth, 1948.
15. Franz, S. I. On the functions of the cerebrum: the frontal lobes, *Arch. Psychol.*, 1907, (2).
16. Franz, S. I. On the functions of the cerebrum: the occipital lobes, *Psychol. Monogr.*, 1911, **13** (4).
17. Gay, J. R., and Gellhorn, E. Cortical projection of proprioception. *Amer. J. Physiol.*, 1948, **155**, 437.
18. Girden, E., Mettler, F. A., Finch, G., and Culler, E. Conditioned responses in a decorticate dog to acoustic, thermal, and tactile stimulation, *J. comp. Psychol.*, 1936, **21**, 367–385.
19. Goldstein, K. *Human nature in the light of psychopathology.* Cambridge, Mass.: Harvard Univ. Press, 1940.
20. Head, H. *Aphasia and kindred disorders of speech.* New York: Macmillan, 1926. Vol. II.
21. Herrick, C. J. *Brains of rats and men.* Chicago: Univ. Chicago Press, 1926.
22. Hunter, W. S. A consideration of Lashley's theory of the equipotentiality of cerebral action, *J. gen. Psychol.*, 1930, **3**, 455–468.
23. Ingebritsen, O. C. Coordinating mechanisms of the spinal cord, *Genet. Psychol. Monogr.*, 1933, **13**, 485–553.
24. Jacobsen, C. F. Influence of motor and premotor area lesions upon the retention of skilled movements in monkeys and chimpanzees, *Proc. Ass. Res. nerv. ment. Dis.*, 1932, **13**, 225–247.
25. Jacobsen, C. F. Studies of cerebral function in primates, *Comp. Psychol. Monogr.*, 1936, **13** (3).
26. Kellogg, W. N., Deese, J., Pronko, N. H., and Feinberg, M. An attempt to condition the chronic spinal dog, *J. exp. Psychol.*, 1947, **37**, 99–117.
27. Kennard, M. A. Alterations in response to visual stimuli following lesions of frontal lobe in monkeys, *Arch. Neurol. Psychiat., Chicago*, 1939, **41**, 1153–1165.
28. Krechevsky, I. Brain mechanisms and brightness discrimination, *J. comp. Psychol.*, 1936, **21**, 405–445.
29. Lashley, K. S. The human salivary reflex and its use in psychology, *Psychol. Rev.*, 1916, **23**, 446–464.
30. Lashley, K. S. Studies of cerebral function in learning: II. The effects of long continued practice upon cerebral localization, *J. comp. Psychol.*, 1921, **1**, 453–468.
31. Lashley, K. S. Studies of cerebral function in learning: III. The motor areas, *Brain*, 1921, **44**, 256–286.
32. Lashley, K. S. Studies of cerebral function in learning: IV. Vicarious function after destruction of the visual areas, *Amer. J. Physiol.*, 1922, **59**, 44–71.
33. Lashley, K. S. Studies of cerebral function in learning: V. The retention of motor habits after destruction of the so-called motor areas in primates, *Arch. Neurol. Psychiat., Chicago*, 1924, **12**, 249–276.

34. Lashley, K. S. *Brain mechanisms and intelligence.* Chicago: Univ. Chicago Press, 1929.
35. Lashley, K. S. The mechanism of vision: V. The structure and image-forming power of the rat's eye, *J. comp. Psychol.,* 1932, **13,** 173–200.
36. Lashley, K. S. Studies of cerebral function in learning: XI. The behavior of the rat in latch-box situations, *Comp. Psychol. Monogr.,* 1935, **11,** 1–42.
37. Lashley, K. S. The mechanism of vision: XIII. Nervous structures concerned in the acquisition and retention of habits based on reactions to light, *Comp. Psychol. Monogr.,* 1935, **11,** 43–79.
38. Lashley, K. S. The mechanism of vision: XV. Preliminary studies of the rat's capacity for detail vision, *J. genet. Psychol.,* 1938, **18,** 123–193.
39. Lashley, K. S. The mechanism of vision: XVI. The functioning of small remnants of the visual cortex, *J. comp. Neurol.,* 1939, **70,** 45–67.
40. Lashley, K. S. Thalamo-cortical connections of the rat's brain, *J. comp. Neurol.,* 1941, **75,** 67–121.
41. Lashley, K. S. The problem of cerebral organization in vision, *Biol. Symp.,* 1942, **7,** 301–322.
42. Lashley, K. S. The mechanism of vision: XVII. Autonomy of the visual cortex, *J. genet. Psychol.,* 1942, **60,** 197–221.
43. Lashley, K. S. Studies of cerebral function in learning: XII. Loss of the maze habit after occipital lesions in blind rats, *J. comp. Neurol.,* 1943, **79,** 431–462.
44. Lashley, K. S. Studies of cerebral function in learning: XIII. Apparent absence of transcortical association in maze learning, *J. comp. Neurol.,* 1944, **80,** 257–281.
45. Lashley, K. S. The mechanism of vision: XVIII. Effects of destroying the visual "associative areas" of the monkey, *Genet. Psychol. Monogr.,* 1948, **37,** 107–166.
46. Lashley, K. S. The problem of serial order in behavior. In Jeffress, L. A. (Ed.) *Cerebral mechanisms in behavior.* New York: Wiley, 1951. Pp. 112–136.
47. Lashley, K. S., and McCarthy, D. A. The survival of the maze habit after cerebellar injuries, *J. comp. Psychol.,* 1926, **6,** 423–433.
48. Lashley, K. S., and Wiley, L. E. Studies of cerebral function in learning: IX. Mass action in relation to the number of elements in the problem to be learned, *J. comp. Neurol.,* 1933, **57,** 3–55.
49. Lorente de Nó, R. Studies on the structure of the cerebral cortex: II. Continuation of the study of the Ammonic system, *J. Psychol. Neurol., Lpz.,* 1934, **46,** 113–177.
50. McGeoch, J. A. *The psychology of human learning.* New York: Longmans, Green, 1942.
51. Mettler, F. A. Physiologic effects of bilateral simultaneous removal of Brodmann's cytoarchitectural areas in the human, *Fed. Proc. Amer. Soc. exp. Biol.,* 1949, **8,** 109.
52. Nielsen, J. M. *Agnosia, apraxia, aphasia: their value in cerebral localization.* Los Angeles: Waverly Press, 1936.
53. Poltyrew, S. S., and Zeliony, G. P. Grosshirnrinde und Assoziationsfunktion, *Z. Biol.,* 1930, **90,** 157–160.
54. Smith, K. U. Bilateral integrative action of the cerebral cortex in man in verbal association and sensori-motor coordination, *J. exp. Psychol.,* 1947, **37,** 367–376.
55. Sperry, R. W. Cerebral regulation of motor coordination in monkeys following multiple transection of sensorimotor cortex, *J. Neurophysiol.,* 1947, **10,** 275–294.
56. Tsang, Yü-Chüan. The function of the visual areas of the cortex of the rat in

the learning and retention of the maze, *Comp. Psychol. Monogr.*, 1934, **10,** 1–56.

57. Walker, A. E. *The primate thalamus.* Chicago: Univ. Chicago Press, 1938.
58. Ward, A. A., Jr., Peden, J. K., and Sugar, O. Cortico-cortical connections in the monkey with special reference to Area 6, *J. Neurophysiol.*, 1946, **9,** 453–461.

Study Questions for Part I

1. Suppose you were a Martian neuroscientist given the task of determining how the human brain works. Your normal eyesight is comparable to what we on Earth would see when examining an object under 120 × magnification. To complicate the problem further, suppose you have no access to any text on human neuroanatomy. First, how would you proceed to determine brain-behavior relationships? In what way might your description of the CNS differ from that of the earthlings?

2. Suppose that one group of animals had been subjected to one-stage bilateral removal of structure (x), whereas a second group underwent similar bilateral ablation of structure (y). Subsequently, it was found that (x) showed marked impairments in learning a visual discrimination, an auditory discrimination, and a tactual discrimination problem. On the other hand, (y) had difficulty with only the auditory discrimination.

From these data, draw a tentative inference about the nature of these two impairments and the types of structures that might be involved. Then construct a research program that would test the validity of your original assumption. You need not feel constrained to creating a single "definitive" experiment. Rather, we suggest that you construct a series of If . . . Then statements (hypotheses), taking into account projected positive and negative findings.

Part II

Learning:
Electrophysiological Aspects

Shortly after the discovery of electricity, scientists of the day began to wonder whether nervous activity could possibly have something to do with current flow. When Volta, in Italy, accidentally discovered that electrical stimulation of frogs' legs caused them to twitch in a predictable fashion, the idea of animal electricity quickly caught on. Up to that time, there were a number of debates on the subject of whether nervous energy consisted of gaseous or liquid factors, but Volta's discovery provided the background for modern neurophysiology and subsequent understanding of how nerves transmit information.

Until the 1930s, when Berger developed the electroencephalograph, systematic investigation of brain electrical activity was not possible. Initially, investigators concerned themselves with measuring and describing the various patterns of EEG activity that could be found at different locations on the skull. It was soon found that certain types of brain damage often, but not always, produced abnormal or paroxysmal, EEG activity. Within a short period of time, it became fashionable to study whether various kinds of behavior could be reflected in changes of the EEG. Soon it became necessary to question some of the assumptions that underlie the use of the EEG in understanding brain function.

The first question one might ask is whether electrical activity as measured by EEG is, in fact, an accurate reflection of CNS state or function. For example, it is not uncommon in clinical diagnoses to find individuals with known behavioral impairments to have normal EEG. Likewise, it has also been shown that individuals with abnormal EEG records can have perfectly normal behavior patterns. In the laboratory, it has been demonstrated that drugs like atropine produce EEG records characteristic of slow-wave sleep; yet the organism is quite active and alert. Some of the readings will deal more specifically with this question later.

Another related point worth considering is the kind of relationship that exists between EEG and behavior. At best, this relationship is correlative rather than causal. Thus, we cannot say for certain that changing electrical activity in a given area *causes* behavioral change. Nor are we in a position to infer that behavioral change *causes* electrical activity of the CNS to change. All we know is that there is a *correlation* between these two events. And indeed, as the above examples have suggested, this correlation is less than perfect.

Another criticism that has been leveled against the EEG is that measurement of "gross" activity in millions of cells, summing over excitation and inhibition, does not really tell us anything about how information is processed in the units themselves. Since one of the articles presented below deals specifically with this question, we will ask you to decide this issue for yourself.

On the positive side, recording of electrical potentials from cortical and subcortical areas, although not necessarily conclusive, has provided us with the only technique for observing activity in a variety of structures *simultaneously*. In our opinion, this is a critical step toward solving the problem of how different components within the system deal with input and generate patterns at any given moment in time. With the aid of computers, it has become possible to study small changes in activity throughout the brain and analyze these simultaneous changes to determine, for example, if there is any consistent relationship between activity in all of the structures comprising the limbic system.

If we place electrodes anywhere on the skull, or if we lower a set deep into the brain, the one thing we can be sure of finding is a continuous state of activity; the brain, in the living organism, is never silent. This general state of activity has often been referred to as background "noise" that has to be overridden in order for a stimulus to be perceived. In the first article, Pinneo discusses the problem of noise in the CNS and suggests that it may provide the *context*, or schema, against which stimulus input must be matched if organized behavior is to occur. Pinneo also takes the position that activity in *all* parts of the brain contributes to the overall pattern that provides the basis for judging the quality of stimulus input. This position is very similar to the notions presented in our earlier chapter on attention.

In Part I we pointed out that transduced information can change the state of the CNS and this change in state is referred to as "learning." The paper by John and Killam presents evidence that indicates that as learning proceeds, systematic changes in evoked potentials of a large number of interrelated structures are observed. Using an avoidance paradigm, the authors conditioned cats to make an avoidance response to a 10-cps flickering light. When the cats had learned this response, they were then given a 6.8-cps light to test for generalization. At first, the response to 6.8 cps was the same as with the 10-cps light, and at this time the evoked potential discharge in the visual cortex was *the same* as for the 10-cps stimulus. John and Killam interpreted their data to suggest that discrimination learning may depend on "matching" the stimulus with the stored representation of previous input. In a subsequent study, the authors showed that when cats make an error in an approach situation in which positive and negative cues are present, the evoked potentials reflect the cps of the incorrect stimulus.

A potential criticism of the evoked potential work is that an "average" waveform does not, in fact, correspond to the kind of activity that can be observed in the firing of a single cell. Further, it may very well be that the compound stimuli that are used to trigger the evoked potential do not produce parallel types of firing when activity is measured in a single cell. The paper by Fox and O'Brien is quite technical and somewhat difficult for the beginner to read, but its main point is that there is a close correspondence between averaged cellular activity and the probability of a single cell firing. The implications are that if a number of systems are involved in CNS activity during learning (as is suggested by John and Killam), then firing in single cells that respond to multisensory inputs may provide the mechanisms for the matching process we briefly mentioned above. This very same activity that provides the context for a "match" may also be the anatomical basis for the electrical activity measured in EEG or evoked potential studies.

Although it would appear that EEG accurately reflects CNS processes associated with information processing and storage, there are studies that provide conflicting evidence. The final article in this section, by Chow, discusses some of the methodological and empirical difficulties involved in attempting to correlate changes in evoked potentials and EEG with changes in learned behavior. Essentially, what Chow found was that changes in EEG recorded from the temporal cortex of the monkey did not follow "the behavioral learning curve." The author also demonstrated that although flicker was critical for the discrimination response, photic driving in the temporal cortex habituated but the monkeys were still capable of solving the behavioral task. This finding appears to contradict the report of John and Killam and suggests that EEG changes may *not* adequately reflect information storage or matching processes in the CNS.

On Noise in the Nervous System

LAWRENCE R. PINNEO

Reprinted from *Psychological Review*, 1966, Vol. 73, No. 3, pp. 242–247.

Two recent theoretical papers have argued that "noise" in the nervous system has interfering effects in discrimination and learning. In one, Treisman (1964) has suggested that three sources of noise limit discrimination: (a) the irreducible physical variability of the stimulus, (b) the "spontaneous" neural background activity to which a stimulus is added, and (c) the neural noise arising from variation in the pathways transmitting messages centrally. Based on these three sources of noise, Treisman has worked out a complicated signal-detection theory to explain the form of the Weber function for visual intensity discrimination and for other sense dimensions.

In the other paper, Hebb (1961) raised the question of the interfering effects of random activity in the nervous system during learning of a specific task. By learning he meant the modification of the direction of transmission in the central nervous system (CNS) at the synapse. He pointed out that a large brain such as a mammal's has many more neurons present than are necessary for learning a specific task. Therefore, random activity in the neurons not involved in learning the task constitutes noise, which Hebb felt must interfere with learning.

These two papers illustrate a widely held misconception of brain function, namely, that the spontaneous, random, or background discharge of neurons has little or no functional value; that is, this activity has no information value for the organism and therefore is noise in the communications sense of the word. In this theoretical note I attempt to show that the *neural* noise to which Treisman and Hebb refer (leaving out Treisman's first category) is not noise at all, that this neural activity does not limit discrimination nor interfere with learning, and that in fact this activity is essential to discrimination and learning.

Arduini (1963) has suggested that there are fundamentally two types of nervous discharge, and he has carefully defined them; his definitions will be used in this paper. Borrowing from the terminology applied to muscle activity, Arduini defines "phasic" activity as a transient increase or decrease in impulse firing rates of neurons that is time locked to a particular stimulus. A familiar example is the evoked response. "Tonic" activity on the other hand is nontransient, or continuous, neural discharge in which the average firing rate is random and constant and is *not* time locked to a stimulus. So-called spontaneous activity (a dubious term at best since it implies the discharge of neurons without benefit of influences external to the neurons), background activity, random discharge, and the like, are familiar examples of tonic activity.

Tonic activity may conveniently be considered as the functional substrate of the nervous system. As Lashley (1951) has pointed out, neurological theory has been dominated by the incorrect belief that neurons of the CNS are inactive for the greater part of the time. According to this view, neurons are always in the resting state where they are linked in the relative isolation of reflex arcs until a particular reaction for which they are specifically associated activates them. Yet, no matter where in the CNS one places an electrode, and no matter what the condition of the organism as long as he is alive, a steady discharge of neurons may always be recorded. In general, level of "arousal" or "activation" increases with the level of tonic activity throughout the brain. And it is against this tonic level that sensory messages are received and motor acts achieved. As Lashley (1951, p. 131) has so well expressed it, "all the cells of the cerebrospinal axis are being continually bombarded by nerve impulses from various sources and are firing regularly, probably even during sleep." And, "in the intact organism, behavior is the result of interaction of this background of excitation with input from any designated stimulus [p. 112]."

The nonspecific attributes of tonic activity are now well documented following the experiments of Moruzzi and Magoun (1949) on the cortical arousing effects of stimulation of the brain-stem reticular formation, and the descending tonic influence of the lower brain stem upon postural tonus as shown by Lindsley, Shreiner, and Magoun (1949). Even tonic motor activity itself increases level of activation and modifies behavior (Pinneo, 1961). But tonic activity also has been shown to have specific functional value in the skeletal and autonomic motor systems for the regulation of movement and the function of visceral organs. Thus, Sherrington (1906) observed that at the level of motor units the intensity of a mechanical effect resulting from a normal tonic discharge depends in large part upon the frequency of tonic impulses. Tower (1949) has carried this concept a little further by suggesting that the tonic nature of the discharging motor neurons is the expression of a central excitatory state (cf. Sherrington, 1906), modulated by a phasic or episodic function which appears as a specific contribution to individual acts.

Stimulation of central tracts and nuclei concerned with regulation of the skeletal and autonomic motor systems illustrates the *fine* control that tonic activity in these systems exerts (see the many chapters devoted to these systems in Field, Magoun, and Hall, 1960). Almost countless locations have been found (for example, in the pyramidal and extrapyramidal systems, cerebellum, and brain stem) in which stimulation with gross electrodes over short and long periods of time appears to initiate and maintain highly integrated and complex patterns of muscle activity. Frequently, it is found that the extent and complexity of movement is directly related to current strength. What moves, however, depends upon the location of the electrode. Since at these levels it is highly unlikely that fibres are excited selectively and in the proper temporal sequence to produce such complex and organized movements, it must be concluded that it is the increase in tonic level brought about by stimulation of the descending tracts that controls the motor activity. The argument (Patton and Amassian, 1960) that many of these movements are reflex results of afferent stimuli by spread of current from efferent tract stimulation to nearby afferent tracts has some validity. However, stimulation of efferent pathways alone can produce the same highly organized movements (Dow and Moruzzi, 1958; Pompeiano, 1959).

In our laboratory we have repeated and extended some of these experiments and have been able to completely reproduce a series of highly integrated movements in the squirrel monkey (*Saimiri sciureus*) by simultaneous and successive stimulation of several critical nuclei in the cerebellum and brain stem (Pinneo, in press—a). First, with a single stimulating electrode pair, we explored various loci in such nuclei as the interpositus, Deiter's, fastigial, and vestibular, and several other nuclei and tracts of the caudal brain stem, to determine the type of movement that could be elicited at each locus and the optimum electrical parameters for obtaining the movement. Then, by chronically implanting up to six pairs of electrodes in chosen sites, and by the proper ordering of stimulation at each electrode pair with respect to the other electrodes, fine coordinated movements were reproduced at our desire.

These effects were obtained whether the motor cortex concerned with the muscular groups in question was intact or not. For example, destruction of the motor cortex for the right arm and hand of the squirrel monkey produces paralysis in that limb, as in man. But, by proper placement and stimulation of electrodes in the homolateral interpositus nucleus, we were able to close the fingers (as in a grasp around an object) and to bring the hand rapidly and smoothly to the mouth; this could be repeated as often as desired. Other possible combinations included extension of the arm outward (as in reaching), backward, and to the side. Other electrode locations were found that produced similar movements in other limbs, opening and closing of the mouth (as in mastication), movement out and in of the tongue (as in licking), and control of rate and amount of respiration, and rate and volume of cardiac output. In all of the locations examined, the mechanical effect was proportional to current strength in the stimulating electrode (and therefore proportional to the level of tonic activity in the tracts or nuclei involved), so that very finely graded movements were obtainable singly or in combination.

The functional value of tonic activity is not limited to the skeletal and autonomic motor systems. In the primary visual pathway of mammals, tonic activity alone is recorded under maintained states of darkness or light (Arduini and Pinneo, 1961, 1962, 1963b; Granit, 1955). In the dark-adapted state a large number of retinal ganglion cells, perhaps most, maintain a relatively high rate of tonic discharge (Arduini and Cavaggioni, 1961; Granit, 1955). With the onset and offset of a prolonged light stimulus, "on" and "off" retinal bursts provide a momentary phasic response throughout the visual system whose size is proportional to the stimulus intensity. Shortly thereafter, however, and for as long as the intensity of the stimulus remains constant, the activity in the primary visual system is tonic (Arduini and Pinneo, 1961, 1962, 1963b). Furthermore, the level of the tonic activity with a steady light was found by Arduini and Pinneo (1962) to be inversely related to the intensity of the light by a power function of a form quite similar to the brightness function described by Stevens (1962) for humans.

Recently, Brooks (1964) has confirmed that the level of tonic activity in the primary visual system is the probable neural basis of brightness vision. Using the classical $\Delta I/I$ versus I paradigm, Brooks trained squirrel monkeys to make brightness discriminations over 4 log units of background light and then recorded the phasic and tonic activity (due to ΔI and I, respectively) from the lateral geniculate nucleus under threshold conditions. Brooks found that (a) the Weber function of the squirrel monkey was very similar to that of man; (b) the tonic and phasic activity changed with illumination of the retina as Arduini and Pinneo (1962, 1963b) had shown for the cat; and (c) brightness discrimination at threshold was inversely proportional to the level of tonic activity in the geniculate. Thus, in primates as in the cat, the noise in the visual system to which Treisman (1964) refers is *highest* during dark adaptation when visual sensitivity is greatest and *lowest* under conditions of high illumination when sensitivity is poorest. It is difficult, therefore, to see how this noise interferes with discrimination.

Perception of flicker fusion and the brightness of an intermittent light at critical fusion frequency (CFF—the Talbot brightness) also have been shown to depend upon the presence and level of tonic activity in the visual system (Arduini and Pinneo, 1963a). Recording from electrodes implanted in human patients for therapeutic reasons, Pinneo (in press—b) and Heath found that CFF, as determined by verbal report, occurred at that frequency of intermittent light where all or most phasic activity in the visual system had disappeared and only tonic activity remained. Furthermore, they found that the level of tonic activity at CFF was the same as that produced by a steady light of the same intensity as the average intensity of the flickering light. Thus, the flicker was perceived as steady because the activity of the visual system responded as though the light were steady; that is, the discharge was tonic, and the level of tonic activity was inversely proportional to the power of the average intensity.

Functional relations also have been found between the level of tonic activity in other primary sensory systems and environmental stimuli, notably the auditory pathway (Galambos and Davis, 1944; Galin, 1964) and the temperature organ (Hensel, 1952; Zotterman, 1953). Though many other examples could be cited, these and the others described above should suffice to illustrate that tonic activity in the nervous system has very specific functional value and therefore is not merely noise.

Analysis of the mode of action of phasic and tonic activity in the CNS as demonstrated by the experiments discussed suggests that phasic activity selects and guides responses while tonic activity controls the fineness and extent of the response. In a given sequence from stimulus to response, the distribution of the two types of activity throughout the CNS may be described as follows:

1. In sensory systems phasic activity is the response to transient stimuli, while the level of tonic activity signals the average intensity of background stimuli.

2. Both phasic and tonic activity in sensory systems modulate the exist-

ing tonic discharge in the brain-stem reticular formation. In this case the state of arousal is modified by the level of tonic activity in the ascending reticular activating system; postural tonus is changed by the tonic discharge of the descending reticular activating system (motor set to respond?), while the phasic discharges probably mediate attention or orienting responses.

3. In the skeletal and autonomic motor systems the phasic activity in specific motor nuclei and tracts selects and initiates movement and modifies visceral function while tonic activity provides the fine control and extent of movements and level of visceral function.

4. Feedback of phasic and tonic activity in all systems—receptor, sensory, motor, autonomic, and activating—to and from the cerebral cortex and subcortical nuclei provides the continued sequence of responses necessary for completion of an act.

It is evident from this analysis that stimuli are always superimposed upon the tonic activity of the *entire* brain, and that the perception and "meaning" of a stimulus must depend upon the relative amounts of tonic activity in the various parts of the nervous system. Discrimination, generalization, and learning occur with repeated exposures under different and similar circumstances with different and similar patterns of tonic activity throughout the nervous system. This is well illustrated by the fact that perception, discrimination, and learning depend upon and may be modified by changes in level of activation, patterns of muscle activity, and states of visceral activity and the activity in other sensory systems, all primarily tonic in nature.

In his thoughtful evaluation of cerebral organization and behavior, Lashley (1958) has given to tonic activity the major role of the neural basis of mind. Though reminiscent of Hebb's (1949) concept of the "cell assembly" and "phase sequence," in that Lashley organizes the brain into a large number of systems where each system consists of the traces of a number of habits or memories, Lashley still ascribes mental function to the tonic activity of these trace systems rather than to a particular set of connections between specific neurons and their patterns of activity. This concept is not only consistent with what is now known of the physiology of the brain, but is also the only explanation that will satisfy the efficiency of behavior following brain damage (e.g., Lashley's laws of "mass action" and "equipotentiality") and the many controversial neurological interpretations of events in perception and learning.

References

Arduini, A. The tonic discharge of the retina and its central effects. In G. Moruzzi, A. Fessard, and H. H. Jasper (Eds.), *Progress in brain research*. Vol. 1. *Brain mechanisms*. New York: Elsevier, 1963. Pp. 184–206.

Arduini, A., and Cavaggioni, A. Attività tonica della retina registrata con semi-microelettrodi. *Bollettino della Società italiana di biologia sperimentale,* 1961, **37,** 1393–1395.

Arduini, A., and Pinneo, L. R. Attività nel nervo ottico e nel genicolato laterale nell'oscurita 'e durante l'illuminazione continua. *Bollettino della Società italiana di biologia sperimentale,* 1961, **37,** 430–432.

Arduini, A., and Pinneo, L. R. Properties of the retina in response to steady illumination. *Archives italiennes de biologie,* 1962, **100,** 425–448.

Arduini, A., and Pinneo, L. R. The effects of flicker and steady illumination on the activity of the cat visual system. *Archives italiennes de biologie,* 1963, **101,** 508–529. (a)

Arduini, A., and Pinneo, L. R. The tonic activity of the lateral geniculate nucleus in dark and light adaptation. *Archives italiennes de biologie,* 1963, **101,** 493–507. (b)

Brooks, B. A. *Neural correlates of brightness discrimination in the squirrel monkey* (Saimiri sciureus). (Doctoral dissertation, Florida State University) Ann Arbor, Mich.: University Microfilms, 1964, No. 65-326.

Dow, R. S., and Moruzzi, G. *The physiology and pathology of the cerebellum.* Minneapolis: University of Minnesota Press, 1958.

Field, J., Magoun, H. W., and Hall, V. E. (Eds.), *Handbook of physiology: Section I. Neurophysiology.* Vol. 2. Washington, D.C.: American Physiological Society, 1960.

Galambos, R., and Davis, H. Inhibition of activity in single auditory nerve fibers by acoustic stimulation. *Journal of Neurophysiology,* 1944, **7,** 283–303.

Galin, D. Auditory nuclei: Distinctive response patterns to white noise and tones in unanesthetized cats. *Science,* 1964, **146,** 270–272.

Granit, R. *Receptors and sensory perception.* New Haven: Yale University Press, 1955.

Hebb, D. O. *The organization of behavior.* New York: Wiley, 1949.

Hebb, D. O. Distinctive features of learning in the higher animal. In A. Fessard, R. W. Gerard, J. Konorski, and J. F. Delafresnaye (Eds.), *Brain mechanisms and learning.* Springfield, Ill.: Charles C Thomas, 1961. Pp. 37–51.

Hensel, H. Physiologie der Thermoreception. *Ergebnisse der Physiologie (biologischen Chemie und experimentellen Pharmakologie),* 1952, **47,** 165–368.

Lashley, K. S. The problem of serial order in behavior. In L. A. Jeffress (Ed.), *Cerebral mechanisms in behavior.* New York: Wiley, 1951. Pp. 112–147.

Lashley, K. S. Cerebral organization and behavior. *Proceedings of the Association for Research in Nervous and Mental Diseases,* 1958, **36,** 1–18.

Lindsley, D. D., Schreiner, L. H., and Magoun, H. W. An electromyographic study of spasticity. *Journal of Neurophysiology,* 1949, **12,** 197–205.

Moruzzi, G., and Magoun, H. W. Brain stem reticular formation and activation of the EEG. *Electroencephalography and Clinical Neurophysiology,* 1964, **1,** 455–473.

Patton, H. D., and Amassian, V. E. The pyramidal tract: Its excitation and functions. In J. Field, H. W. Magoun, and V. E. Hall (Eds.), *Handbook of physiology: Section I. Neurophysiology.* Vol. 2. Washington, D.C.: American Physiological Society, 1960. Pp. 837–861.

Pinneo, L. R. The effects of induced muscle tension during tracking on level of activation and on performance. *Journal of Experimental Psychology,* 1961, **62,** 523–531.

Pinneo, L. R. Electrical control of behavior by programmed stimulation of the brain. *Nature,* in press. (a)

Pinneo, L. R. Neurology of brightness vision. *Scientific American,* in press. (b)

Pompeiano, O. Organizzazione somatotopica delle risposte flessorie alla stimolazione elettrico del nucleo interposito nel gatto decerebrato. *Archivio di scienze biologiche,* 1959, **43,** 163–176.

Sherrington, C. S. *The integrative action of the nervous system.* New Haven: Yale University Press, 1906.

Stevens, S. S. The surprising simplicity of sensory metrics. *American Psychologist,* 1962, **17,** 29–39.

Tower, S. S. The pyramidal tract. In P. C. Bucy (Ed.), *The precontrol motor cortex.* Urbana: University of Illinois Press, 1949. Pp. 149–172.

Treisman, M. Noise and Weber's law: The discrimination of brightness and other dimensions. *Psychological Review,* 1964, **71,** 314–330.

Zotterman, Y. Special senses: Thermal receptors. *Annual Review of Physiology,* 1953, **15,** 357–372.

Electrophysiological Correlates of Avoidance Conditioning in the Cat[*]

E. R. JOHN AND K. F. KILLAM[†]

Reprinted from *Journal of Pharmacology and Experimental Therapeutics,* 1959, Vol. 125, pp. 252–274.

At present much information has been accumulated concerning the electrical activity of the central nervous system and an equally large amount relative to learned behavior. Yet relatively little is known about the relationships between the electrical activity of the brain and the adaptive behavior which it presumably directs. From studies of animals with brain lesions, much knowledge has been gathered concerning the central neural structures necessary for the acquisition or retention of certain responses. Less well understood is the manner in which activity in these structures modifies and interacts with incoming information to generate adaptive behavior. Some indication of these processes should be obtainable, however, by direct observation of the electrical activity from brain structures during the acquisition and performance of behavioral responses. Reviews of the extensive literature in this field have been published recently by Yoshii, Matsumoto and Hori (1957) and Rusinov and Rabinovich (1958).

A major difficulty in this approach has been the identification of relevant signals in the midst of generalized brain activity. This paper reports an attempt to solve this problem by the use of a "frequency-tagged" conditioned stimulus in experiments in which frequency discrimination formed a requirement of the conditioning procedure. The recurrent conditioned stimulus has been termed a "tracer conditioned stimulus" (TCS) because the neural signals evoked may

* Part of this material was presented before the American Society for Pharmacology and Experimental Therapeutics, Baltimore, Maryland, September, 1957.

† This investigation was supported in part by a Senior Research Fellowship (Keith F. Killam) from the United States Public Health Service and by grant G-3354 from the National Science Foundation.

be followed through the brain somewhat as a radioactive tracer can be followed through a chemical process. Correlates of learning were identified by searching the records of electrical activity, obtained from several parts of the brain during the acquisition of the conditioned response, for brain potentials whose frequency was correlated with that of the TCS.

Since the appearance of electrical potentials at the TCS frequency was to be used to identify structures that were handling the information at any given stage of training, it was necessary to avoid changes which might be associated with the animal's adaptation to the TCS alone. Therefore, before avoidance training was initiated, the animals went through a period of familiarization during which the TCS was repeatedly presented, unpaired with any consequence. When no further changes in the recorded electrical responses were observed in a series of presentations of the TCS, avoidance training was begun.

During the acquisition of a conditioned avoidance response (CAR) a progression of changes in electrical responses was noted, terminating in an electrical response pattern specific for the performance of the CAR, once it had been acquired. Despite the fact that these electrical changes developed in parallel with behavioral changes, suggesting that they were related to learning, additional exploration of the coincidence of the behavioral responses with the appearance of the electrical pattern was undertaken by manipulating the animals' behavior with psychological or pharmacological techniques. The former included tests of *generalization* of the CAR to stimuli of the same modality but other frequencies, as well as to stimuli of the same frequency but another modality; *transfer* of the CAR to a TCS of the same frequency but another modality, but now associated with reinforcement; and *extinction* of the CAR. The pharmacological manipulation to be reported here consisted of the administration of reserpine in sufficient dosage to block the CAR.

Methods

Recording electrodes were implanted in 6 cats under pentobarbital anesthesia. All animals were subjected to CAR training and 4 also received conditioned approach training. In all 6 essentially the same progression of electrical changes was observed during CAR training. This report will be restricted to the detailed analysis of the electrical changes observed with the 2 animals subjected only to CAR training. In both animals, stainless steel screws resting lightly on the dura were placed over the cortical visual and auditory areas, while bipolar electrodes were oriented stereotaxically into the lateral geniculate body, the superior colliculus and the mesencephalic reticular formation. In one animal, additional electrodes were implanted in anterior and posterior hippocampus and in the lateral portion of the amygdaloid complex; in the other, electrodes were placed in fornix, septum and nucleus ventralis anterior of the thalamus.

These placements were chosen to monitor electrical activity in the classical afferent system: cortical placements, superior colliculus and lateral geniculate; in the extralemniscal system: midbrain tegmentum and ventralis anterior of the thalamus; and in the rhinenecephalic forebrain: fornix, septum, hippocampus and amygdala.

In both cats, all electrode placements were confirmed by histologic examination at the conclusion of the experiments. The maximum variation in placements common to the 2 animals was 0.5 mm in geniculate and superior colliculus. The electrodes implanted in the deep structures of the brain consisted of two 32 gauge insulated stainless steel wires laminated to a coated 22 gauge steel strut. The electrodes were trimmed off at the tip of the strut, so that recordings were taken from the cross-section of the 2 wires separated by the width of the strut.

Procedures were carried out in a sound-resistant, shielded, two-compartment hurdle box, one wall of which consisted of a one-way vision mirror which enabled observation of the animal. The tracer visual stimulus was provided by a fluorescent tube in the rear wall of the apparatus which flickered at 10 flashes per second. The same tube provided steady light of identical intensity between periods of flicker. Other flicker frequencies were used as indicated for generalization studies. The light intensity was moderate but sufficient to illuminate the entire interior of the hurdle box. The presence of a mirror as one wall and the use of glossy white paint on the others minimized variations in intensity inside the box. The auditory tracer stimulus, used in transfer studies, consisted of 10 per second clicks from an 8 inch speaker driven by 9 V, 0.5 millisecond pulses from a Grass stimulator.

Following an initial healing period after surgery of 10 days to 2 weeks, electrical recordings were taken, using a Grass model 111B electroencephalograph, at all daily sessions throughout the experimental procedures which are described below. Throughout the various procedures, periodic attempts were made to assure that the responses observed were not due to artifacts introduced by the equipment used. The fluorescent tube was covered, masking the light but not shielding electric radiations into the box or blocking out any possible auditory cues. No sound accompanied the on-off of the tube. The photocell used to monitor the flashing light was also removed to avoid radiation of signals when it was energized. The leads were moved to other terminals on the input terminal box. Records were taken with the apparatus as normal except that a 10,000 ohm resistance was substituted for the animal. Finally the experimenter would cover the animals' eyes with his hands. Under all the conditions described, no evidence of artifacts could be discerned.

Experimental Procedures

A. FAMILIARIZATION.   Twenty 15-second periods of flicker (10/sec) were presented daily for 20 days. The time interval between flicker periods randomly varied from 15 to 75 seconds so that on the average there occurred 1 flicker period per minute over a total time of 20 minutes.

B. TRAINING.   After familiarization, a conditioned avoidance response (CAR) was established to 10-second flicker using 20 randomly spaced flicker periods daily. Fifteen seconds after onset of each flicker period, intermittent shocks at an intensity of 0.2 to 0.4 mA were delivered to the feet of the animal once every 5 seconds until it crossed the hurdle (escape), at which time shock was terminated and the flicker replaced by steady light. If crossing occurred within 15 seconds after the onset of flicker (CAR), the flicker was replaced by steady light and no shock was delivered. The time interval between the onset of the flicker (TCS) and CAR was recorded as the "response latency." This training procedure was continued daily until crossing occurred in 15 seconds or less in all 20 TCS presentations on a single day, that is, until no shock was delivered to the animal throughout an entire day's training session (100% CAR).

C. GENERALIZATION.   After criterion was reached (100% CAR) to 10-second flicker, other flicker frequencies ranging from 6.8 to 13/sec were presented. If crossing of the hurdle occurred in 15 seconds or less, flicker was terminated and replaced by steady light. If crossing did not take place, the flicker was terminated at 15 seconds and replaced by steady light. *In no case was shock administered.* Thus, while CAR was reinforced by termination of the presumably aversive stimulus, failure was not punished. Crossing responses to flicker frequencies other than 10 per second therefore constitute evidence of generalization rather than of new learning.

Following completion of tests for generalization to other flicker frequencies, 10/sec clicks were presented for 20 15-second periods in the presence of steady fluorescent light. Failure to cross the hurdle within 15 seconds was not punished by shock; the clicks were terminated either on performance of the CAR or at the end of 15 seconds without CAR.

D. TRANSFER TRAINING.   After (C) was completed, training was initiated to transfer the CAR to 10/sec clicks which were now paired with shock. The procedure was completely analogous to that used in (B) except that silence rather than steady sound replaced the clicks at the termination of each stimulus period.

E. EFFECTS OF RESERPINE.   After transfer was achieved, 70 μg/kg of reserpine was injected intramuscularly. Recording of the electrical activity and behavioral performance, both to the original and transferred TCS, was taken every other hour for 8 hours and then periodically until the behavioral response returned to criterion (100% CAR).

F. EXPERIMENTAL.   One of the animals suffered an accidental injury and died at this stage. In the remaining animal, after the above procedures were concluded, the CAR to 10/sec flicker was experimentally extinguished. The extinction procedure on each day was as follows: 1) Twenty flicker periods were presented and the latency of crossing was measured. If the crossing did not occur within 15 seconds after the onset of the flicker, the flicker was terminated and no shock was delivered. 2) Fifteen minutes of continuous flicker was presented and the number of crosses of the hurdle were recorded. Crossing was not reinforced by the termination of the TCS, nor were shocks delivered. 3) Twenty flicker periods were delivered as in 1) above. This extinction procedure was continued until no CAR's were obtained during the 2 sessions of 20 15-second flicker periods on a single day and until no evidence of autonomic response to the TCS could be observed, e.g., pupillary dilation and alteration in respiration. Electrical recordings were taken during the 15/sec flicker sessions.

G. EFFECT OF EXTINCTION ON A TRANSFERRED RESPONSE. After extinction of the CAR to 10/sec flicker was achieved, 10/sec clicks were presented to see whether the CAR to the auditory stimulus had also been extinguished. The latency of the CAR's was measured as usual. Flicker periods were then interspersed with click periods to see whether the extinguished CAR to flicker would rebound if the CAR was elicited by clicks.

Analysis of Data

During the procedures outlined above, a sequence of changes was observed in the electrical activity associated with the learning of the CAR. Of necessity only discrete points in this continuum can be illustrated. In order to analyze the data 4 procedures were carried out. First, various stages in the learning curve were designated from the behavioral protocols. Second, a section of record was selected that was typical of the series of TCS presentations at each stage. Third, the selected records were characterized for the dominant electrical patterns and the patterns for successive stages were compared. Since electronic frequency analysis equipment was not available, frequency measurements were made with calipers and overlays. Finally, in an effort to inject more continuity into this method of presentation, the recordings obtained on the day before and the day after each illustration were scored for similarity or dissimilarity to the example. For each figure presented to illustrate changes during conditioning, the percentage of "similar" recordings is indicated on the day from which the example was selected and a comparison is made with the preceding and succeeding days.

Results

Observations during the long period of familiarization, training generalization, transfer and subsequent stabilization consisted for each animal of 45 to 60 minutes of electroencephalographic recordings at each of 48 daily sessions. Further studies during psychological and pharmacological manipulation of the learned behavior involving an additional 79 hours of recording over 45 days for one animal and 32 hours over 5 days for the other. The mass of data accumulated revealed a complex sequence of changes in the electrical activity of various brain structures emitted spontaneously and in response to the repeated presentations of the TCS. Since similar acquired responses appeared at approximately the same stages of learning in both animals, the figures presented are composites which depict typical changes in electrical activity in structures common to both animals as well as electrical activity recorded from other electrodes in each animal.

Familiarization

The familiarization period for each animal lasted for 21 days. Upon repeated presentations of the same 10/sec flicker a diminution of the central electrical response was observed, not only within a given daily session of 20 trials but also progressively from day to day. On initial presentation of the

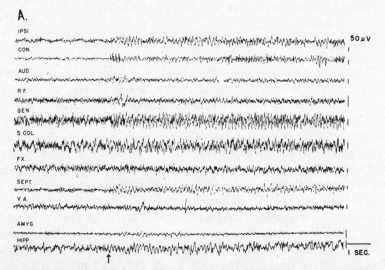

FIGURE 1. *Note:* Percentages refer to all responses for both animals, recorded on the day the illustrated records were obtained, which displayed the essential characteristics of the example. Plus or minus denotes whether the records which differed from the example were characterized consistently by more or less pronounced labeled responses. The annotation "a" indicates that due to either sudden, quick movements of the animal or the appearance of shorting artifact from a broken cable the records were too obscured to allow analysis.

A. Electrical response to the TCS recorded at the beginning of the familiarization period. IPSI (100%)—bipolar derivation from the same optic gyrus; CON (100%)—bipolar transcortical (visual) derivation; AUD (73%+)—auditory cortex; RF (65%+)—midbrain tegmentum (reticular formation); GEN (50%−)—lateral geniculate body; COLL (95%)—superior colliculus; FX (100%)—fornix; SEPT (100%)—septum; VA (100%)—nucleus ventralis anterior of the thalamus; AMYG (67%)—lateral amygdaloid complex; HIPP (100%)—hippocampus. Records obtained on the day after the illustrated responses showed a generalized slight diminution in labeled responses, with the decrement most marked in SEPT, AMYG and HIPP.

flickering light, high-voltage, frequency-specific responses * were observed in visual cortex (IPSI and CON),† lateral geniculate body (GEN), superior colliculus (S. COLL.) and hippocampus (HIPP). Occasional labeled potentials might also be seen in the tegmentum (RF), septum (SEPT) and amygdala (AMYG) (Fig. 1*A*). The labeled responses disappeared first from the amygdala and then from the hippocampus.

The pattern of disappearance of frequency-specific responses in the visual pathway was of particular interest. After 6 days (120 repeated presentations of the flickering light), an intermediate stage was observed in which the lateral geniculate responses waxed and waned during the flicker rather than maintaining their earlier constant amplitude (Fig. 1*B*). During the periods when no geniculate response was apparent, labeled potentials were still recorded in the reticular formation and in the visual cortical derivations. As the familiarization period was continued, the cyclical diminution of geniculate responses became more frequent and more marked (Fig. 1*C*) until, after 19 to 21 days of flicker

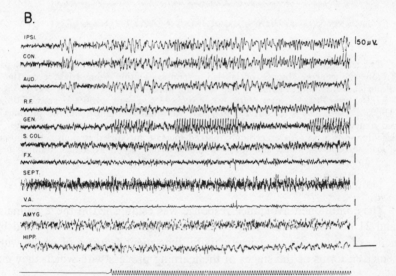

B. Electrical responses to the TCS recorded in the middle of the familiarization procedure. Note the pronounced waxing and waning in the lateral geniculate response (GEN) and the presence of labeled responses in various structures, including RF, during the waning phase: IPSI (95%), CON (95%), AUD (90%), RF (95%), GEN (50%−), COLL (95%), FX (95%), SEPT (95%), VA (95%), AMYG (100%), HIPP (100%). Recordings obtained the day before those illustrated were essentially comparable to the figure with somewhat more labeled responses visible in SEPT, AMYG and HIPP and with less pronounced waxing and waning in GEN. Little change was observed the next day except for more pronounced GEN fluctuations.

*The term "evoked potentials" is used to denote electrical activity induced by the presentation of the TCS. Evoked potentials at the same frequency as the TCS, or at multiples or submultiples thereof, are referred to as "labeled responses," "frequency specific responses" or "following."

† "IPSI" refers to records between 2 electrodes on the same hemisphere, and "CON" to transcortical records.

presentation, the high-amplitude, frequency-specific responses dropped out completely. When the final vestige of this response was no longer evoked by flicker, avoidance training was initiated.

C.

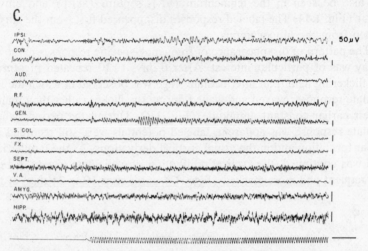

C. Electrical responses to the TCS recorded at the end of the familiarization procedure. Note the general absence of labeled responses. During some trials, even the low amplitude labeled responses visible in GEN were not apparent: IPSI (73% +), CON (93% +), AUD (97%), RF (90% +), GEN (80% --), COLL (93% a), FX (100%), SEPT (70% +), VA (100%), AMYG (80% a), HIPP (90% a). Recordings obtained on the previous day showed somewhat more pronounced labeled responses in cortical derivations and GEN, and appreciably more in RF. An exceedingly marked increase in labeled responses was observed in all leads except VA, AMYG and HIPP on the next day, when avoidance training began.

Training

The conditioned avoidance response was established in the 2 animals in 19 and 21 days of training respectively. This learning was accompanied by a sequence of changes in electrical activity, the salient features of which will be presented in terms of the stages of the learning process with which they coincided.

A. INITIAL EFFECTS OF SHOCK.   At the initiation of training, the association of shock with the TCS led to an overall increase in background activity and to the return or increase of labled electrical responses (Fig. 2).* High-voltage, frequency-specific waves were recorded from optic cortex, lateral geniculate, superior colliculus, fornix and septum. The potentials from the fornix and septum became similar, in contrast to earlier and later stages. Occasional bursts of frequency-specific potentials were seen in records from the auditory cortex. The hippocampus, however, did not exhibit "following" of the TCS until 80 shock trials had been presented.

* Editor's note: Figures 2–14 have been deleted from the text of this article. The reader is referred to the original source for these illustrations.

B. DISCRIMINATION OF THE TCS.   As pairing of TCS and shock continued, animals gave evidence of discrimination of the TCS by exhibiting behavior reminiscent of the "conditioned emotional response," i.e., at the onset of flicker, the animals cringed, growled and defecated. This behavior was well established by the fifth day of training when no avoidance responses had yet been made.

During this period marked changes occurred in electrical recordings from various brain structures (Fig. 3). First, the generalized, high-amplitude responses seen after the first shock experiences diminished, and then were replaced by marked and persistent frequency-specific responses in visual cortex, reticular formation and hippocampus. There was a striking absence of evoked potentials in superior colliculus and auditory cortex. The similarity of the potentials recorded from the fornix and septum persisted.

The labeled potentials recorded from the lateral geniculate body were markedly reduced over those seen during the early pairing of TCS with shock. The most extreme example, characteristic of one animal, is depicted in Figure 3. In both animals, as well as in subsequent animals, this decrement in response approximated that seen in the terminal stages of the familiarization period before CAR training began. In many instances there was even a decrease in the responses beyond that obtained during the familiarization period. This pattern became evident with the appearance of behavior resembling the conditioned emotional response and persisted in the recordings from the geniculate body until a significant number of CAR's were elicited. At this time a decrease was observed in frequency-specific potentials recorded from the midbrain tegmentum and hippocampus as the labeled potentials returned to the recordings from the lateral geniculate body (discussed below).

C. EARLY CONDITIONED AVOIDANCE RESPONSES.   The earliest avoidance responses to the TCS occurred at a stage when there was an increased incidence of spontaneous hurdle crossing. At this point only relatively minor alterations were observed in the electrophysiological recordings during TCS (Fig. 4). An evoked response in the auditory cortex appeared and amygdaloid activity showed an increase in amplitude. Frequency-specific responses remained in the optic cortex and hippocampus and began to appear sporadically in superior colliculus, although they were still not recorded from the lateral geniculate body. The response of the reticular formation, however, became less discrete and regular, while the apparent synchronization between fornix and septum was accentuated during the TCS.

In contrast to these small quantitative changes in the responses to TCS observed during the first avoidance responses, a number of important qualitative changes appeared when a significant level of CAR performance had been reached (Fig. 5). By the 24% performance level, stable, high-voltage potentials appeared in the lateral geniculate body at the TCS frequency, while high-voltage slow waves were observed in superior colliculus with superimposed low-voltage, TCS-frequency activity. The frequency-specific potentials were no longer marked from visual cortical recordings taken transcortically (*con vis*), although they remained present in records taken from electrodes on the same hemisphere (*ipsi vis*). Outside of the visual system, changes were also observed. Following of the TCS lessened in the auditory cortex and the reticular formation. Fornix and septal recordings became disassociated and some indications of frequency-specific responses appeared in fornix. These subsequently became more marked and then diminished again by the time 65% CAR was reached. No tracings were obtained from the hippocampus or amygdala at the 24% CAR level of performance.

D. WELL ESTABLISHED CAR.   When performance reached 65% correct responses (Fig. 6), electrical responses to the TCS became stable in many brain structures and appeared to be characteristic of the fully trained animal. In the visual system, high-voltage, frequency-specific responses consistently appeared in the lateral geniculate body and high-voltage, slow activity was even more evident in the superior colliculus. The visual cortex, however, showed a markedly different response from that obtained earlier; evoked responses appeared at a multiple of the TCS frequency, at 20 or 30/sec. Auditory cortex showed TCS following only sporadically. Activity in the reticular formation was decreased in amplitude relative to that seen at earlier stages and included little labeled response. Again, as during the 24% CAR stage, fornix and septum showed no relationship although some frequency-specific response to the TCS, most marked in fornix, was visible in the recordings from both structures. Somewhat higher amplitude activity was seen in the amygdala than in previous recordings. Frequency-specific responses no longer appeared in the tracings obtained from the hippocampus, although the amplitude of activity was higher.

When criterion was reached (100% CAR), the most marked changes noted were in the activity of the amygdala, which displayed bursts of 40/sec waves during the TCS, and in nucleus ventralis anterior of the thalamus, which for the first time acquired a marked frequency-specific response to the TCS (Fig. 7). Electrical patterns from visual cortex were only slightly altered. The evoked cortical responses tended to appear more often at 20/sec than at 30/sec and tracings from the 2 visual derivations were more often different than alike, with respect to TCS following. Frequency-specific responses showed increased amplitude in the lateral geniculate body and the slow waves from the superior colliculus were also enhanced.

Responses at the TCS frequency were further decreased in reticular formation and were no longer recorded from the auditory cortex, fornix, septum and hippocampus. The overall amplitude of background activity in these structures also decreased markedly.

E. CHANGES IN SPONTANEOUS ELECTRICAL ACTIVITY DURING TRAINING. During the training period spontaneous activity in many brain structures, recorded in the absence of the TCS, became strikingly modified to include features of the acquired electrical response to the TCS characteristic of the particular stage of learning (Fig. 9). These rhythms dominated the spontaneous activity recorded during early stages of acquisition of the CAR, but became less evident as training progressed. When the CAR was established at the 100% criterion, spontaneous activity was very different from that recorded at 0%, but activity resembling responses evoked by the TCS occurred primarily in the amygdala (40/sec bursts of high voltage waves), in the superior colliculus (slow wave activity) and in visual cortex (20 to 30/sec potentials).

During intervals between conditioning trials, animals in the conditioning apparatus demonstrated a set of behavioral changes parallel to the alterations in spontaneous electrical activity of the brain just described. During initial training, affective responses were shown throughout the experimental period including almost continuous growling and vocalizing and frequent defecation. As training continued, these responses diminished but the level of motor activity was increased and the incidence of spontaneous crossings of the hurdle rose sharply. When the CAR was well established, the incidence of spontaneous hurdle crossing became very low and few signs of affective response were present. Of particular interest was the high correlation of spontaneous electrical activity patterns reminiscent of acquired responses to the TCS, particularly in amygdala and visual cortex, with spontaneous crossing of the hurdle at this stage.

The patterns of electrical changes occurring during the acquisition of the CAR and the patterns preceding the performance of the CAR in the fully trained animals were not seen in untrained animals or in animals being subjected to the familiarization procedure. Labeled electrical responses to the flashing light were observed in the untrained animals as the animals crossed the barrier in the course of the random motor activity associated with exploratory behavior as well as when the animals were not moving about. Occasionally there would appear in a recording from a single area a fleeting response that in comparison to the electrical changes described as occurring during training would be considered similar, e.g., a short burst of multiple-frequency responses in the visual cortical leads. However, during such activity the records from the other central nervous system structures were dissimilar to the records obtained during the training procedure.

It has not been possible from these studies to delineate any particular structure that could be considered to generate the conditioned avoidance behavior. Rather it has been observed that, associated with the generation of the behavior, electrical activity appears in many structures. Undoubtedly there are additional structures involved in the performance of the conditioned behavior that were not monitored in this study. Whether activity in the structures monitored in this study is common to the generation of other types of conditioned behavior will need to be ascertained.

Generalization

After 100% performance of the CAR had been established to light flickering at 10/sec, initial presentation of flicker at a frequency of 6.8/sec elicited the CAR. However, central electrical responses to the new stimulus remained bound to the original TCS frequency; for example, 20 to 30/sec in visual cortex (Fig. 10*A*). After repeated presentations of the 6.8/sec stimulus without reinforcement, however, electrical activity of the brain showed a 7/sec basic frequency, and avoidance responses were no longer elicited. At this stage, re-presentation of the original TCS (10/sec flicker) elicited 7/sec potential responses in the brain and no behavioral avoidance response was obtained (Fig. 10*B*). After further presentation of the 10/sec TCS, the electrical responses characteristic of a trained animal returned to the electrical records and the animals again performed conditioned avoidance responses. Similar data were obtained during tests of generalization to 13/sec flicker.

Transfer

In both animals trained to 100% CAR with 10/sec flickering light, presentation of 10/sec clicks did not evoke frequency-specific potentials in the electrical records nor was the CAR elicited (Fig. 11*A*). Shock was then paired with the clicks, using a procedure parallel to that used in earlier training to flicker. Only 2 reinforced presentations of the 10/sec clicks in 1 animal and 4 reinforced presentations in the other were required to establish fully the CAR to 10/sec clicks. In both cases, the electrical activity evoked at central sites by 10/sec clicks then bore a remarkable resemblance to that evoked by 10/sec flicker (Fig. 11*B*), particularly with respect to the incidence of 20 and 30/sec activity in visual cortex, the high voltage slow waves in the superior colliculus and the 40/sec bursts in the amygdala.

The Effects of Reserpine

Six hours after reserpine (70 μg/kg, i.m.) the animals evidenced no avoidance responses and 8 hours after reserpine, no escape responses. Reduction of spontaneous crossings of the hurdle, together with the characteristic decay of the behavioral response and its subsequent return in 3 days, are shown in Figure 12. Following administration of reserpine, the alterations in the behavioral responses paralleled alterations in the acquired electrical responses; and the electrical responses returned with the return of the CAR

The EEG recordings after the disappearance of the CAR are typified by Figure 13. The frequency of the evoked potentials recorded from the visual cortex is that of the TCS, 10/sec, rather than 20 to 30/sec as just before the test. Marked labeled potentials reappear in the reticular formation and fornix. The high voltage, slow waves disappeared from the superior colliculus and there was a decay in the responses in the lateral geniculate recordings. The 40/sec burst activity in the amygdala was no longer present. These findings resemble a regression to records obtained around the 25% performance level of the CAR during training. The alteration of electrical changes after reserpine approximated a reversal of the training progression in a telescoped fashion.

Furthermore, after reserpine, at any given behavioral performance level the electrical recordings were similar to those seen at the same level of performance during the acquisition of the CAR. Three to 4 hours after administration of the drug, the behavioral performance level was 70 to 80% correct responses. At this time, frequency-specific responses were no longer present in the records obtained from the nucleus ventralis anterior of the thalamus, and the 40/sec burst activity was not observed in the records from the amygdala. Six to 8 hours after the drug was administered, when the CAR was completely suppressed, the transcortical visual records were relatively isopotential, whereas records obtained from the 2 electrodes on the same optic gyrus exhibited frequency-specific following. The high voltage slow activity disappeared from the superior colliculus records.

With the disappearance of escape behavior, approximately 8 hours after the drug was administered, frequency-specific potentials appeared in the records from the reticular formation and in both visual cortical leads. The responses in the lateral geniculate became more irregular but frequency-specificity was observed over short periods of time. Of interest is the fact that evoked potentials did not return in the hippocampal leads, although they could be seen in records from the fornix. As the drug action waned, the electrical patterns characteristic of the trained animal reappeared in approximately the reverse order. An additional phenomenon of interest, observed after reserpine, was a marked hypersynchrony in the visual system which could be evoked or could appear spontaneously. This hypersynchrony, which was not associated with seizure discharge in the rhinencephalic structures, will be described in detail in a forthcoming paper.

Throughout the period in which the CAR was blocked by reserpine the animals reacted to the presentation of the TCS by growling, crouching, defecating and by vigorously attempting various routes of anticipatory evasion other than the appropriate one of crossing the hurdle. Between presentations of the TCS, the reserpinized animals displayed the behavior usually described as "tranquilized." Throughout the duration of action of reserpine, they exhibited side effects characteristic of the drug action.

Experimental Extinction

After the extinction procedure was initiated, the first electrical response to wane from the pattern characteristic of the trained animal was the 40/sec burst activity in the amygdala. This response was quite labile, in that it would occasionally reappear during the extinction period, sometimes for no apparent reason, but usually in association with a CAR. At a later stage, flinching and growling were once more seen in response to the TCS and marked multiple frequency responses in the visual cortical recordings persisted as long as the animal exhibited these overt responses. Interestingly, some indication of frequency-specific responses could again be observed in the hippocampus during this phase. As the extinction procedure continued, visual cortical following at

10/sec first appeared for short periods, during the typical multiple frequency responses, and then gradually occupied more and more of the visual cortical records. Frequency-specific responses gradually diminished in the lateral geniculate. The amplitude of activity recorded from the amygdala decreased, the slight following previously seen in the hippocampus diminished, and occasional brief periods of following appeared in the reticular formation. As the behavioral extinction criterion was reached, the electrical activity recorded from all structures became essentially identical with that which had been observed earlier in the advanced stages of the familiarization procedure. While frequency-specific responses could still be observed occasionally in various structures, they persisted only briefly and did not resemble those of the trained animal before extinction (Fig. 14).

After the CAR to 10/sec *flicker* was completely extinguished, presentation of the nonextinguished TCS, 10/sec *clicks,* still evoked conditioned avoidance responses. Accompanying the CAR to 10/sec clicks, evoked potentials similar to those seen before extinction of the CAR to the flicker stimulus appeared in the visual cortical tracings. When a balanced, randomly mixed series of 10/sec flicker and click stimuli was presented to the animal, performance of the CAR to flicker returned to a performance level of 30%. The accompanying electrical responses were comparable to those seen at corresponding performance levels during training. On the following day a series of only the visual stimulus was repeated and neither conditioned avoidance nor associated electrical responses were elicited.

Discussion

These experiments were designed to enable the identification of electrical events in the brain which were correlated with the acquisition and retention of an overt conditioned response. A series of changes was observed in both the form and central distribution of electrical responses to a "tracer," repetitive conditioned stimulus, during the acquisition of a conditioned avoidance response. Since the alterations in electrical responses developed as a continuous process, the attempt to present discrete features so as to categorize the responses at different stages of learning inevitably oversimplifies the observations. Stages of the learning process have been selected, however, at which marked changes in activity could be seen to occur in certain brain areas, although in other regions changes were only gradual. However, it is urged that this description be considered at best as providing only a preliminary outline of central events taking place during avoidance learning.

It was our assumption that the appearance of evoked potentials, particularly at the frequency of the tracer conditioned stimulus or a multiple thereof, indicated the arrival of information about the peripheral event at a central structure. We have termed such responses as "labeled" for the purpose of this discussion.

The data revealed that presentation of a novel TCS, in the form of flickering light, resulted in labeled electrical responses not simply in the classical visual system (lateral geniculate, superior colliculus and optic cortex), but in the extralemniscal sensory pathway (reticular formation) and in the rhinencephalon (hippocampus and amygdala) as well. As the familiarization procedure progressed, labeled electrical responses gradually disappeared and it became exceedingly difficult to tell from the recorded activity when the flashing light was turned on or off. The phenomena are reminiscent of the process of "habituation" described by other workers (Hernández-Peón and Scherrer, 1955; Galambos et al., 1956; Sharpless and Jasper, 1956) and considered to be an active function of the reticular formation. Whereas prior workers have observed this phenomenon after the continued presentation of periodic stimuli for long intervals, the present results show that marked diminution of responses can take place in a cumulative fashion, over a number of weeks, with relatively brief periods of irregularly spaced stimulus presentations separated by 24 hours. The order of disappearance of central responses (rhinencephalon, reticular formation and superior colliculus, visual cortex and finally thalamic relay nucleus) suggests that, if the process is an active one, the several participating systems display a differential susceptibility, with the classical afferent path being the most resistant.

When avoidance training was initiated and the TCS paired with shock, an increased degree of arousal in the animals was associated with an immediate return of the previously diminished labeled electrical responses in some, but not all, of the monitored structures. Of particular interest, however, is the fact that responses did not reappear in the hippocampus, which furnishes evidence that reversal of the whole familiarization process did not occur with this increased arousal. Furthermore, subsequent changes in recorded electrical responses in the various structures during training appeared independent of the simple consequences of arousal since certain labeled responses which reappeared after initial shock again diminished despite continued pairings of the TCS and shock during training. The findings (Hagbarth and Kerr, 1954; Killam and Killam, 1957) indicating that increased reticular outflow causes active blockade in sensory relays further support the view that increased reticular formation activity leading to arousal would not per se cause a reappearance of electrical responses previously diminished during familiarization.

As the animals began to associate onset of flicker with the imminence of shock (when shock had been paired with the TCS about 80 times), behavioral evidence of discrimination of the TCS was observed without appropriate avoidance behavior. This coincided with an abundance of labeled potentials in relay nuclei of the visual pathway while cortical receiving areas showed clear labeled responses to the TCS. It is not yet possible to decide whether, at this discrimination phase of learning, signals were being transmitted to the cortex by extralemniscal pathways, though the impressive responses then recorded in the reticular formation support this view. While there is considerable evidence for corticopetal projections from the reticular formation (Moruzzi and Magoun,

1949; Lindsley, Bowden and Magoun, 1949), their distribution is usually inferred to be more generalized than in the present instance. It is conceivable, alternatively, that elements of the relay nuclei responded so massively that no potential difference occurred between the bipolar recording electrodes. At the same stage, labeled responses appeared in the hippocampus.

After a surprisingly long "stimulus discrimination phase," perhaps related to the familiarization of the animals to the TCS prior to training, the CAR gradually became established. As the animals began to manifest CAR and moved into what might be called the "stimulus-response association phase" of learning, a new pattern of electrical responses emerged and those most characteristic of the stimulus discrimination phase diminished. As the activity waned in the reticular formation and hippocampus, labeled electrical responses appeared in the lateral geniculate body and superior colliculus. It is possible that the frequency-specific response in the reticular formation was previously instrumental in the suppression of similar frequency-specific responses in the visual pathways. Whatever the mechanism, the stimulus-response association phase began with the apparent establishment of a previously nonoperative afferent pathway for the signal. As the CAR performance improved from 25 through 65%, the gradual shift in labeled responses from reticular formation to specific relay nuclei of the visual system continued and the rhinencephalic system ceased to respond to the TCS. The latter change might be related to a diminution of affective reaction to the TCS as the incidence of failure and consequent shock decreased. Further experiments will be necessary to establish whether this inverse relationship between reticular formation and hippocampus on the one hand and relay nuclei on the other is functional or fortuitous.

Another major alteration in electrical activity during this part of the learning process was the departure from frequency-specificity in the evoked responses of the visual system. The slow wave in the colliculus, first observed in the stimulus-discrimination phase, became more pronounced while visual cortical responses became double or triple the TCS frequency. The precise frequency observed in the cortex suggested that 2 or 3 events occurred at each flash of light. Whether the first event is evoked by activity in the primary afferent pathway and later events by activity in more circuitous routes, or whether the presentation of the TCS evoked a repetitive cortical discharge, still remains to be determined. Whatever the explanation, this alteration in response appeared closely associated with final stages of learning.

Throughout these stages of discrimination and association, spontaneous electrical activity was observed similar to or even identical with the labeled responses evoked by the TCS. These changes, also reported by Livanov *et al.* (1951) and Yoshii *et al.* (1956), were described as "assimilation of rhythm." The fact that, at later stages of training, spontaneous performance of the CAR frequently followed the appearance of such spontaneously emitted, acquired patterns of central activity suggests their possible relation to "memory." One must certainly consider the possibility that such spontaneous repetition of the acquired electrical response to the TCS might serve in the formation of stable new associations and enable them to be carried over from session to session. Most speculations on the neural mechanisms underlying learning have in fact postulated some mechanism which enabled the central representation of a transient event to persist for a period of time while a more permanent "trace" was developed.

During the final stages of conditioning, the animal perfected motor aspects of the CAR and reduced its latency. The new central events recorded during this period were the appearance of 40/sec bursts of high voltage activity in the amygdala and the occurrence of labeled responses to the TCS in the nucleus ventralis anterior of the thalamus. Similar amygdala burst activity has been previously described by Lesse (1957) as recorded from the lateral portion of the amygdala. Histological examination of electrode placements in the current study revealed that electrode tips were in the lateral portions of the amygdaloid complex. The bursts of activity in the amygdala were almost invariant preludes to performance of the CAR, whether evoked by the TCS or spontaneously emitted. Their relevance to the final, stable, 100% performance level was further attested by their disappearance during abolition of the CAR by reserpine or experimental extinction.

Confirming evidence for the significance of the electrical response observed after the final establishment of the CAR was obtained by studies of generalization. Essentially, a test for generalization asks whether 2 different stimuli are equivalent in their ability to elicit some common response. The data presented suggest that when an animal responds with similar conditioned behavior to 2 different frequencies of flickering light, the central electrical responses to the 2 stimuli are basically the same. Thus, in the generalization trials, the initial presentation of 7/sec flicker evoked both the CAR and electrical responses comparable to those evoked by 10/sec flicker admixed with electrical responses related to the frequency of the presented stimulus. When generalization no longer occurred, evoked central responses reflected only the frequency of the new stimulus. Similarly, when subsequent 10/sec flicker was at first represented centrally with predominantly a 7/sec electrical response, no CAR occurred. After several trials, the central responses again corresponded to the frequency of the TCS, and the CAR returned. Throughout the generalization procedure, neither 7 nor 10/sec flicker was reinforced by shock.

On the presentation of 10/sec clicks, neither the criterion of conditioned response nor that of central electrical response indicated the existence of any stimulus equivalence across sensory modalities. The transfer of training, however, occurred at a remarkable rate; the CAR to the pulsed auditory stimulus was fully established after only 2 to 4 reinforcements. Further, following this transfer of training, the *auditory* TCS evoked potentials in the visual system similar to those elicited by the *visual* TCS.

These data suggest that transfer of training resulted in the establishment of central stimulus equivalence. However, after experimental extinction of the CAR to the visual TCS, when it was no longer effective in eliciting either the CAR or its acquired electrical correlates, an interesting phenomenon was observed.

The auditory TCS still retained the capacity to elicit the CAR and part, but not all, of the acquired electrical correlates were manifested. A subsequent temporary restitution of the ability of the visual TCS to elicit both the CAR and labeled electrical responses was observed. This suggests that all of the electrical correlates evoked in the visual system by the auditory TCS after transfer are not essential to the performance of the CAR, and also indicates that the "extinguished" responses to a particular stimulus can be reactivated by another stimulus with appropriate characteristics.

The primary purpose of the various psychological procedures which have been described was to evaluate the significance of the observed labeled responses in mediating the conditioned behavior. In the course of carrying out these procedures, a number of phenomena were observed which may be considered to provide evidence about mechanisms underlying the organization of afferent input to the central nervous system. During the process of familiarization, it was observed that central electrical responses to a stimulus were suppressed. Generalization tests indicated that under certain circumstances the electrical responses evoked by a particular stimulus may have the characteristic form of responses acquired to a prior different stimulus of the same modality. The phenomena observed during transfer of training indicate that a stimulus in one modality, with the appropriate characteristics, may come to evoke the electrical responses previously established to a similar stimulus over a different modality.

A single mechanism can be postulated which might account for these 3 phenomena. During repeated experience with a stimulus, an extralemniscal system may be organized which is in some fashion "tuned" to the characteristics of the stimulus in such a manner that this system can interact with classical afferent systems and exert an inhibitory or facilitatory influence. Interaction of this tuned system with a specific afferent system in an inhibitory fashion could result in the selective suppression of afferent input with certain characteristics, as observed in familiarization. Conversely, interaction in a facilitatory fashion, stabilized during conditioning, could result in the production of electrical responses in the specific system which bore the characteristics imposed by the tuned system rather than those related to the afferent input, as observed in generalization. Presentation of a new stimulus in a different modality, but with the appropriate characteristics and in the proper context, might result in the activation of the tuned system. Subsequent facilitatory action of the tuned system might result in the production of electrical responses in an afferent system different from that of the new stimulus, as observed in transfer and in the resurgence of response in the visual system after extinction when the auditory TCS was presented.

To some extent, this hypothesis is supported by the data obtained by Chow *et al.* (1957) who showed that functional equivalence is not achieved by a procedure which only establishes stimulus equivalence with respect to *cortical* electrical responses.

The relationship between the acquired central electrical responses and the CAR was investigated further by observing the consequences on both of the administration of reserpine. As the performance of the CAR deteriorated after reserpine, the acquired electrical responses disappeared in essentially the reverse order to that seen during acquisition of the CAR. As drug effects wore off, the sequence of changes in electrical response to the TCS basically recapitulated those seen during initial acquisition of the CAR. Finally, experimental extinction of the learned behavioral response resulted in a parallel gradual disappearance of the acquired electrical activity.

These various observations support the conclusion that the acquired electrical responses are neurophysiological correlates of avoidance conditioning. Perhaps more important, these experiments present a novel method of investigating the neurophysiological mechanisms mediating learning and the effects of drugs on the central nervous system.

Summary

Central electrical responses to a flickering light (TCS) have been recorded from cats having electrodes chronically implanted in cortical and subcortical areas during a) initial presentation of the stimulus, b) familiarization, c) acquisition and performance of a conditioned avoidance response (CAR), d) generalization to other frequencies of flickering light, e) transfer to pulsed auditory stimulation, f) blockade of the CAR by reserpine and g) extinction of the CAR.

Frequency-specific responses (labeled responses) recorded from visual cortex, auditory cortex, lateral geniculate, superior colliculus, amygdala and hippocampus upon first presentation of the TCS waned and disappeared during the familiarization process.

With the initial pairing of shock with TCS, labeled responses reappeared in all structures except the amygdala and hippocampus. The responses were modified in form and amplitude in the different areas of the brain in different phases of learning. Of particular interest was the shift in location of labeled responses from the classical visual pathway to the extralemniscal ascending system and then back to the major visual path again during successive stages of avoidance training.

At 100% CAR 40/sec burst activity in the amygdala and multiples of the TCS frequency in the cortical responses were characteristic features.

Evidence of the functional relevance of the electrical responses observed in certain central structures was obtained by studies of generalization, of transfer and of the effects of reserpine.

References

Chow, K. L., Dement, W. C. and John, E. R.: *J. Neurophysiol.* **20:** 482, 1957.
Galambos, R., Sheatz, G. and Vernier, V. G.: *Science* **123:** 376, 1956.
Hagbarth, K. E. and Kerr, D. I. B.: *J. Neurophysiol.* **17:** 295, 1954.

Hernández-Peón, R. and Scherrer, H.: *Fed. Proc.* **14:** 71, 1955.

Killam, K. F. and Killam, E. K.: *Reticular Formation of the Brain,* Little Brown & Co., Boston, 1958.

Lesse, H.: *Fed. Proc.* **16:** 79, 1957.

Lindsley, D. B., Bowden, J. W. and Magoun, H. W.: *Electroenceph. clin. Neurophysiol.* **1:** 475, 1949.

Livanov, M. N., Korolikova, T. A. and Frenkeli, G. M.: *Jur. Vysh. Nervn. Deyat.* (*Russ.*) **1:** 521, 1951

Moruzzi, G. and Magoun, H. W.: *Electroenceph. clin. Neurophysiol.* **1:** 455, 1949.

Rusinov, V. S. and Rabinovich, M. Y.: *Electroenceph. clin. Neurophysiol.* Suppl. 8, 1958.

Sharpless, S. and Jasper, H. H.: *Brain* 79: 655, 1956.

Yoshii, N., Gastaut, H. and Pruvot, P.: *Communications,* XX International Physiological Congress, Brussels, p. 985, 1956.

Yoshii, N., Matsumoto, J. and Hori, Y.: *Communications,* First International Congress of Neurological Sciences, Brussels, 1957.

Duplication of Evoked Potential Waveform by Curve of Probability of Firing of a Single Cell

STEPHEN S. FOX AND JAMES H. O'BRIEN

Reprinted from *Science,* Feb. 19, 1965, Vol. 147, pp. 888–890. Copyright 1965 by the American Association for the Advancement of Science.

The relation between evoked potentials and the electrical activity of single cells in brain is still not well understood, and sustained interest and a considerable amount of data have resulted in a number of contrasting points of view (*1*). Most interpretations of this relation have been based on single and multiple superimposed oscilloscope traces, but such small variable samples can yield only impressions of the pattern of single-cell firing and make agreement regarding the relation to the evoked potential difficult to reach. Although the use of nonphysiological (electrical) stimulation to produce synchronously evoked potentials provides better control of the stimulus and response and reduces the variability of the relationship, the probabilistic nature of the relation between the evoked potential and the single cell, which is characteristic of physiologically evoked responses, makes interpretation of oscilloscope data difficult.

Despite frequent disagreement as to which wave components of an evoked potential are attributable to which level of the cortex or cellular mechanism, it is generally agreed that different neural elements sequentially activated relate to the sequential appearance of various components of the waveform of the

electrically evoked potential. By means of a computer we have attempted to
clarify the relation between the probability of firing of single cortical cells and
the components of the waveform of the evoked potential recorded from the
same microelectrode. In this way, quantitative data from a large number of
single oscilloscope sweeps could be stored in the computer and summed while
the original time relations were maintained.

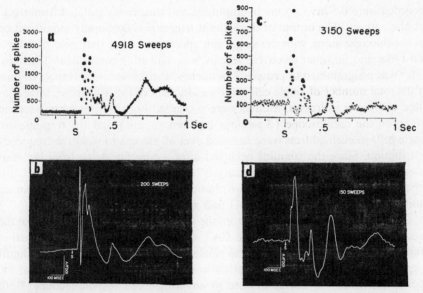

FIGURE 1. Relation between probability of firing of a single cell and evoked potential
waveform. (*a*) Frequency distribution of spikes from a single cell in the visual cortex of a
cat after stimulation with 4918 flashes; (*b*) averaged evoked potential (200 oscilloscope
sweeps) recorded from the same microelectrode, after cell death ($r = .60$; $p < .001$).
Similarly, spike distribution for a single cell is shown in (*c*) (3150 sweeps) and the corresponding averaged evoked potential in (*d*) (150 sweeps) ($r = .51$; $p < .001$). Ordinate
(for unit distributions): number of times the cell fired in response to light flash. Abscissa (for
unit distributions): time, in 100-msec divisions.

If the suggested relation of individual cell spikes to evoked potentials
(concluded from previous studies in which electrical stimulation was used)
also applied to asynchronous evoked potential and single cell responses to
physiological stimuli, then individual cells should show high probabilities of
firing corresponding uniquely to specific components of the evoked potential
complex (unimodal distribution). However, if a high frequency of firing by
individual cells does not correspond uniquely to any single component of the
evoked potential complex, but corresponds to a number of components (mul-
timodal distribution), then this would suggest that the entire evoked potential
complex is related probabilistically to each cell.

Forty cats were operated on under ether anesthesia; they were then
curarized and maintained by means of artificial respiration. The exposed tissue
margins were treated with procaine and the eyes were treated with atropine

regularly. After 3 to 5 hours, spikes from single cells were recorded from a glass microelectrode, filled with KCl (0.5- to 2 μ-tip), placed on visual or somatic sensory cortex. One microelectrode was used to record both the evoked potential and single cell responses, and these two types of response were differentiated by separate amplifiers set at appropriate frequencies.

In addition the spikes from a single cell activated a Schmitt trigger which provided digital input for one channel of a computer (2). The single cell spikes recorded were 0.5 mv to 5 mv in amplitude and thus easily isolated from background activity. The output of the Schmitt trigger was constantly monitored on an oscilloscope along with the single cell spikes to ensure that only the single cell spike and no other electrical activity was activating the trigger. The computer was programmed to provide a frequency distribution with respect to time of the total number of single cell responses in each of the 400 consecutive 2.5-msec computer addresses. Stimuli were presented once during each 1-second sweep on the oscilloscope (3 seconds between sweeps) and the responses of single cells in each address were summed over all sweeps to yield the frequency distribution. Since the stimulus occurred after a constant delay from the start of each sweep, and the computer analysis began at the start of each sweep, this procedure provided a frequency distribution composed of the spikes from an individual cell both before (control) and after stimulation.

Evoked potentials recorded from the microelectrode were averaged in the usual analog-to-digital mode of the CAT 400-B, after mechanical destruction (tapping on the microdrive) of the related cell. Observation of the Schmitt trigger monitor while evoked potentials were being averaged indicated that the evoked potential did not contribute to any single cell response count. Both frequency distributions of responses of single cells and the evoked potential averages were photographed from a "slave" oscilloscope and punched out on paper tape for processing by a general purpose computer (3). The computer program for the analysis of the data provided both an overall and a dynamic (moving window) cross-correlation for each single cell frequency distribution and evoked potential average recorded from the same microelectrode site.

Data collected from 100 cells which responded to stimulation (light or somatic) and from their related evoked potentials indicate that the probability of firing for any single cell is to a great extent given by the waveform of the evoked potential recorded from the same microelectrode; that is, the function of the best fit to the frequency distribution of response of any cell following a sensory stimulus is given by the evoked potential. Expressed somewhat differently, a single cortical cell, given enough stimulus presentations, will generate a frequency distribution over time which duplicates the entire evoked potential.

The curve in Figure 1A shows the (frequency-time) distribution of the responses of a single visual cortical cell stimulated 4918 times with a 10-μsec light flash. The averaged evoked potential from the same electrode and location, recorded after destruction of the cell which produced the data in Figure 1A, is given in Figure 1B (average of 200 sweeps). The fit of the averaged evoked potential to the distribution of the responses of the single cell is apparent. Most interesting, perhaps, is the consistency with which the single cell frequency distribution duplicates in detail even the very late (500 to 800 msec) components of the evoked potential. Comparison of Figure 1C and 1D shows that the probability of firing for another visual cortical cell after 3150 stimulations with a light flash is accurately reproduced by the shape of the averaged evoked potential (average of 150 sweeps) recorded from the same microelectrode. Since these distributions are simply counts of single-cell spikes from 4918 or 3150 multiple superimposed sweeps, little or no indication of such distribution is ever seen in single traces or in a few superimposed traces.

Overall correlations (total sweep) of single-cell spike distributions with their respective evoked potential waveforms yielded significant correlation coefficients for 66 percent of the pairs. Correlation coefficients ranged from 0.14 to 0.88 with 58 percent significant at the .001 level, 6 percent at the .01 level, and 2 percent at the .05 level of probability.

Components of the evoked response in which there are deflections both negative and positive to the baseline are duplicated by a single-cell frequency distribution only if the spontaneous firing rate is greater than zero. The relation described here between the probability of firing of a single cell and the waveform of the evoked potential holds in general for responses of single cells to both visual and somatic stimuli recorded from a number of sensory and association cortical areas, for the cerebellar vermis, and for responses of single cells to two sensory stimuli separated by a short interval. That is, if a cell responds to more than one sensory stimulus, the probability of response to each stimulus is given by the respective waveform of the evoked potential.

We conclude from these data that no component (positive or negative, early or late) of the asynchronous evoked potential recorded in this way is uniquely related to responses of specific cell populations or to specific portions of cells, since from each cell a probability curve can be obtained which closely resembles the waveform of the entire evoked response. This outcome suggests, therefore, that whatever potential sources contribute to the evoked potential, they are directly related to or reflected in the firing of a single cell.

The data appear to support at least two interpretations of evoked potential electrogenesis: (i) the evoked potential may consist of summated and asynchronous discharges from cell bodies, with cells in a given localized area having approximately the same probability of firing, or (ii) the evoked potential may be compounded of electrical activity from a number of sources either local or distant, for example, apical, somatic, or basal dendritic postsynaptic potentials and local potentials associated with electronic spread from dendrites.

Although our records for both cells and waves are from microelectrodes deep in the cortex, some more specific conclusions can be drawn. It appears, for example, that either the recorded evoked potentials do not reflect dendritic activity at all and that both positive and negative waves recorded are local in origin, or that there is, in fact, an important relation between dendritic activity and the production of spikes from the cell body.

Whatever mechanisms actually underlie the observed correlation between probability of firing of single cells and the waveform of the evoked potential, it is certain that, contrary to conclusions from other studies (4), knowledge of the waveform of the evoked potential does, to a great extent, enable prediction of the response pattern of a particular cortical cell.

References and Notes

1. G. H. Bishop and M. H. Clare. *J. Neurophysiol.* **15**, 201 (1952); *ibid.* **16**, 418 (1953); C. L. Li, C. Cullen, H. Jasper, *ibid.* **19**, 111 (1956); C. L. Li, *J. Cell. Comp. Physiol.* **61**, 165 (1963); L. Widen and C. Ajmone-Marsan, *Arch. Ital. Biol.* **98**, 248 (1960); D. P. Purpura and H. Grundfest, *J. Neurophysiol.* **19**, 573 (1965); H. Grundfest, *Electroencephalog. Clin. Neurophysiol. Suppl.* **10**, 22 (1958); *N.Y. Acad. Sci.* **92**, 877 (1961); D. P. Purpura and R. J. Shofer, *J. Neurophysiol.* **27**, 117 (1964); ———, F. S. Musgrave, *ibid.* **27**, 133 (1964).
2. Mnemotron Computer of Average Transients, model 400-B.
3. Digital Equipment Corporation. PDP-1.
4. R. Jung, *Electroencephalog. Clin. Neurophysiol. Suppl.* **4**, 57 (1953); G. L. Gerstein and N. Y-S. Kiang, *Exptl. Neurol.* **10**, 1 (1964).
5. This research was supported by NSF grants G21446 and GB1711.

Changes of Brain Electropotentials During Visual Discrimination Learning in Monkey [*][†]

KAO LIANG CHOW

Reprinted from *Journal of Neurophysiology*, 1961, Vol. 24, pp. 377–390.

Many recent studies have demonstrated electroencephalographic (EEG) [‡] alterations during the formation of conditioned responses in dogs and cats. This literature has been reviewed recently by several authors (3, 5, 16, 23, 27), as well as being the subject of the Moscow Colloquium (15). Generally

[*] This research was supported by grant B-801 (C4) from the National Institute of Neurological Diseases and Blindness, NIH, and the Wallace C. and Clara M. Abbott Memorial Fund of The University of Chicago.

[†] Some of the data have been reported at the American EEG Society meetings, Atlantic City, 1959 (4), and the Montevideo Symposium on Brain Mechanisms and Learning (6).

[‡] The term EEG is used here to denote electrical recordings from the cortex and subcortical regions by permanently implanted electrodes.

speaking, the reported EEG changes differ from study to study, apparently being dependent upon a variety of factors such as the condition of the animal, the conditioned and unconditioned stimuli (CS and US), and the training procedure. What happens in these kinds of experiments is that the CS induces specific EEG waves which become an established response. During the conditioning procedure in which the CS is paired with the US, these same or new waves appear. This event is considered an electrical correlate of conditioning. The EEG responses elicited by the CS during an experiment may take any one of the following forms: generalized activation, generalized evoked potentials, augmented background waves, and slow waves; or, if the stimulus is an intermittent stimulus (a train of light flashes or clicks within limits), the EEG may show stimulus-bound rhythmic waves. These changes occur widely in the brain in many structures beside the sensorimotor systems of the CS and US. They do not persist throughout the conditioning period; rather, they tend to disappear when the conditioned responses (CR) are well established. The EEG alterations may appear in some neural structures and at the same time disappear in others. Thus, with a few exceptions (2, 13, 18, 26, 28, 29), the time course of these alterations is not simply or directly correlated with behavioral modifications that are expressed in learning curves. The EEG recording technique has been used most frequently to establish functional localization, i.e., to detect what neural structures are involved during the formation of a particular CR. A few studies have attempted to analyze the underlying neural mechanisms (1, 21, 22, 24).

Others have evaluated the methodological problems involved and the significance of the results obtained. John (16) upheld the potentialities of this technique of relying on EEG alterations, and considered it as providing the most intimate insight into the intricate processes during the course of conditioning. Diamond and Chow (3), on the other hand, voiced a more cautious and less enthusiastic point of view.

The present report represents an extension of earlier work to a different kind of learning situation, i.e., visual discrimination learning. The middle and inferior temporal gyri of monkey have been shown to be important for learning and remembering visual tasks. Monkeys with bilateral ablations of this area require more trials to learn visual discrimination problems than do normal animals and they also forget the pre-operatively learned solution to visual problems after such a lesion. This detrimental effect fulfills the criterion of double dissociation (25); that is, removals of other cortical areas do not affect the performance on visual discriminations, and temporal ablations do not affect the acquisition and retention of non-visual discrimination tasks. Furthermore, the participation of the temporal lobe in visual learning is confined to the cortex, and it communicates with the visual areas through cortico-cortical pathways. (For a review of the literature, see 3.) Thus a functional localization, visual discrimination to temporal neocortex, is established. The present study was designed to find out whether any systematic EEG changes occur in the temporal cortex and the visual systems of monkeys during the learning of

visual discrimination problems. Electrographic recordings were also obtained
in other regions that previously have not been implicated in visual learning.

Methods

Four male and five female young adult monkeys (seven *Macaca mulatta,*
two *Macaca ira*) were used. Their body weight at the time of sacrifice ranged
from 3.0 to 6.5 kg. The animals were kept in separate monkey chairs throughout the five to six months' experimental period. They were held loosely in the
chair, and could move around, lift their legs to scratch their backs, etc. They
continued to grow and remained in good physical condition.

A taming period of about two months preceded surgery. During this
period, the animals were adapted to the testing situation. They learned to wait
for the removal of the opaque screen, to push open the door of the stimulus
box, etc. They were specifically trained to be quiet before each trial. This prolonged taming was necessary in order to eliminate extraneous factors that
might affect the animals' behavior. It was essential that the animal be relaxed
during the test session so that the EEG baseline would serve as a stable reference for evaluating possible changes during learning.

Eight pairs of bipolar electrodes were implanted aseptically in each
monkey. These electrodes were made with 30 gauge nichrome wire, insulated
up to 1 mm. from the tip. The distances between the electrodes varied from
1 to 3 mm. The subcortical electrodes were placed stereotaxically. Two sub-
miniature plugs (Winchester) connecting the electrodes were fixed on the
skull with dental cement. Two male plugs with Microdot wires connected the
animal to the EEG.

Training on the visual tasks commenced seven days after the operation.
Two types of visual problems were used: a two-choice, successive visual discrimination problem and conditional reaction task. The successive visual discrimination problems consisted of a red vs. a green square, then a black
triangle vs. a black circle, and finally black and grey vertical striations vs.
black and grey horizontal striations. The first stimulus of each pair was the
positive stimulus and the other was the negative stimulus. One visual stimulus
was presented on each trial. Correct responses were recorded if the monkey
pushed open the stimulus box for food reward within 5 sec. when the positive
stimulus was present or did not reach for the door for 5 sec. when the negative stimulus was present. Incorrect responses were recorded when monkeys
failed to perform in this manner to a positive or a negative stimulus. A small
piece of food was handed to the animal if it refrained from reaching for the
door when the negative stimulus was presented three trials in succession.
Thirty trials were presented each day with the positive and negative stimuli
being presented an equal number of times. Criterion for learning was 90%
correct responses in a one-day session. Training was conducted in a darkroom
and the monkey chair was covered with opaque screens on all sides except the

bottom. The testing situation has been illustrated elsewhere (6). Briefly, the experimenter sat in front of the monkey chair within easy reach of the flickering light and the EEG controls. A specially constructed photic stimulator was used (8). The light was continuous between trials but changed to flashes (4 10 c./sec.) before each trial. Hence the stimulus was illuminated by the flickering light, which has been thought of as a "tracer" stimulus (17). At the start of each trial, the opaque screen was lowered in front of the stimulus box so as to conceal the visual stimulus. When the EEG showed a wave form indicating a relaxed state, the light was changed to intermittent, and the opaque screen was removed, thereby exposing the stimulus. The stimulus box was beyond the monkey's reach for 2 sec. Then it was pushed forward to allow the monkey to respond. The EEG was recorded for each trial by means of either a Grass 4-channel model III or an Offner 6 channel model T machine.

The testing arrangement for the conditional reaction learning was similar to that for the discrimination problems. The monkey was first given a visual discrimination problem consisting of a triangle vs. circle. The triangle was the positive stimulus and the flickering light was 4 c./sec. (condition 1). When the animal reached the criterion of 14 correct out of 15 trials (either the first half or the second half of a 30-trial daily session), the flashes were changed to 10 c./sec. and the circle became the positive stimulus (condition 2). After the monkey reached the same criterion on condition 2, the light flashes were reversed back to 4 c./sec. and the triangle was once again positive. Training was continued in this fashion, reversal after reversal, until four consecutive reversals were made at criterial performance. Two additional days of testing with 25 trials each were given. During these two days, the conditions were mixed from trial to trial in a balanced order. Thus, whether the same triangle was the positive or the negative stimulus depended on the rate of light flashes. Successful solution of this problem is contingent upon its conditional aspect, i.e., the background light flashes.

At the completion of training, the monkeys were employed in another study (7) and were subsequently sacrificed. The placements of the surface electrodes were recorded with the aid of a camera lucida. The sub-cortical placements were verified histologically.

Results

I. Visual Discrimination Learning

All nine monkeys were trained on the red vs. green discrimination problem. In addition, two animals each were given either the triangle vs. circle discrimination task or the horizontal vs. vertical striations problem. Another two monkeys learned both these two problems. The animals took 90–180 trials (including criterion trials) to reach the criterion of learning. The percentages of correct responses on successive daily sessions for each discrimination showed a positively accelerated learning curve. The EEG records of 14 out of a total of 17 discrimination problems given to all animals were examined.

A. TEMPORAL NEOCORTEX.   Bipolar electrodes were placed on the temporal cortex bilaterally in seven monkeys and unilaterally in two monkeys. The positions of the electrodes were bounded by the superior temporal sulcus dorsally, the base of the skull ventrally, the level of the central fissure rostrally, and about 5 mm. in front of the inferior occipital sulcus caudally. None of the electrodes reached the ventral surface of the temporal lobe. The background EEG pattern of the temporal cortex between trials showed the low-voltage, high-frequency activation pattern intermingled with the 4–5 c./sec. waves of relaxation. In addition, there were periodic bursts of 12–16 c./sec. 100 μV. waves which appeared regularly in all temporal leads. Figures 1A and 3A illustrate these bursts. Photic driving rarely occurred in the temporal tracings.

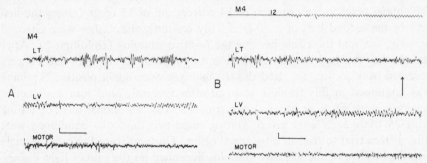

FIGURE 1. EEG records of monkey M4. A: Record taken between trials to show the 12–16 c./sec. bursts in temporal cortex, alpha waves of visual area, and low-amplitude, high-frequency waves of motor area. B: EEG of trial 12, 3rd reversal, during conditional reaction training. Temporal EEG shows reduced amplitude during presentation of stimulus (break in upper tracing of light flashes indicates exposure of stimulus), and visual area, photic driving. There is no change in motor area tracings. Arrow indicates monkey's response to this negative trial. LT, left temporal; LV, left visual area; calibration, 50 μV. and 1 sec.

When the visual stimulus was presented during training, the only recognizable change of the temporal neocortical EEG was a disappearance of the 12–16 c./sec. bursts accompanied by a reduction in amplitude. In most instances this change occurred when the negative stimulus was presented (Figs. 1B, 2; trials 12, 14), yet in other instances of negative stimulus presentation no such changes were seen (Figs. 2, 3B). This lack of consistency is illustrated in the tracings shown in Figure 2. These three trials were taken from the record of monkey M7 on the second day of training a red vs. green discrimination task. The animal made 53% correct responses on that day. These were negative stimulus trials. The monkey made incorrect responses, i.e., it reached for the stimulus as indicated by the arrow. Breaks in the first tracing of light flashes denote the time at which the visual stimulus was exposed. The

M 7   R·G   53%

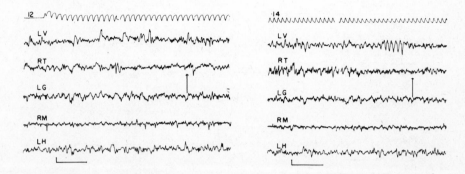

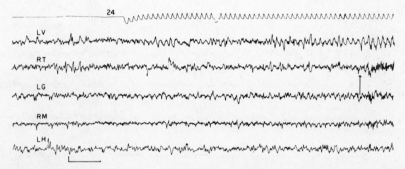

FIGURE 2. EEG records of three negative trials taken from second day of training. Monkey M7 made 53% correct responses on red and green discrimination on that day, but responded incorrectly (arrow) to these three trials. Trials 12 and 14 show reduced amplitude of temporal EEG. Trials 14 and 24 show photic driving of visual area. Photic driving also appears in lateral geniculate body and reticular formation in trial 24. LV, left visual area; RT, right temporal; LG, left lateral geniculate body; RM, reticular formation; LH, left hippocampus; calibration, 50 μV. and 1 sec.

electrographic changes of the temporal neocortical tracings were clear in trials 12 and 14 but not in trial 24. Similar records could have been chosen from positive stimulus trials or from other animals, some of which have been included in a preliminary report (4). Thus it was difficult to reach any conclusion on the basis of a few sample trials. The data of two monkeys on the red vs. green discrimination problem is represented quantitatively in the upper graphs of Figure 4. The number of trials (solid line) that showed EEG changes when the negative stimulus was presented is plotted against 15-trial daily sessions. The percentage of correct responses for each day is indicated at the bottom of the graph. The temporal tracings of monkey M7 indicated an increased number of negative stimulus trials showing EEG changes during the middle portion of the learning process. When the animal reached the criterion of learning, the number of trials showing EEG alterations returned to the initial level. The graph of monkey M6 did not show any consistent trend

M6

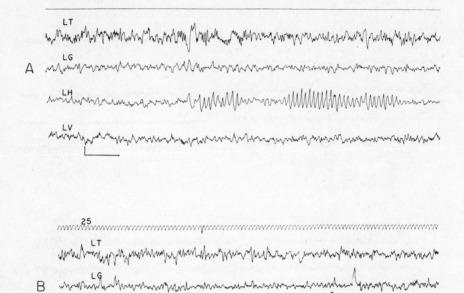

FIGURE 3. EEG records of monkey M6. A: Record taken between trials to show the 5–8 c./sec. theta waves of hippocampus, and relaxation waves in visual area. B: EEG of trial 25, 8th reversal, during conditional reaction training, taken from same session as A. Monkey made correct response (arrow) to this positive trial. EEG shows photic driving in hippocampus only. LT, left temporal; LG, left lateral geniculate body; LH, left hippocampus; LV, left visual area; calibration, 50 μV. and 1 sec.

of EEG changes associated with the learning process. Graphs of negative stimulus trials showing EEG changes similar to that of M7 were apparent in 11 out of 14 visual discrimination problems. The number of daily positive stimulus trials showing a decreased amplitude in temporal EEG is indicated by crosses in Figure 4. For positive trials, no consistent trend of electrographic changes was detected in any of the 14 discrimination tasks. It is concluded that the only systematic temporal cortical EEG changes during the acquisition of visual discrimination is a transient increase of the number of trials showing a diminished amplitude in response to the negative stimulus.

B. VISUAL AREA.   Bipolar electrodes were implanted in either one or both visual areas in each monkey. These electrodes were placed on the lateral surface, caudal to the lunate sulcus. The normal EEG of the visual area showed the activation and relaxation patterns. Occasionally, alpha rhythms similar to those described by Kennard (19) were seen (Fig. 1*A*).

Rhythmic waves synchronized with light flashes during exposure of visual stimulus were present in the visual area EEG. Usually this photic driving appeared during negative stimulus trials. It occurred in some trials (Figs. 1*B;* 2, trials 14, 24) but not in others (Figs. 2, 3*B*). Again, the three trials of Figure 2 illustrate this point. Data of two monkeys on two visual discrimination problems are represented in the lower graphs of Figure 4. The number

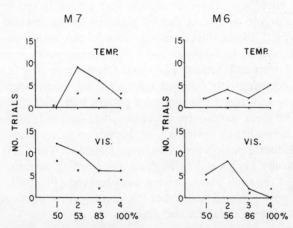

FIGURE 4. Graphs of monkey M7 on triangle and circle discrimination and monkey M6 on red and green discrimination to indicate number of trials of temporal EEG (TEMP) showing a reduced amplitude, and of visual area records (VIS) showing photic driving. Solid lines indicate negative trials and crosses, positive trials. One to 4 refer to successive daily sessions of 30 trials each, with corresponding percentages of correct responses indicated below.

of negative stimulus trials that showed photic driving (solid line) are plotted against daily session. In M7 the photic driving decreased as learning progressed. This habituation process was the common finding. The graph of M6 shows an increased photic driving during the middle portion of the learning process. This type of EEG change occurred in only three out of 14 cases. The crosses indicate photic driving that was observed in the positive stimulus trials, which usually appeared in few trials and habituated subsequently. In general, establishment of the photic driving induced by the background flickering light constitutes the visual area EEG change during visual discrimination learning.

C. LATERAL GENICULATE BODY.   Electrodes were placed in the lateral geniculate body of four monkeys, in the middle of the nucleus at the F5 plane of the stereotaxic coordinates. EEG records from these electrodes were available on four visual discrimination problems. The normal EEG of the lateral geniculate body showed the activation pattern and irregular slow waves (Fig. 3*A*).

The only electrographic response during learning was the appearance of photic driving in response to the flickering light. The photic driving appeared infrequently, ranging from 0 to 8 trials in a 30-trial session. It was present in some trials (Fig. 2, trial 24) but not in others (Figs. 2, trials 12, 14; 3*B*).

These trials were scattered randomly throughout, and no systematic trend was observed. The occurrence of photic driving in the lateral geniculate body did not coincide with that in the visual area. Hence photic driving may be present in one structure but absent in the other during the same trial.

D. HIPPOCAMPUS.   Four monkeys had electrodes implanted in the hippocampus bilaterally. These electrodes were placed in the region of CA2 and CA3 of Lorente de Nó, at the F7 plane of the stereotaxic coordinates. The normal EEG of the hippocampus showed the activation pattern and irregular slow waves. In addition 5–8 c./sec. theta waves, similar to those described by Green and Arduini (12) and Grastyán *et al.* (11), were seen. These waves occurred only between trials, and then only when the animals looked vacantly and their EEG showed a pattern indicative of a relaxed state (Fig. 3*A*). The theta waves were never observed during behavioral alertness nor immediately before or during a trial. Hippocampal electrographic records on five visual discrimination problems were available. The EEG tracings remained practically unchanged throughout the learning process. On approximately 10% of the trials photic driving was observed (Fig. 3*B*). Its presence, however, was not correlated with either the learning curve or the photic driving of lateral geniculate body and visual area.

E. MIDBRAIN RETICULAR FORMATION.   Bipolar electrodes were placed in the midbrain reticular formation of three monkeys. The electrodes were situated lateral to the central grey, medial to the posterior tip of the median geniculate body, and at the FO plane of the stereotaxic coordinates. Activation and relaxation patterns constituted the normal EEG of the reticular formation.

Electrographic records of five visual discrimination problems contained reticular formation tracings. Aside from the activation pattern, photic driving during the exposure of the visual stimulus was the only EEG alteration (Fig. 2, trial 24). The total number of trials showing photic driving in a 30-trial session ranged from 0 to 18, occurring equally between positive and negative trials. The time course of these trials resembled that found in the visual area; i.e., at the beginning a large number of trials showed photic driving which subsequently became habituated. For example, M7 learned the red vs. green discrimination task in four days. The number of daily trials showing photic driving in reticular formation EEG was 13, 9, 2, and 3. This decreased trend of photic driving occurred in three of the five visual tasks. The photic driving in the reticular formation did not, however, always occur at the same time as that in the visual system (Fig. 2).

F. MOTOR CORTEX PULVINAR.   In one monkey bipolar electrodes were placed in the arm region of the motor cortex contralateral to the hand used. In another animal, electrodes were implanted in the posterior n. pulvinaris medialis. Electrographic records on one visual discrimination problem each were obtained. The findings were inconclusive and are reported here to complete the record. The motor cortex EEG showed low-amplitude, high-frequency waves throughout (Fig. 1). The burst of high-frequency waves (50–80 c./sec.) described by Kruger and Henry (20) were not seen. The pulvinar EEG contained mostly irregular slow waves with short periods of activation pattern. Photic driving was observed in the pulvinar in 13 out of 120 trials.

II. Conditional Reaction Learning

Three monkeys were trained on this problem, requiring 630, 750, and 855 trials (including criterion trials), and 10, 13, and 10 reversals to reach the criterion. They made 88, 84, and 78% correct responses in 50 trials when the two conditions were presented in a mixed but balanced order.

Electrographic alterations during conditional reaction learning were essentially the same as that found for visual discrimination learning. In the temporal EEG, the number of trials (both positive and negative stimulus trials) showing a reduced amplitude increased transiently during the middle portion of a reversal. When the animal learned the problem at the criterial reversals, the number of such trials returned to the initial low level. For the visual area EEG, a sharply increased photic driving was apparent at the beginning of each reversal with a rapid subsequent decrease. This descending curve of photic driving in the visual area contrasted with the ascending curve of the number of correct responses of the behavioral learning curve. Again, during the criterial reversals, the number of trials with photic driving returned to the initial low level. Figure 5 depicts the data of monkey M5. The top graph describes the learning curve, i.e., the number of correct responses in 15-trial blocks. The temporal EEG tracing in the middle graph shows the number of trials with reduced amplitude. The bottom graph indicates the trials with photic driving in visual area. Similar results were obtained from the other two monkeys; the data of one of them were included in a preliminary report (6). When the animals were tested with the 50 mixed trials (conditions 1 and 2 were mixed in a balanced order), the number of trials showing reduced amplitude in the temporal EEG averaged eight trials, and photic driving in visual area tracings averaged 14 trials. Thus, when the animals learned the visual task well, the electrographic alterations occurred only sporadically.

Hippocampal electrographic tracings were obtained in three monkeys. There was occasional photic driving during the exposure of the visual stimulus. The number of trials showing photic driving was less than 5%. These trials seemed to be concentrated, at least for two animals, in the earlier part of the learning process. For example, in the record of M5 (compare Fig. 5) photic driving appeared 24 times in the first three reversals, but only seven times during the rest of training. Otherwise, the EEG showed only activation and irregular slow waves. Photic driving appeared also in the lateral geniculate body of two monkeys, but these trials were rare (less than 3%) and showed no systematic trend. They also had no relationship with the photic driving which occurred in the visual area.

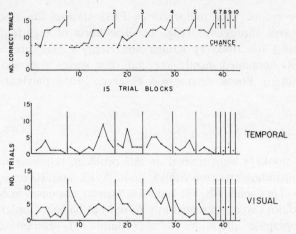

FIGURE 5. Graphs of monkey M6 on conditional reaction learning. Top curve shows learning data. Number of correct responses in 15-trial blocks are plotted. Numbered vertical lines indicate number of reversals. Middle graph is number of trials showing a reduced amplitude in temporal EEG. Bottom graph shows number of trials with photic driving in visual area EEG.

Discussion

The present study demonstrated a transient electrographic change in monkey's temporal cortex during the acquisition of visual discriminations. This EEG change, a reduction of EEG amplitude in response to the stimulus, did not follow the behavioral learning curve. On the contrary, the EEG modification became prominent only in the middle portion of the learning process. It probably is not a direct reflection of whatever neuronal modifications are responsible for this type of learning. Since ablation studies have established the temporal area as being uniquely related to visual learning, inadequacy of the test used will not permit resolution of this result. It may be argued, however, that this transient EEG change indicates a certain phase of visual learning, which may be complex and composed of many interlocked neural processes. Both the behavioral and the electrographic indices are too crude to reveal these subtle neural processes. It is also possible that the electrographic waves could be incidental, indicating a state of the animal during learning, but not a reflection of the process itself. More specifically, when the monkey started to sense the solution, it had to concentrate to make a choice. Once it knew the problem, little effort was needed to respond correctly. The fact that this EEG change most frequently occurred during negative trials supports this contention. For in this particular situation what the monkey essentially had to learn was to refrain from reaching for the negative stimulus.

Electrographic records taken from the visual area showed a steadily diminishing photic driving in response to the light flashes during the acquisition of visual discrimination. It is especially noteworthy that habituation also occurred during conditional reaction learning. This task was designed to integrate the background flickering light into the solution of the problem; the animal had to attend to the light flashes in order to make correct responses. If photic driving has any significance for learning, the hundreds of trials needed to master this difficult task provided ample time for revealing systematic EEG changes. This habituation of rhythmic waves in the sensory area induced by the CS is also a common finding in the formation of instrumental conditioned responses (9, 10, 11, 13, 17). However, habituation has been reported to occur whenever repetitive sensory stimuli are presented (14). Clearly, this EEG modification does not specify the learning process.

Of the several sub-cortical regions studied, the findings of the midbrain reticular formation suggests the only noticeable trend of EEG alterations. Nevertheless, habituation of photic driving in response to flickering light occurred. Photic driving was observed infrequently in the hippocampus * and the lateral geniculate body. Its presence was not correlated with the learning process. In contrast, Galambos, John and Killam, Yoshii, and others (1, 10, 11, 13, 18, 28, 29) reported striking EEG alterations induced by the conditioned stimulus in the same sub-cortical structures during the formation of conditioned responses in dogs, cats, and monkeys. These EEG changes were said to correlate with the various phases of the conditioning paradigm. The discrepancy between this study and those of others probably is not due to the different species used. It may indicate that the neural mechanisms underlying the conditioned response and those operative in visual discrimination learning are basically different. Another possible explanation for the difference between these results and those reported by others is a difference in the emotional states of the animals. Under the procedure of Pavlovian and instrumental conditioning, the animals are generally apprehensive and mentally set to react promptly, especially when shock is the US. In this study, the monkeys were trained to relax and were less intense in their responses. Results from other studies in which cats and monkeys were required to press a lever in response to the CS to get food or to avoid shock provide suggestive evidence (13, 18). The rhythmic waves induced by the intermittent CS (clicks, tones, or light flashes) in almost all sub-cortical structures showed rapid habituation during instrumental conditioning. However, the same waves became widespread and pronounced when a differential conditioning procedure was used. A similar increase of EEG-evoked responses was evident also during Pavlovian conditioning procedure (18, 28, 29).

The largely negative findings of the present study point to some methodological limitations in using the electrographic technique at the present time. First, the electrodes may not be placed in the structures where crucial neural events take place. Even though the temporal cortex is concerned with visual

---

* The hippocampus in cat consists of a dorsal and a ventral division which may have structural and functional significance. Electrographic changes during learning were recorded from the dorsal hippocampus. It is not certain whether the electrodes in the monkey's hippocampus of this study were placed in the region comparable to that of cat.

learning, the few electrodes used may miss the critical location. Second, the EEG records obtained are too gross to reveal subtle neuronal alterations. Whether implanted microelectrodes offer a better resolution remains to be shown. Third, the tracing may contain significant EEG trends which are not detected by visual inspection. Some suitable data analysis devices are needed to test this possibility. Fourth, when electrographic correlates of learning have been established, there still remains the task of ascertaining that the EEG alterations are indeed reflections of neural events of the acquisition processes and not incidental by-products. Notwithstanding the reservations raised, this technique offers a useful tool for locating the place where neural changes occur at different stages of the learning process. Data of this sort provide fresh information on the intricate relations between structure and function. Whether the electrographic data will provide insight into the mechanisms of learning at a cellular and molecular level depends ultimately on the elucidation of the genesis of EEG.

Summary

Nine monkeys (seven *Macaca mulatta* and two *Macaca ira*) were trained on two-choice, successive visual discrimination problems. The discriminations used were red vs. green square; triangle vs. circle; and horizontal vs. vertical striations. Light flashes (4–10 c/sec.) provided the background illumination, so that the animals saw the stimuli only through the flickering light. Three of the animals were taught a conditional reaction problem; i.e., the triangle was positive and the circle negative when the light flashed at 4 c./sec. but the triangle became negative and the circle positive when the 10 c./sec. flashes constituted the background light. Electroencephalographic records of every trial throughout the learning process were obtained by means of gross electrodes implanted in various neural structures.

Electrographic records were taken from the temporal cortex of nine monkeys. The only apparent EEG alteration was a transient increase of the number of trials showing a reduced EEG amplitude during the animals' acquisition of a solution to the visual tasks. This EEG change occurred in 11 out of 14 visual discriminations and in all three conditional reaction learning.

The visual area of the nine monkeys showed only rhythmic waves in the EEG in response to the light flashes during learning. Photic driving usually was habituated during the course of acquisition of visual discrimination and the conditional reaction problem. At the beginning of each new problem, however, there was a reappearance of the photic driving.

Electrographic records obtained from the midbrain reticular formation of three monkeys also showed an habituation of the photic driving in three of five visual discriminations.

The EEG of the lateral geniculate body and the hippocampus contained occasional photic driving trials. They were infrequent and scattered, bearing no consistent relationship to the learning process. The 5–8 c./sec. theta waves of the hippocampus were observed only when the monkey was in a behaviorally relaxed state.

The significance of the EEG findings and the methodological problems involved in studying the electrographic correlates of learning were discussed.

References

1. Adey, W. R., Dunlop, C. W., and Hendrix, C. E. Hippocampal slow waves. Distribution and phase relationships in the course of approach learning. *Arch. Neurol., Chicago,* 1960, **3:** 96–112.
2. Beck, E. C., Doty, R. W., and Kooi, K. A. Electrocortical reactions associated with conditioned flexion reflexes. *EEG clin. Neurophysiol.,* 1958, **10:** 270–289.
3. Diamond, I. T. and Chow, K. L. Biological psychology: the biological methods for the study of behavior with special reference to learning. In: Koch, S., ed. *Psychology: a study of a science.* New York, McGraw-Hill, 1961 (in press).
4. Chow, K. L. Brain waves and visual discrimination learning in monkey. Pp. 149–157 in: Wortis, J., ed. *Recent advances in biological psychiatry.* New York, Grune and Stratton, 1960.
5. Chow, K. L. Brain functions. *Ann. Rev. Psychol.,* 1961, **12:** 281–310.
6. Chow, K. L. Anatomical and electrographical analysis of temporal neocortex in relation to visual discrimination learning in monkey. In: Delafresnaye, J. F., ed. *Brain mechanisms and learning.* Oxford, Blackwell Scientific Publishers, 1961 (in press).
7. Chow, K. L. Effect of local electrographic after-discharges on visual learning and retention in monkey. *J. Neurophysiol.,* 1961, **24:** 391–400.
8. Chow, K. L., Dement, W. C., and John, E. R. Conditioned electrocorticographic potentials and behavioral avoidance response in cat. *J. Neurophysiol.,* 1957, **20:** 482–493.
9. Galambos, R. Electrical correlates of conditioned learning. Pp. 375–415 in: Brazier, M. A. B., ed. *The central nervous system and behavior.* Transactions of the first conference. New York, Josiah Macy, Jr. Foundation, 1959.
10. Galambos, R., Sheatz, G., and Vermeer, V. G. Electrophysiological correlates of a conditioned response in cats. *Science,* 1956, **123:** 375–376.
11. Grastyán, E., Lissak, K., Madarasz, I., and Donhoffer, H. Hippocampal electrical activity during the development of conditioned reflexes. *EEG clin. Neurophysiol.,* 1959, **11:** 409–430.
12. Green, J. D. and Arduini, A. A. Hippocampal electrical activity in arousal. *J. Neurophysiol.,* 1954, **17:** 533–557.
13. Hearst, E., Beer, B., Sheatz, G., and Galambos, R. Some electrophysiological correlates of conditioning in the monkey. *EEG clin. Neurophysiol.,* 1960, **12:** 137–152.
14. Hernández-Peón, R. Neurophysiological correlates of habituation and other manifestations of plastic inhibition. Pp. 101–114 in: Jasper, H. H. and Smirnov, G. D., eds. *The Moscow Colloquium on Electroencephalography of Higher Nervous Activity. EEG clin. Neurophysiol.,* 1960, **Suppl. 13.**
15. Jasper, H. H. and Smirnov, G. D., eds. *The Moscow Colloquium on Electroencephalography of Higher Nervous Activity. EEG clin. Neurophysiol.,* 1960, **Suppl. 13:** 1–420.

16. John, E. R. Higher nervous functions, brain functions and learning. In: *Ann. Rev. Physiol.*, 1961 (in press).

17. John, E. R. and Killam, K. F. Electrophysiological correlates of avoidance conditioning in the cat. *J. Pharmacol. exp. Ther.*, 1959, **125**: 252–274.

18. John, E. R. and Killam, K. F. Studies of electrical activity of brain during differential conditioning in cats. Pp. 138–148 in: Wortis, J., ed. *Recent advances in biological psychiatry*. New York, Grune and Stratton, 1960.

19. Kennard, M. A. and Nims, L. F. Changes in normal electroencephalograms of *Macaca mulatta* with growth. *J. Neurophysiol.*, 1942, **5**: 325–334.

20. Kruger, J. and Henry, C. Electrical activity of rolandic region in unanesthetized monkey. *Neurology*, 1957, **7**: 490–495.

21. Morrelli, F., Barlow, J., and Brazier, M. A. B. Analysis of conditioned repetitive response by means of the average response computer. Pp. 123–137 in: Wortis, J. ed. *Recent advances in biological psychiatry*. New York, Grune and Stratton, 1960.

22. Rabinovich, M. The electrical activity in different layers of the cortex of the motor and acoustic analysers during the elaboration of conditioned defensive reflexes. *Pavlov J. Higher Nervous Activity*, 1958, **8**: 507–519.

23. Rusinov, V. S. and Rabinovich, M. Y. Electroencephalographic researches in the laboratories and clinics of the Soviet Union. *EEG clin. Neurophysiol.*, 1958, **Suppl. 8**: 1–36.

24. Stern, J. A., Ulett, G. A., and Sines, J. O. Electrocortical changes during conditioning. Pp. 106–122 in: Wortis, J., ed. *Recent advances in biological psychiatry*. New York, Grune and Stratton, 1960.

25. Teuber, H. L. Physiological psychology. *Ann. Rev. Psychol.*, 1955, **6**: 267–296.

26. Verzilova, O. V. Changes in the cortical electrical activity of the dog in the region of the auditory and motor analysers during the formation and reversal of motor defensive reflex. *Pavlov J. Higher Nervous Activity*, 1958, **8**: 410–420.

27. Yoshii, N., Matsumoto, J., Maeno, S., Hasegawa, Y., Yamaguchi, Y., Shimokochi, Y., Shimokochi, M., Hari, Y., and Yamazaki, H. Conditioned reflex and electroencephalography. *Med. J. Osaka Univ.*, 1958, **9**: 353–375.

28. Yoshii, N. and Maeno, S. An electroencephalographic study of conditioned salivary reflex. *Folia Psychiat. Neurol. Jap.*, 1958, **12**: 296–316.

29. Yoshii, N., Hasegawa, Y., and Yamazaki, H. Electroencephalographic study of defensive conditioned reflex in dog. *Folio Psychiat. Neurol. Jap.*, 1959, **13**: 320–367.

Study Questions for Part II

1. When electrodes are implanted throughout the brain, we can see that changes in activity in any one area produces changes throughout the entire CNS. Yet we also know that lesions in a specific portion of the brain tend to produce specific types of impairments. Do results from lesion and electro-physiological studies tend to contradict one another? How would you resolve the following problems? Suppose you have a patient who shows bizarre behavior patterns, but who has a perfectly normal EEG? Suppose you have a patient with a bizarre and abnormal EEG, but whose behavior is apparently quite normal? In view of these contradictions, how would you evaluate the use of EEG as a research and diagnostic instrument?

2. An auditory stimulus will not ordinarily produce an electrical response in the visual cortex. Yet some investigators have been able to demonstrate that if the auditory input is paired with a visual input for several trials, the visual cortex will respond to the onset of the sound alone. But if the sound is then presented by itself for several additional trials, the visual area ceases to respond, only to begin responding again when the pairing is resumed (see Morrell *).

Some people have argued that this phenomenon represents the cortical equivalent of classical conditioning. What relationship might this phenomenon have to classical conditioning? In what sense are they similar? From the information provided in this chapter, write either a defense or criticism of the above interpretation.

---

* F. Morrell: Effect of anodal polarization on the firing pattern of single cortical cells. *Ann. N.Y. Acad. Sci.,* 1961, **92:** 860–876.

Part III

Memory:
Information Transfer and Storage

Probably one of the most important questions to physiological psychologists is how and where is information stored in the central nervous system? As we mentioned in a previous section, the type of training a person has will often shape his beliefs and attitudes regarding the best approach to finding the elusive "engram." In this section, we will deal with a molecular or chemical approach to the study of learning and memory.

There would seem to be at least three reasons for the increasing popularity of biochemical manipulations of behavior as evidenced in recent years. First, psychologists have historically shown proclivity for adopting the models and procedures of other disciplines in an attempt to bring new insights to the field. For example, consider Hull's attempt to adapt the deductive methods of Newtonian physics to learning theory or recent computer simulation models of information processing.

Second, biologists and biochemists have shown increasing interest in the relationship of the organism to its environment (ecological investigation). Considering this relationship, it soon became evident that one would have to study the mechanisms by which the organism adapts and modifies his response to the environment. This led, in turn, to the study of the biochemistry of learning and memory.

Third, recent developments in the field of molecular biology and genetics suggested that models of information storage and coding used to explain genetic inheritance might be relevant or applicable to psychological explanations of learning *and* memory.

The articles in this section will deal with only one of several possible biochemical and pharmacological methods. Specifically, these studies all involve introducing a chemical agent into an experimental subject and observing concomitant behavioral changes. Although this approach has served to increase our appreciation of the complexity of the coding process, it is not without its difficulties.

129

One crucial consideration in all drug research is "how much is enough" to produce a desired change in behavior. Rarely does one find a linear relationship between the amount of drug and the magnitude of the observed response. This leads us to a necessary consideration of the dose-response curve for any particular agent.

Often, finding the appropriate dose needed to produce a desired response, such as facilitation of learning, is a matter of chance. Further, the appropriate dose will often vary as a function of sex and strain differences. Another important problem related to the "right" dose level is that drugs that affect neural activity often have a U-shaped function. That is, a low dose may produce a desired effect as well as a high dose, but all concentrations in between the two extremes have no discernible effect on the response in question.

In any drug or chemical study that attempts to manipulate learning, we must be able to demonstrate that any changes in observed behavior are not transient results or "side effects" of the compounds being studied. For example, drug A is thought to facilitate memory and is injected prior to a learning task. We notice a marked improvement in performance; can we assume that the animal's memory has been facilitated? Unless we could demonstrate that attention, arousal, level of motivation, and emotion were not affected, we could not conclude that we had improved memory since all of the above variables can change *performance* of a learned response.

Another point to consider is that when the animal is under the influence of the drug, the altered state of CNS activity becomes part of the overall context against which information has to be processed, stored, and retrieved. When the subject is tested at some later time after the effects of the drug have dissipated, the environmental cues must be integrated against a *different* contextual state. The confusion that arises is due to the problem of trying to distinguish whether or not the drug exerted any long-term effects on learning or memory. Although permanent changes in brain chemistry may have been produced, it may be necessary to reintroduce the drug as a "priming" device to reestablish the context of activity under which learning had occurred. However, when this is done, the experiment is then subjected to the criticism raised above, namely, that performance factors such as attention, motivation, and so forth cannot be separated from those variables affecting learning. The article by McGaugh attempts to provide a solution to this difficult problem, and it would be best to arrive at your own conclusions.

In most systematic psychopharmacology, the purpose of the experiments is to determine the *mechanism of action* of various drugs on behavior. Obviously, almost anything in sufficient quantity can produce *some* effect, but the critical question is whether changes in behavior can be traced to *specific* alterations in brain chemistry. The difficulty here is that usual relationships are often very elusive. For example, let's say drug A causes a marked decrease of serotonin in the hypothalamus. It is also observed that discrimination learning is markedly impaired. Can we conclude that drug A impairs learning or even that depletion of serotonin impairs learning? The actual impairment may result from a long chain of events initially triggered by lowered levels of serotonin and in a part of the brain far removed from the hypothalamus. Because of the potentially large number of changes produced by administration of a drug, we think it is important for any investigator to have a specific hypothesis regarding the effects of the agent on the CNS and resulting behavioral change, rather than simply "let's see what happens if . . . "

Each of the following articles in this section attempts to test a specific hypothesis about the biochemical and pharmacological bases of learning and memory. The first paper, by Babich et al., provoked one of the most exciting controversies of the decade and generated a great deal of research; however, after four years, little light seems to have been shed regarding the issue of whether it is possible to transfer information from one organism to another via tissue extract.

The first three articles in this chapter deal with the molecular basis of memory transfer. In their paper, Babich et al. present the thesis that stored information can be transferred by injection of a brain extract, from a trained animal to a naïve recipient. This implication is that "memory" is encoded in a biochemical substrate labile enough to be modified by experience yet stable enough to withstand reduction and extraction procedures. Because of the importance of this finding, many investigators rushed to their laboratories in an attempt to replicate these results and they met with varying degrees of success.

The next paper, by Luttges et al., describes a series of sophisticated experiments designed to obtain evidence of interanimal memory transfer but that were unsuccessful. The authors point out some of the methodological difficulties encountered in their research and conclude that the RNA hypothesis of Babich et al. is untenable.

The third article, by Frank et al., attempts to provide an alternative explanation for the phenomenon of interanimal memory transfer. Typically, failure to replicate the original reports of Babich et al. ended up confirming the null hypothesis (i.e., no significant differences among experimental groups). However, many factors can account for lack of significance between groups, and if a particular hypothesis is inadequate, one demonstrates this by providing a better, or more simple, explanation of an observed event. This was the goal of the paper by Frank and colleagues. Some of their findings are surprising and unexpected, but the results are sufficiently clear for you to draw your own conclusions on this somewhat "messy" subject.

The review article by Flexner and his co-workers approaches the biochemistry of learning and memory from a different tack. In this paper, the authors argue that protein synthesis plays a critical role in information storage, and they describe a series of elegant experiments that demonstrate that when protein synthesis in the brain is blocked, selective and specific impairments in memory (not learning) can be observed.

By and large, the first four articles deal with the question of biochemical processes occurring *within* the cell that may be involved in memory storage. In addition to this approach, there is another active area of investigation in which researchers have tried to study changes occurring at the level of the *synapse* that may be involved in memory storage and retrieval. The papers by Banks and Russell and by Deutsch explore what happens to learning and retention when levels of transmitter substances at the synapse are modified by injections of anticholinesterase drugs. The apparent implication of this research is that communication *between* cells may be more critical for memory storage than intracellular forms of activity; however, one should not accept this conclusion without a great deal of additional thought and evidence. It may be the case (and indeed it is likely) that intra- *and* extracellular processes are critical for neural activity underlying formation and utilization of information.

The final article, by McGaugh, reviews a number of recent findings regarding temporal factors in memory storage. McGaugh's major thesis is that the "memory trace" goes through various stages of consolidation from very labile (short-term memory) traces that are easily obliterated to very stable traces that form the basis for long-term memory. McGaugh describes how memory is susceptible to manipulation by drugs and electroconvulsive shock at certain stages of learning, but not others, and this is taken as evidence for support of the notion that storage of information in the CNS is the result of finite processes that are likely to have some of the characteristics described in the various articles presented in this section.

Transfer of a Response to Naive Rats by Injection of Ribonucleic Acid Extracted from Trained Rats

FRANK R. BABICH, ALLAN L. JACOBSON,
SUZANNE BUBASH, AND ANN JACOBSON

Reprinted from *Science*, 1965, Vol. 149, pp. 656–657. Copyright 1965 by the American Association for the Advancement of Science.

Although there has been abundant theorizing of late which implicates ribonucleic acid (RNA) in the process of memory storage (*1*), direct experimental evidence in support of this contention has been scanty. Hydén and Egyhazi (*2*) reported changes in the ratio of bases in the nuclear RNA of vestibular neurons of rats after the animals had performed a wire-climbing task. In further work (*3*), Hydén and his associates extended their biochemical analyses and studied an additional training paradigm involving reversal of handedness in rats. In the most recent of these experiments, they reported that different types of neural RNA are produced during the early, as compared with the later, stages of learning. Preliminary experiments with planarians (*4*) indicate that, if RNA from trained animals is injected into naive animals, the naive animals respond more than do controls upon subsequent testing. In the present study with rats we used a direct test similar to that used for the planarian experiments.

We used 50- to 60-day-old male Sprague-Dawley rats, each weighing approximately 250 g. Eight rats received magazine-training in a standard Grason-Stadler Skinner box—that is, they were trained to approach the food cup upon hearing the distinct click produced by operation of the pellet dispenser. Magazine training was accomplished as follows. On the first day, a rat deprived of food for 48 hours was placed in the Skinner box and allowed to eat two 45-mg Noyes pellets which had been placed in the cup. Then, while the rat was investigating the cup, the food magazine was operated a number of times in succession, producing each time a distinct click and delivery of a single 45-mg pellet. As training progressed, the click was withheld until the rat moved first a short, and later a longer distance from the cup. During this time, the rat was permitted a number of interspersed cup investigations which were not preceded by the click and hence were not rewarded with food.

Each of the rats was given 200 food-reinforced approaches to the food cup per day for 4 days and 100 such trials on the 5th day. No additional food was given to these rats. By the end of training, each rat approached the food cup promptly and swiftly from any part of the box when the click was sounded, and rarely or never approached the cup in the absence of the click. Control rats were fed daily an amount of Purina Lab Chow equivalent in weight to the amount of food received by the experimental animals.

On the day of completion of magazine-training, each of the eight experimental rats was killed with ether, and the brain was removed as quickly as possible. A posterior cut was made on a line joining the superior colliculus to the rostral end of the pons. An anterior cut was made which removed the frontal areas and the olfactory bulbs. The tissue posterior to the posterior cut and the tissue anterior to the anterior cut were discarded. The selection of this portion of the brain was based on preliminary work showing that (i) this portion was sufficient to give the effect observed in the present experiment, and (ii) this amount of tissue was convenient for our techniques. The average weight of the tissue retained was 1.0 g. We then extracted RNA from this tissue by the following procedure. The tissue was placed in a cold mortar with 5 ml of phenol (90 percent) and 5 ml of isotonic saline and was ground with purified sand for approximately 3 minutes. The mixture was then centrifuged at 18,000 rev/min for 30 minutes at 0°C. The aqueous phase was carefully drawn off to avoid contamination with phenol or with the interphase. The aqueous phase was then brought up to a concentration of $0.1M$ $MgCl_2$, and 2 volumes of cold ethanol were added to precipitate the RNA. Precipitation time was 15 minutes. The suspension was centrifuged at 6000 rev/min for 15 minutes, after which the supernatant liquid was poured off. The remaining ethanol was evaporated off, and the RNA was dissolved in 1.0 to 1.5 ml of isotonic saline. The amount of RNA was determined from the optical density at 260 mμ ($\epsilon^p = 7450$ in $0.2M$ NaCl). The yields were in the range of 0.7 to 1.1 mg per gram of tissue. Tests for protein with biuret (5) and for DNA with diphenylamine (6) were negative. The RNA seemed to be relatively undegraded as measured by Sephadex chromatography.

We also extracted, in the same manner, RNA from nine control (untrained) rats. Approximately 8 hours after extraction, the RNA from each of the rats, experimental or control, was injected intraperitoneally with a 1.8-cm, 22-gauge needle into an untrained rat (the xiphoid process was used as a guide for the injection). Before being injected, each of these untrained rats had been adapted to the Skinner box for 5 days, 15 minutes per day; during each session the magazine had been operated two separate times, producing a distinct click each time. No food was ever given to these animals during the adaptation series, although food powder was sprinkled lightly over the grid floor to keep the animals active and to counteract any tendency on the part of the rats to approach the food cup on the basis of residual odor.

Seventeen rats in all were injected with RNA; eight of them received RNA from trained rats and nine received RNA from untrained rats. These 17 rats were assigned code letters, and all testing from this point on was conducted "blind"; the testers did not know the group to which each rat belonged until the completion of testing.

A session of testing consisted in placing an animal in the Skinner box, permitting 2 minutes to elapse, and then delivering a series of clicks (produced by operation of the empty food magazine) spaced no less than 1 minute apart. Five such testing sessions were given, at 4, 6, 8, 22, and 24 hours after injection. Each test animal thus received a total of 25 trials. At the beginning of testing, all rats had been deprived of food for approximately 28 hours. After the third test session, all rats were fed 4 to 5 g of Purina Lab Chow.

A response on a test trial consisted of the rat's placing its nose inside a demarcated area, 63-cm^2, surrounding the food cup, within 5 seconds of the click. The food cup was located in one corner of the box, the floor of which had an area of 670 cm^2. That is, the rat had to approach to within a certain specified distance of the cup in order for a response to be counted. Further restrictions were placed upon the test trials as follows: Two judges scored all trials independently, and a response was counted only if their tallies agreed; and trials were given only when the animal was facing away from the cup by more than 90° and was located at least a body length from the cup. During testing, as during the adaptation period before testing, food powder was sprinkled lightly over the grid floor.

A comparison of the two judges' tallies revealed that they agreed on 370 out of 375 trials—that is, on 98.7 percent of the judgments. Table 1 presents the score for each test animal in terms of the number of cup approaches, as defined earlier, out of the 25 trials during which clicks were presented (7). The mean number of responses for the experimental rats was 6.86; the mean for the control rats was 1.00. By a Mann-Whitney U-test (8), the difference between the groups was significant at $p<.002$ (one-tailed test). Total scores of the seven experimental rats for the separate test sessions, in order, were: 5, 13, 9, 12, 9; corresponding scores for the eight control rats were: 3, 2, 1, 1, 1.

Table 1.
Total number of responses per animal on the 25 test trials.

Experimental rats	Control rats
1	0
3	0
7	0
8	1
9	1
10	1
10	2
	3

Thus the experimental animals showed a significantly greater tendency than controls to approach the cup area when the click was presented. In order to understand this phenomenon more precisely, further analysis is required to determine, for example, how general or specific the effect is and the range of behavioral situations in which the effect will occur. Moreover, although it appears most reasonable that the observed effect was produced by RNA, the possibility should not be overlooked that other substances in the extract might have been involved.

If the effect can be shown to depend on associative learning rather than on something more general (for example, sheer amount of stimulation), and if this effect can be definitely ascribed to RNA, then the problem arises of what modifications in RNA are produced by the training situation, such that the present result could occur. Several possible coding mechanisms have been proposed, such as changes in the linear sequence of bases, changes in the helical structure, or changes in the overall configuration or composition of the RNA molecule (*3, 9*). Whatever the coding mechanism, an additional problem remains: namely, how the injected material acts to affect the behavior of the recipient animal (*10*).

References and Notes

1. J. Gaito and A. Zavala, *Psychol. Bull.* **61,** 45 (1964); T. K. Landauer, *Psychol. Rev.* **71,** 167 (1964).
2. H. Hydén and E. Egyhazi, *Proc. Nat. Acad. Sci. U.S.* **48,** 1366 (1962).
3. ———, *ibid.* **49,** 618 (1963); **52,** 1030 (1964); H. Hydén and P. Lange, *ibid.* **53,** 946 (1965).
4. C. Fried and S. Horowitz, *Worm Runner's Digest* **6,** 3 (1964); A. Zelman, L. Kabat, R. Jacobson, J. V. McConnell, *ibid.* **5,** 14 (1963).
5. E. Layne, in *Methods of Enzymology,* S. P. Colowick and N. O. Kaplan, Eds. (Academic Press, New York, 1957), vol. 3, p. 450.
6. W. C. Schneider, *ibid.,* p. 680.
7. Two injected rats were discarded during test trials because they persistently froze in one corner and thus could not be tested. One of these rats was a control and the other an experimental animal. In contrast, all the other 15 injected rats typically roamed around the box freely during test sessions. The discarded control rat was replaced, but the experimental rat was not: hence *N* was unequal in the two groups.
8. S. Siegel, *Non-parametric Statistics for the Behavioral Sciences* (McGraw-Hill, New York, 1956).
9. W. Dingman and M. B. Sporn, *J. Psychiat. Res.* **1,** 1 (1961).
10. Since this research was completed, we have learned of a similar experiment recently conducted in Copenhagen [E. J. Fjerdingstad, Th. Nissen, H. H. Røigaard-Petersen, *Scand. J. Psychol.* **6,** 1 (1965)]. Despite several differences in procedure, the results of the two studies appear to corroborate each other.

An Examination of "Transfer of Learning" by Nucleic Acid

MARVIN LUTTGES, TERRY JOHNSON, CLAYTON
BUCK, JOHN HOLLAND, AND JAMES McGAUGH

Reprinted from *Science*, Feb. 18, 1966, Vol. 151, pp. 834–837. Copyright 1966 by
the American Association for the Advancement of Science.

A recent article (*1*) clearly indicates the excitement currently generated in
neurobiology by the discoveries in the field of molecular genetics. As pointed
out, the application of such findings to an understanding of some of the long-
existing problems of biological memory seems very promising. The research
activities of many individuals attest to the current efforts directed toward a
grasp of the relationships between nucleic acids, proteins, and biological
memory (*2*). There are reports (*3*) that "transfer of learning" effects have
been accomplished through the extraction of nucleic acid from the brains of
trained animals and its subsequent injection into naive animals. Such a finding
would, indeed, seem to furnish the first direct relation between nucleic acids
and biological memory. We have used many different testing devices over a
wide range of conditions and now report our unsuccessful attempts to find
"transfer of learning" effects.

In the first study 20 mice (male Swiss-Webster albino, approximately
60 days of age) were trained on a two-choice brightness discrimination task
to swim to the nonpreferred, darker alley. Ten additional animals were trained
always to turn left regardless of the light's position. A raised platform in the
correct alley allowed the mice to escape from the water (18°C). Each trial
began when the platform was submerged, so that the mice were forced to
swim to the appropriate one of the two remaining alleys. An error was recorded whenever the "dark-trained" animals entered the lighted alley or the
"left-turn" animals entered the right alley. Every animal was given six training
trials each day for 11 days. The intertrial interval was 30 seconds. After the
training, the dark-trained animals were divided into two groups: group I consisted of ten animals that made no more than one error on the last 18 training
trials; and group II consisted of ten animals that made as many as four errors
out of the last 18 training trials.

Two groups of dark-trained animals, the left-turn group, and a group
of untrained mice were killed, and their brains were quickly removed. The
brains from each group were placed in cold phenol containing 0.15M NaCl
(1:1) and homogenized with a tissue grinder. The aqueous phase was removed
after centrifugation, and the nucleic acids were precipitated with two volumes
of ethanol. The precipitate was collected by centrifugation and dried in a
stream of air. The total nucleic acid collected for each group was then resus-

pended in 2.0 ml of $0.15M$ NaCl (4). A group of ten test animals served as recipients of each extract; each animal received intraperitoneal (I.P.) injections of 0.2 ml of the appropriate preparation. Ten mice were injected with $0.15M$ NaCl to serve as additional controls. In this and subsequent studies all animals were coded at the time of injection, and testing was completed without knowledge of the animals' prior treatments.

Eighteen hours after injection, the spontaneous activity of each animal was determined automatically for a 2-minute test interval. The activity was tested in a rectangular apparatus with a floor of metal plates that, when bridged by a mouse, activated an electromagnetic counter. Two hours later, the experimental animals were given six trials in the water maze with the same procedures described. The activity measures and the discrimination tests are presented in Table 1A. There were no significant differences between any of the experimental groups on either of the two behavioral measures.

Since the preceding study failed to produce any evidence of "transfer of learning," the extraction procedure was altered slightly to follow more closely one procedure reported to have given "transfer of learning" effects (3). This involved the addition of $MgCl_2$ to the nucleic acid before precipitation (5). Male Swiss-Webster mice were trained in the water "Y" maze. The procedures were the same as described except that all 20 mice were given six trials on a light-dark discrimination daily for 7 days. By the end of training, none of the trained animals had committed more than one error out of the last 12 trials. The mice were divided into two matched performance groups of ten animals each. A group of ten naive mice was also used. The brains were removed and processed in the usual manner, except that for the extraction of the brains of the naive group and one trained group, ethanol plus $0.1M$ $MgCl_2$ was used for precipitation (3). All of the resulting precipitates were resuspended in $0.15M$ NaCl to a final volume of 5 ml. The ten animals in each of the three groups injected (I.P.) with nucleic acid and the group injected with $0.15M$ NaCl were tested for a 2-minute spontaneous-activity sample 15 hours after injections. At 16 hours after the injections, all animals were given six trials in the water "Y" maze. Subsequently, six test trials were given at 12-hour intervals (Table 1B). The addition of $MgCl_2$ before precipitation of the nucleic acids affected neither the activity nor the discrimination test scores.

In a further attempt to test the ability of brain nucleic acids to "transfer learning" to naive animals by way of I.P. injections, male rats (Sprague-Dawley derived, approximately 150 days of age) were trained on a light-dark discrimination in an automated shuttle-box discrimination apparatus. Two chambers were separated by a central partition with two plexiglass doors. On each trial the rats were required to push open a lighted door and shuttle to the other compartment in order to escape from a grid-delivered foot shock (1 ma). Selection of the dark, locked door resulted in a foot shock delivered by a small grid in front of that door and in the automatic recording of an error. The 30-second intertrial intervals and changing of the correct door positions were automatically controlled by electronic progamming. Trials and

Table 1.

Spontaneous activity scores and correct choices made in the first block of six test trials in the water "Y" maze. Additional blocks of six test trials each were given at 24-hour intervals (A) or at 12-hour intervals (B) but neither produced additional information. There were ten animals in each group. Results are given as means ± S.D. NA, nucleic acid; S, saline.

Injection	Training	Activity measures	Correct* trials
	A. 24-HOUR INTERVAL		
S		79.1 ± 15.9	2.2 ± 1.4
NA	Naive	75.9 ± 19.2	2.1 ± 1.4
NA	Left-turn	69.9 ± 23.1	2.7 ± 1.4
NA	Dark trained (group I)	75.8 ± 19.4	2.8 ± 1.8
NA	Dark trained (group II)	74.7 ± 16.9	2.5 ± 1.4
	B. 12-HOUR INTERVAL		
S		86.1 ± 13.1	2.1 ± 1.4
NA	Naive (Mg Cl₂)	77.3 ± 23.1	2.1 ± 1.1
NA	Dark trained (Mg Cl₂)	74.4 ± 23.9	3.0 ± 2.4
NA	Dark trained	86.9 ± 22.2	2.4 ± 1.3

* Statistically, an analysis of variance yielded scores which did not approach critical values of "F."

errors were also automatically recorded. Ten male rats were trained daily to a criterion of nine correct choices out of ten consecutive trials. After 10 consecutive days of criterion performance the animals attained the performance criterion within the first ten training trials on each day. The ten trained and ten naive rats were killed with chloroform, and their brains were immediately homogenized in a mixture of phenol and 0.15M NaCl. The nucleic acid was prepared as described and was suspended in a solution of 0.15M NaCl containing 0.1M MgCl₂ The test animals were injected I.P. with the appropriate nucleic acid preparation. Approximately 18 and then 42 hours after injection, each rat was given 20 test trials in the discrimination apparatus. The two test groups did not differ significantly on performance on the test trials (Table 2A).

In a second experiment with rats the same techniques were used except that the "donor" animals received twice as much training (20 consecutive days of criterion performance). The recipient animals were tested at 8, 16, and 40 hours after they had been injected I.P. with 0.6 ml of the appropriate nucleic acid preparation (Table 2B). The changes in procedure were not effective in producing differential effects.

Table 2.

Error scores of rats in the automated light-dark discrimination apparatus following I.P. injections of nucleic acid solutions. Results are given as means ± S.D. of the number of errors.

Training	Trials		
	1–20	21–40	41–60
A. TEST 18 AND 42 HOURS AFTER INJECTION			
Naive	12.9 ± 5.6	12.0 ± 6.5	
Light	11.8 ± 3.4	11.1 ± 5.0	
B. TEST 8, 16, AND 24 HOURS AFTER INJECTION			
Naive	11.9 ± 4.0	8.1 ± 4.3	5.8 ± 2.8
Light	9.7 ± 3.2	7.2 ± 3.6	4.7 ± 3.4

Since earlier reports of successful "transfer of learning" were based upon "donor" animals which had been trained in an appetitive situation (3, 6), an appetitive task was used in the next experiment. Male mice (60 days old. Swiss-Webster) that were deprived of water (that is, maintained at 80 percent of body weight) were first trained for 8 days to run a straight alley for a water reward. The mice were given a single daily trial in a modified Lashley III maze. Errors were scored whenever a mouse entered blind alleys. After 18 days of training, eight mice that had exhibited no more than one error throughout the last 3 days of training and eight naive animals were killed, and their brains were removed. The extraction procedures were the same as described. The resulting precipitate was resuspended in 0.15M NaCl containing 0.1M MgCl₂. The solutions were injected I.P. (0.5 ml) into two groups of eight mice that had received only "straight-alley" training to water. A control group that also received this prior training was injected with the 0.15M NaCl containing 0.1M MgCl₂ solution. After injections, the mice were given single test trials in the Lashley III maze every 8 hours. The three groups did not differ in performance on the test trials (Table 3).

Table 3.

Initial errors in the Lashley III maze at 8, 16, and 24 hours after injection of nucleic acid (NA) solutions into water-deprived mice. Eight animals in each group; results are means ± S.D. S, saline solution; N, naive; T, trained.

Injection	Training	Initial errors		
		8-hr	16-hr	24-hr
S		5.6 ± 3.4	3.6 ± 2.6	2.6 ± 2.2
NA	N	4.4 ± 2.5	4.1 ± 2.9	2.6 ± 2.0
NA	T	4.8 ± 2.8	3.4 ± 2.5	2.1 ± 2.4

Since the studies just described used a stringent performance criterion, a less complex task was employed subsequently. Fifty mice (60 days old, male Swiss-Webster) were trained in a shuttle box to approach either the light (Group A) or the dark (Group B) in order to avoid a grid foot shock (1 ma). Two groups of 25 mice each were given ten trials daily for 8 days. When the stimulus light switched from one side of the apparatus to the other (every 30 seconds), the animals could avoid a foot shock by moving to the appropriately lighted side of the apparatus within 5 seconds. By the 8th day of training, animals successfully avoided foot shock on 60 percent or more of the trials. On the remaining trials, escape responses were very rapid and efficient. After the training period, the brains were removed from the two groups of trained mice and from a control group of 25 naive mice.

The nucleic acid precipitates were prepared in the usual manner except that the $MgCl_2$ was omitted in resuspension with $0.15M$ NaCl. The final preparations were injected I.P. into eight experimental mice per "donor" group. Thus, the test mice were injected with the equivalence of brain nucleic acid collected from three "donor" animals. A control group of eight mice received an injection of $0.15M$ NaCl. Four hours after injections, each animal was tested in the shuttle box. The testing began with the animals on the lighted side, and stimulus lights changed sides every 30 seconds. No foot shock was given. An activity floor consisting of electrically conductive square sections was placed over the grid floor. During the 5-minute, 10-test trial session, the amount of time spent in the lighted side of the apparatus was measured. Spontaneous activity exhibited by each animal under both the light and the dark conditions was measured. Finally, the number and direction of shuttle responses on each trial were recorded (Table 4). Even with the modest performance demands of this task and the enhanced likelihood of transfer with the larger amount of nucleic acid injected, no evidence of "transfer of learning" was observed.

Table 4.
Illumination preferences, activity measures, and shuttle responses collected from mice tested in the shuttle box. Eight animals in each group; NA, nucleic acid; S, saline.

In-jection	Train-ing	Mean time in light (sec)	Activity		(No.) Shuttle responses	
			In light (mean)	Total (mean)	Light to dark	Dark to light
S		172.0	130.7	212.4	24	41
NA	Naive	158.3	123.9	204.1	26	40
NA	Dark	184.0	140.6	209.8	16	50
NA	Light	166.3	129.3	203.1	23	42

Since we could not detect a transfer of learning when the crude nucleic acid preparations described above were injected I.P., we thought it imperative to determine whether the RNA contained in these preparations could cross the blood-brain barrier and be detected in the brain. Accordingly, RNA in brain was labeled in vivo by the injection of P³² orthophosphate directly into the intraventricular cavity. In addition, P³²-labeled RNA was prepared in mouse L cells propagated in tissue culture. The RNA was extracted as from the tissue described except that the resulting material was reprecipitated, in the presence of 0.001M ethylenediaminetetraacetate (EDTA), at least ten times to remove the bulk of ethanol-soluble P³². Sprague-Dawley rats were then injected I.P. with 10⁶ count/min of labeled RNA (approximately one-half brain per recipient animal). Animals were killed at various times, and the radioactivity was measured in the animal's peritoneal fluid, blood, and brain (Fig. 1). The early

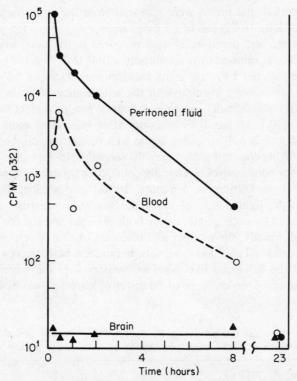

FIGURE 1. Fate of P³²-labeled RNA after I.P. injection into rats. RNA from rat brain and mouse L cells was injected I.P. (10⁶ count/min) and portions of peritoneal fluid, blood, and brain were removed at the times indicated. The amount of radioactivity in each sample after phenol extraction was determined with a Nuclear Chicago gas-flow counter. The results are a composite of three experiments and are presented as the number of counts per minute recovered in 1 ml of peritoneal fluid, 1 ml of blood, and the total brain (cerebrum and cerebellum).

high concentrations of radioactivity were rapidly cleared from the peritoneum and blood, and no significant amounts of radioactivity could be found in the brain. However, most of the radioactivity was excreted in the feces and urine.

In view of the finding that little, if any, nucleic acid passes the blood-brain barrier after I.P. injection, a final attempt to induce "transfer of learning" was made by directly injecting the nucleic acid into the ventricles of the brain. Initially, 60 Swiss-Webster male mice approximately 55 days of age were prepared as "donors." Thirty mice were given inhibitory (or "passive") avoidance training on a "step-through" apparatus. The mice were trained to remain on a small platform mounted in front of a hole leading to a darkened box. Entries were punished with a momentary 4-ma foot shock. Each mouse was given massed training trials with a 30-second intertrial interval until it remained on the platform for 30 seconds. All animals were retrained to the same criterion every 12 hours for a total of seven training periods. At the time of training, each of the other 30 animals was paired with a trained animal in such a way that it received comparable foot shock in a small lucite box with a grid floor each time an experimental mouse was shocked.

After training, 12 trained and foot-shock control pairs of animals were randomly selected from the two groups. A group of 12 naive mice was also used for controls. The mice were then killed, and their brains were removed and placed into ice-cold Hanks balanced salt solution. The brains of each group were then placed in a solution of phenol, 0.15M NaCl, and 1 percent sodium dodecyl sulfate (SDS) at 60°C and homogenized with a tissue grinder. After two successive precipitations, the nucleic acid was dried and resuspended in 0.15M NaCl to a total volume of 0.5 ml. Five groups of 12 test animals each were used either as nucleic acid "recipients" or as control groups. Bilateral intraventricular injections of 20 μl of solution were made with 27-gauge hypodermic needles while the mice were lightly anesthetized. One control group received intraventricular 0.15M NaCl, and the other received no injection but was etherized. The remaining 18 animals in each of the "donor" groups were used to provide comparisons for the five experimental groups. At 18 hours after injections, all animals were given inhibitory avoidance training as described. The amount of time each animal stayed on the small platform before entering the darkened hole was recorded on each of two test trials. The latencies of the recipients of "trained" RNA did not differ significantly from those of animals in the other groups (Table 5). In contrast, it should be noted that with the exception of but one animal, those animals which were originally trained demonstrated criterion performance on the two retention tests.

In conclusion, the numerous variables which provided unsuccessful attempts to demonstrate "transfer of learning" should be summarized. First, several training and testing tasks have been used in both the preparation of the "donor" animals and the subsequent assay for "transfer of learning" effects. As may be judged from the number of trials required for original learning by "donor" animals, these tasks cover a wide range of relative difficulty. Spontaneous activity measures and response latency scores were included to provide an assay of more general transfer effects that might not necessarily be associated with learning. Motivational variables manipulated included foot shock, water deprivation, and cold-water immersion. Additional variables included the use of two species of animals, the degree of "donor" training, and the inclusion of testing intervals longer than those previously reported (*3, 6*). Under

Table 5.

Response latencies of test animals on the step-through apparatus after intraventricular injections of the appropriate nucleic acid preparations. NA, nucleic acid; S, saline. Results are means ± S.D.

Injection	Training	Number of animals	Response latencies (in seconds)	
			1st trial	2nd trial
S		12	13.2 ± 5.7	17.8 ± 6.1
None	(Ether control)	12	5.7 ± 2.7	17.2 ± 5.7
NA	Naive	12	7.3 ± 8.9	17.3 ± 7.7
NA	Foot-shock	12	6.8 ± 6.4	13.5 ± 7.2
NA	Trained	12	9.0 ± 6.8	17.9 ± 8.7
None*	"Donor" trained	18	29.9 ± 0.4	30.0 ± 0.0
None*	"Donor" foot-shock	18	10.3 ± 7.5	22.6 ± 11.2

* These animals were from the same groups of animals that were prepared as "donor" animals. They were retested at the time of testing of the injected experimental animals.

these diverse conditions, the results provided no evidence of "transfer of learning." The nucleic acid extraction and administration procedures were selected to minimize the possibility of losing any fraction that might be responsible for the "transfer of learning." Cold phenol extractions and precipitations with and without $MgCl_2$, as well as hot phenol extraction with SDS, failed to yield an "active" fraction of nucleic acid. Because of the lack of evidence that nucleic acid crosses the blood-brain barrier after I.P. administration, the nucleic acids were introduced directly into the brain by intraventricular injections. Yet, even under these conditions, there was no evidence for a "transfer" effect. Finally, the amount of total nucleic acid injected into the test animals was varied from the equivalence of nucleic acid from one brain to the equivalence from three brains. Still no "transfer" effect was found.

Although the training schedules and devices used have proven very effective in other studies of conditions affecting learning and memory, findings of "transfer of learning" via RNA reported by others (3, 6) were not corroborated in our laboratories. Rather detailed replications of those procedures originally reported as successful (3) have also failed to produce "transfer of learning" effects (7). Such negative findings suggest that the reported "transfer" effect, if it exists, is either a very limited phenomenon or a very difficult one to reproduce.

References and Notes

1. Francis O. Schmitt, *Science* **149**, 931 (1965).
2. W. Dingman and M. B. Sporn, *J. Psychiat. Res.* **1**, 1 (1961); R. W. Gerard, T. J. Chamberlain, G. H. Rothschild, *Science* **140**, 381 (1963); H. Hydén and E. Egyhazi, *Proc. Nat. Acad. Sci. U.S.* **49**, 618 (1963); D. E. Cameron and L. Solyom, *Geriatrics* **16**, 74 (1961); B. W. Agranoff and P. D. Klinger,

Science **146**, 952 (1964); J. B. Flexner, L. B. Flexner, E. Stellar, *ibid.* **141**, 57 (1963).
3. F. R. Babich, A. L. Jacobson, S. Bubash, A. Jacobson, *Science* **149**, 656 (1965); A. L. Jacobson, F. R. Babich, S. Bubash, A. Jacobson, *Science* **150**, 636 (1965).
4. The average wet weight for a mouse brain was 310 mg, and the average nucleic acid yield was 0.24 mg. For rats the average wet weight was 1430 mg, and the average nucleic acid yield was 1.20 mg. The amount of nucleic acid was determined by spectrophotometer measurements at 260 mμ.
5. The addition of $MgCl_2$ during ethanol precipitation rendered the nucleic acid precipitate nearly insoluble in $0.15M$ NaCl.
6. E. J. Fjerdingstad, Th. Nissen, H. H. Røigaard-Petersen, *Scand. J. Psychol.* **6**, 1 (1965).
7. C. G. Groves and F. M. Cory, *Science* **150**, 1749 (1965).
8. Supported by research grant GB 2301 from NSF and MH 10261 from NIH and postdoctoral fellowships (1-F2-A1-23-167-01, 1-F2-A1-13.382-01) from the NIAID. We thank H. Alpern, D. Lerner, and W. Sparks for technical assistance.

Interanimal "Memory" Transfer:
Results from Brain and Liver Homogenates

BONNIE FRANK, DONALD G. STEIN, AND
JEFFREY J. ROSEN

Reprinted from *Science*, July 24, 1970, Vol. 169, pp. 399–402. Copyright 1970 by the American Association for the Advancement of Science.

Babich *et al.* (*1*) found that RNA extracts taken from the brains of trained donors and injected into naive recipients facilitated performance of the latter when compared to animals receiving homogenates from untrained donors. This was interpreted as a demonstration of memory transfer. In the many attempts to replicate these results, there have been reports of both successes (*2*) and failures (*3*). This raises a question about the validity of the original interpretation. The discrepancy between successful and unsuccessful replications may involve the type of task used in each; "successes" have frequently employed passive avoidance tasks, and "failures" generally employed positive reinforcement situations. In the avoidance task, an increase in latency of recipients when compared with those of donors is taken as evidence of interanimal memory transfer. But such changes in latency could be the result of performance variables completely unrelated to learning, such as increased emotionality, fatigue, or stressful side effects of the particular experimental procedure. Thus, while these variables may have a pronounced effect on latencies, they may have only a marginal effect on either trials to criterion or error scores, the most common dependent measures in positive reinforcement tasks. These uncontrolled variables could account for the ambiguous results in the literature and raise the issue of whether the results of Babich *et al.,* and others, were due to (i) a specific memory transfer, possibly involving mediation by RNA (*4*) or large protein molecules (*5*), or (ii) the transfer of some factor affecting performance (*6*), such as stress. The present experiments were designed to separate these possibilities by contrasting the hypothesis that memory can be transferred from a trained to an untrained animal, with the hypothesis that "apparent" interanimal transfer in an aversive situation is mediated by nonspecific stress substances.

The subjects were 180 male albino mice, of the CD1 strain from the Charles River Laboratories, weighing 25 to 30 g. The subjects were divided into three groups, each comprised of 20 donors and 40 recipients. Each donor was randomly assigned to two recipients, one for brain homogenate and one for liver homogenate. The liver injection served to provide high concentrations of nonspecific RNA, and also to control for volume of foreign matter injected into the intraperitoneal cavity.

The behavioral apparatus was a rectangular box, 42.5 by 12 by 11 cm, one half of which was painted white and the other black, with the two sections separated by a center partition. The floor consisted of a grid of 0.2 by 12 cm brass rods placed 0.3 cm apart. The black side had a removable opaque cover, and the white side was illuminated with a high-intensity lamp producing 3300 lu/m^2 at the top of the box. The dependent variable for the donors was the number of seconds the subjects took to enter the black section from the white section through an opening in the center partition. Each donor was given only one trial in the apparatus, after which the maze was first cleaned with "Windex" spray containing ammonia and then distilled water to remove any odor-producing steroids which might affect subsequent animals. On the basis of previous research, all prospective donors taking longer than 30 seconds to enter the black section were discarded as atypical (this amounted to five animals across all three groups).

The shock-group donors received 5 seconds of scrambled shock (1.2 ma a-c) after entry into the black section of the box. The procedure for donors in the no-shock group was identical to that of shocked donors except that the former were not shocked while detained in the black section.

The stressed, control donors were placed in a ventilated glass jar, 5.5 cm in diameter and 7 cm tall, and rolled back and forth five times across a distance of approximately 15 cm.

Immediately following the procedures described above, each donor was decapitated, and the brain and liver quickly removed, weighed, and individually homogenized with an equal weight of distilled water. The entire liver was used in that homogenate, whereas the brain preparation did not include the olfactory bulbs and the cranial nerves. Next, a single injection of either brain or liver substance was given intraperitoneally in the upper left abdominal area of the appropriate recipient, who was first lightly anesthetized with ether to reduce pain. The volumes of the two homogenates from each donor were equated on the basis of volume obtained for the brain substance, and ranged between 1 and 1.5 ml per injection. The entire procedure, from initial test of donor to intraperitoneal injection of recipient, was completed within 5 minutes.

On the basis of preliminary work, we observed that injected recipients walked with difficulty and seemed lethargic for periods of up to 2 hours. After 3 hours, we noted that in all cases normal home cage activity resumed. Therefore, each recipient was tested 6 hours after injection to permit unequivocal recuperation from any temporary disabling effects of the injections. Recipient testing was identical to that described for the donors given experience in the straight alley, except that no shock was administered upon entry into the black section. All testing was done by an experimenter who was naive as to which recipients had been given brain homogenate and which had been given liver.

Statistical analyses revealed a treatment effect significant at $P < .05$ ($F = 3.29$, $d.f. = 2/54$) (7). We found longer latencies in subjects receiving homogenates from the shocked and stressed donors than in subjects receiving homogenate from the nonshocked donors. In addition, we noticed consistently longer latencies in the recipients of homogenates from donors in the nonspecific stress group than in recipients of homogenates from shocked donors. The mean latencies of brain and liver recipients are summarized in Table 1.

Table 1.

Mean latency of response (seconds) for recipients in experiments 1 and 2.

Recipients of	Source of injection		
	Shocked donors	Non-shocked donors	Stressed donors
EXPERIMENT 1			
Brain	16.05	9.2	18.62
Liver	12.95	13.59	14.82
EXPERIMENT 2			
Brain	18.7	11.35	26.45
Liver	31.0	20.1	30.55

The data from the groups that received brain homogenate from shocked and unshocked donors, respectively, could be interpreted as supporting the hypothesis that a specific memory is transferable from trained donors to naive recipients. As expected, subjects receiving brain homogenates from donors who were shocked in the testing apparatus generally remained outside the black section longer than subjects receiving brain homogenates from nonshocked donors. However, when data from recipients of homogenates from the non-specific stress group are considered, our results suggest that the increased latencies in recipients of homogenates from trained subjects cannot be adequately explained by the memory transfer hypothesis. This hypothesis, as proposed by Rosenblatt (8) or Unger (9), would not be able to account for the long latencies observed in the subjects whose donors were given no experience with relevant learning cues, that is, donors in the nonspecific stress group. However, this occurrence is understandable as a result of transfer of an as yet unidentified stress substance affecting general activity.

As behavioral testing proceeded, we noticed that some of the recipients were slower than their donors, while others had latencies almost identical to those observed in the donor mice. Because of this rather extensive variance, we decided to determine whether "fast" or "slow" subjects, so designated by inspection of the data, were differentially affected by the treatments. For the purpose of this analysis, subjects whose latencies were above the median of their respective group were called "slow," and those below, "fast" (10).

Of the mice whose latencies were above the median, those receiving brain homogenate from the shocked donors had significantly longer latencies than recipients of brain homogenate from unshocked mice ($P < .01$). In addition, the mice receiving homogenates from stressed donors had longer latencies than those receiving from no-shock donors ($P = .025$ for brain and $P < .05$ for liver homogenates). Other comparisons among groups were not significant.

In the below-median latency groups, the recipients from stressed mice took significantly longer to enter the dark side of the box than recipients from shocked mice, given either brain ($P < .01$) or liver ($P < .05$) homogenates. The other comparisons were not significant.

A chi-square analysis was also used to determine the percentage of subjects having response latencies longer than 20 seconds (Table 2). We chose this baseline figure because it represents approximately twice the mean of all donor latencies (11.65 seconds) in our experiment. The results paralleled the latency data; recipients of brain homogenate from the no-shock group were significantly faster than recipients from shocked donors and recipients from stressed donors. No significant differences were found for the recipients of brain from shocked and stressed donors, respectively, or in any liver comparisons.

The individual differences in recipient latencies, and the stressful nature of the experimental situation, suggested that there might be an interaction between emotionality and memory transfer in the cases of similar scores for the donor and recipient. This interference could result from injecting substance from highly emotional donors into nonemotional recipients, and from nonemotional donors into emotional recipients. Because of the possibility of this interaction, it seemed necessary to perform a second experiment before reaching any definite conclusions about the accuracy of our general stress hypothesis. Consequently, mice for the next experiment were pretested on two independent measures of emotionality with the intention of creating groups consisting of three emotionally similar animals, one donor and two recipients. It was expected that this matching would decrease the overall variance.

Table 2.

Percentage of subjects in each group with latencies greater than 20 seconds. (This baseline represents approximately double the mean of all donor latencies, from both experiments.)

Recipients of	Source of injection		
	Shocked donors	Non-shocked donors	Stressed donors
EXPERIMENT 1			
Brain	25	15	33
Liver	20	20	25
EXPERIMENT 2			
Brain	45	10	35
Liver	50	30	50

The subjects were 180 male albino mice, of the CD1 strain from the Charles River Laboratories, weighing 25 to 30 g. These were assigned to the three groups described in the first experiment.

Two independent tasks were used to match triad members. The apparatus consisted of a straight alley and an open field maze. The first was painted a medium gray; it measured 103 by 11.5 by 16 cm, and had a free-flowing water spout at one end. The open field maze measured 46 by 46 by 15.5 cm and was demarcated into 36 squares.

For the 2nd through 5th days following arrival in the laboratory, the mice were placed on a 23 hour 45 minute water-deprivation schedule, and received water only in the straight alley. On the 6th day, each mouse was allowed to run to water ten times. A mean of the latencies for these ten trials was recorded for each animal.

Approximately 3 hours after testing in the straight alley, each mouse was permitted 3 minutes of exploration in the open field maze. A count was made of the squares traversed during that time.

The mean latencies and the open field scores constituted the measures according to which the members of each triad were selected. Within each triad, the difference between the shortest and longest mean latencies was limited to 1.5 seconds (group mean latency = 6.26 seconds, S.D. = 2.84), and the difference between the lowest and highest open field scores was limited to 25 squares (group mean = 255.93, S.D. = 53.33).

The training, injection, and test and data-analysis procedures were identical to those described in the first experiment. Our analysis of the data revealed a significant difference between subjects receiving brain injections and liver injections ($P < .05$, $F = 4.30$, d.f. $= 1/57$). Thus, for the brain recipients, the longest latencies were found in recipients from the nonspecific stress donors, the shortest, in recipients from the no-shock donors, and those in recipients from the shocked donors were intermediary. For the liver recipients, the latencies in recipients from no-shock donors were also the shortest, and the latencies in recipients from stressed and shocked donors, respectively, were virtually the same. Within each treatment group, the liver recipients had significantly longer latencies than their respective brain-recipient counterparts. The mean latencies are summarized in the lower half of Table 1.

As in the first experiment, the data were analyzed with the Mann-Whitney U-test, for above-median and below-median latency scores.

Of the brain recipients with above-median scores, recipients from shocked and stressed donors, respectively, had significantly longer latencies than recipients from the no-shock donors ($P < .01$ and $< .025$, respectively). Similar findings were obtained for the liver recipients; that is, recipients from shocked and stressed donors, respectively, had longer latencies than recipients from the no-shock donors ($P < .05$ *and* $< .025$, respectively). The two remaining comparisons were not significant.

Of the recipients with below-median latencies, there were also four significant differences observed. For brain recipients from shocked and stressed donors, respectively, the latencies were longer than those of recipients from unshocked donors ($P < .025$ and $< .01$, respectively). For the subjects receiving the liver homogenate, recipients from shocked donors had longer latencies than both recipients from the no-shock donors ($P < .025$) and recipients from the stressed donors ($P < .01$). The other differences were not significant,

The results of the chi-square analysis for frequency of subjects with response latencies greater than 20 seconds revealed that recipients from shocked donors took significantly longer than recipients from no-shock donors, in the case of both brain recipients and liver recipients. Recipients from stressed donors also took significantly longer than recipients from no-shock donors, in the case of both brain recipients and liver recipients. No significant differences were found between recipients from shocked or stressed donors for both brain and liver injections.

In addition, Pearson correlation coefficients were obtained between the paired donor pretest scores and the recipient testing latencies for recipients from shocked, no-shock, and stressed donors, respectively; the purpose of this was to determine if the two pretests could predict performance in the test apparatus, as had been intended. These correlations were very low, ranging from $- .26$ to $+ .25$, and were not significant.

The results of these two experiments indicate that support for the hypothesis of specific memory transfer may require further study with additional controls for stress-related substances. Although we obtained increased latencies in subjects receiving homogenates from the shocked donors of our experiment, we observed even greater increases in the recipients from the nonspecific stress donors; furthermore, increased latencies were observed for all recipient groups, regardless of whether the homogenate injected was from brain or liver. At this point, one could ask if two independent agents are active in producing the observed effect, a specific memory substance in the brain, and some hormonal stress element in the liver. This possibility is negated by our finding that substantial increases in latency occurred with injections of brain homogenate taken from subjects given the nonspecific stress treatment. These recipients, whose donors were stressed in a part of the laboratory far removed from the testing apparatus, had the longest latencies of all experimental animals receiving brain homogenates.

If the specific memory hypothesis is questionable, what alternative explanations would provide better understanding of this phenomenon? On the basis of our experimental findings, we would tentatively suggest that a general stress factor may be responsible for the observed increases in latency. Furthermore, it seems necessary to take into consideration individual differences in emotional reactivity. Such individual differences, produced by environmental and genetic variables, have been shown by several investigators (11) to be important factors in predicting an animal's responses to different experimental treatments. Although we attempted to predict emotionality in the second experiment by using various pretests thought to assess arousal, we were unable to obtain significant correlations between the scores of the donors on the pretests (the open field maze and the straight alley) and the appropriate recipient latencies in the test apparatus. However, by matching donors with recipients, our results became less variable even though our measures of emotionality did not correlate perfectly. Future studies of interanimal transfer should seriously consider the prominent role of emotionality and arousal in determining recipient behavior. Therefore, the finding of pretests capable of designating a well-defined range of emotional types is of primary importance at the present time.

Since our studies were done with either whole brain or liver homogenates, no statement can be made regarding the effect of injections of pure RNA extract in interanimal transfer studies (2, 3). We have shown, however, that an effect similar to that obtained with RNA can be demonstrated with stress-affected whole brain or liver substance. Thus, if controls are not made for such factors as stress, it seems inappropriate to conclude that the RNA specific memory hypothesis is adequate, or even accurate.

References and Notes

1. F. R. Babich, A. L. Jacobson, S. Bubash, A. Jacobson, *Science* 149, 656 (1965).
2. E. J. Fjerdingstad, Th. Nissen, H. H. Røigaard-Petersen, *Scand. J. Psychol.* 6, 1 (1965); G. Ungar and C. Oceguero-Navarro, *Nature* 207, 301 (1965); F. Rosenblatt, J. T. Farrow, W. F. Herblin, *Nature* 209, 46 (1966).
3. M. Luttges, T. Johnson, C. Buck, J. Holland, J. McGaugh, *Science* 151, 834 (1965); W. L. Byrne *et al., ibid.* 153, 658 (1966).
4. J. Gaito, *Psychol. Rev.* 70, 471 (1963).
5. F. Rosenblatt, J. T. Farrow, S. Rhine, *Proc. Nat. Acad. Sci. U.S.* 55, 787 (1966).
6. J. A. Dyal, A. M. Golub, R. L. Marrone, *Nature* 214, 720 (1967).

7. In both experiments described in this report, fixed-factor analysis of variance was used to test the significance of our transformed group latency scores. The form of the transformation was $\log_{10}(X + 1)$, and two-tailed tests were used to assess significance.

8. F. Rosenblatt and R. G. Miller, *Proc. Nat. Acad. Sci. U.S.* **56**, 1683 (1966).

9. G. Ungar, *Perspec. Biol. Med.* **11**, 217 (1968).

10. The analysis of above- and below-median scores was based upon the Mann-Whitney U-test, in both experiments reported here. Since we predicted recipient scores to be the same as, or longer than, donor latencies, levels of significance were determined with reference to one-tailed tests. It was not possible to compare scores of individual recipients to scores of their respective donors across all three groups; the design of the experiment could not allow for obtaining latency scores in the test apparatus from the non-specific-stress donors.

11. V. H. Denenberg, *Neurophysiology and Emotion*, D. C. Glass, Ed. (Rockefeller Univ. Press, New York, 1967), pp. 161–190; W. H. Teichner, *Psychol. Rev.* **75**, 271 (1968).

12. This research was carried out under NSF grant GB-7041. We wish to thank Drs. D. Stevens, M. Weiner, and N. Rankin for their thoughtful criticisms of this manuscript, and K. Gans, F. Watkins, J. Galla, M. McIntyre, and D. Cooper, without whose efforts this research would have been impossible.

Memory in Mice Analyzed with Antibiotics

LOUIS B. FLEXNER, JOSEFA B. FLEXNER, AND RICHARD B. ROBERTS

Reprinted from *Science*, March 17, 1967, Vol. 155, No. 3768, pp. 1377–1383.
Copyright 1967 by the American Association for the Advancement of Science.

Memory is thought to consist of overlapping stages. In the first stage the essential process is believed to be the electrical activity of those nerve cells which participate in a learning procedure. In this stage memory can be destroyed by electroconvulsive shock which disrupts this selective electrical activity. The period when memory is vulnerable to electroconvulsive shock in the mammal varies greatly, with a minimal value of less than 1 minute (*1*).

The learning process also leads to changes of a permanent kind so that in man, for example, memory of an event in childhood may persist for life. Thus long-term memory appears to be a relatively stable condition reached as the outcome of events occurring in a period of consolidation. In this period electrical activity is transformed into a more permanent record. Halstead (*1*) in 1951 suggested that the durability of memory may depend upon changes in neuronal nucleoprotein. The past several years have seen a surge of interest in this area and numerous efforts are being made to evaluate the roles of RNA and protein in the function of the brain.

Further clues to the nature of the learning process and memory can be obtained by considering instinctive or inherited behavior. Such behavior must be attributed to certain stable patterns of gene expression which become established during the development of the individual. These patterns of gene expression are dictated by the sequence of nucleotides in the DNA and are manifested during the complicated and mysterious process known as differentiation.

Behavioral patterns acquired by learning or training are so similar to instinctive ones that they are often difficult to distinguish. Accordingly it is reasonable to assume that well consolidated, long-term memory has the same fundamental basis as instinctive behavior, that is, it is the manifestation of a stable pattern of gene expression. Nature frequently uses the same mechanism for a variety of purposes. According to this view, the difference between the two situations is that the instinctive pattern develops from precursor patterns in response to some of the multitude of interactions which comprise differentiation, but the learned pattern is derived from an earlier quasi-stable pattern in response to the chemical events which are initiated by the learning experience.

Although the detailed mechanisms of differentiation remain obscure, there is little doubt that they involve repression and derepression of genes, as differences in the RNA components have been demonstrated in different organs and in different stages of development. Control of the rate of protein synthesis and of the final behavior of the proteins themselves is also likely to play an important role. Interactions within the cell, between one cell and its neighbors, and with distant organs are all parts of the process. Furthermore, the stability of the patterns which persist in the adult organism depends on the stability of a dynamic state. Individual molecules, cellular substructures, or complete cells can be degraded and replaced if synthesis and degradation remain in balance.

In accord with these principles it seems reasonable that the changes in the patterns of gene expression which result from learning will be accompanied by changes in the kinds and quantities of RNA and proteins (as well as small molecules) which are produced by the brain cells. Furthermore, interference with these synthetic processes by inhibitors might prevent the establishment of new patterns of expression or might upset patterns which were partially (or even completely) established.

Whether or not these broad speculations are valid, it is desirable to identify what, if any, macromolecular events are essential for the maintenance of memory. We hoped to approach this goal by injecting into the brain antibiotics which inhibit the synthesis of a specific macromolecule and then testing the effect of this inhibition on established memory. An antibiotic may also provide a way of differentiating different stages in the formation of memory and of indicating molecular events necessary for learning and for its fixation. This article will be concerned with these several aspects of memory and learning in mice.

Procedure

We use a simple behavioral situation. Mice are trained in a Y-maze with a grid floor through which shock can be applied. The mouse is placed in the stem of the Y. If it fails to move out of the stem within 5 seconds (error of avoidance) it is shocked. If it fails to enter the selected arm of the Y (error of discrimination) it receives shock until it moves to the correct arm. Training is continued in one session (usually lasting 15 to 20 minutes) until the mouse has achieved nine correct responses out of ten attempts (the criterion). The same procedure is used to test for memory of the training experience (retention testing); shock is given for errors of performance. Memory is evaluated in the retention tests in terms of the percentage savings of trials and errors. These percentages are calculated by subtracting the number of trials or errors to criterion in the retention tests from the number to criterion in training, dividing by the number in training, and multiplying by 100. Savings of 100 percent indicate perfect memory; zero savings, complete loss of memory.

In our biochemical studies we have so far been concerned only with changes in the rate of cerebral protein synthesis after injection of antibiotics. At various times after treatment, a constant amount of radiovaline is injected subcutaneously. The mouse is killed 40 minutes later, since the rate of incorporation of labeled essential amino acids into cerebral proteins is practically constant during this interval. Protein precipitates are prepared from the following parts of the brain which are separated by dissection: the hippocampus, amygdala, thalamus, corpus striatum, temporal cortex (including entorhinal cortex), and the parietal and frontal portions of the neocortex (Fig. 1). The rate of synthesis of protein is calculated from the amount of radiovaline incorporated into protein and from the specific radioactivity of the valine pool.

Intracerebral injections are placed so as to expose the hippocampus, the entorhinal, and the neocortex to relatively high concentrations of the antibiotics. In our early efforts the spread of injected material was estimated from intracerebral injections of fluorescein, which is easily identified with ultraviolet light. These injections, each of 12 microliters, were made through small holes in the skull and at a depth of 2 mm from the surface of the skull. From one to three injections were made in each hemisphere. Bilateral injections, designated frontal injections, were made near the midline in the forward part of the skull. Ventricular injections were made near the midline well behind the frontal injections. Temporal injections were made below and behind the ventricular injections (2). Frontal injections of fluorescein heavily stained the forward third of the neocortex; ventricular injections stained all of the hippocampus and the caudal half of most of the neocortex, but importantly, spared the entorhinal cortex; and temporal injections stained all of the hippocampus and the caudal third of the cortex including the entorhinal cortex (Fig. 1). The staining obtaining from combinations of these three types of injections was essentially additive.

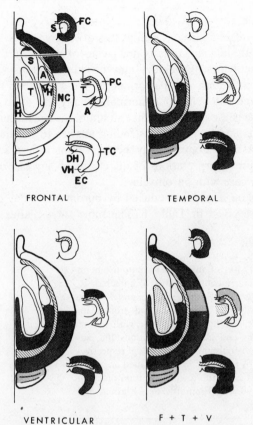

FRONTAL   TEMPORAL

VENTRICULAR   F + T + V

FIGURE 1. Spread of fluorescein after it is injected intracerebrally. The diagrams at the left indicate structures viewed from the top after removal of a horizontal section of the hemisphere; at the right, cross (frontal) sections of the hemisphere at the level indicated in the diagram for frontal injections. Relative intensity of staining is indicated by relative density of stippling. A, Amygdaloid nucleus; DH, dorsal hippocampus; EC, entorhinal cortex; FC, frontal cortex; NC, neocortex; PC, parietal cortex; S, corpus striatum; T, thalamus; TC, temporal cortex; VH, ventral hippocampus; F + T + V, frontal + temporal + ventricular injections. (*From Flexner, Flexner, and Stellar (2).*)

Effects of Puromycin

Our initial choice of an antibiotic was determined by the possibility that maintenance of memory might depend upon protein sustained above a critical level by continuing synthesis. We proposed to drastically reduce the rate of synthesis of cerebral protein for several hours and then to test the ability of mice to remember their training in the Y-maze. At that time Yarmolinsky and de la Haba (3) had found that puromycin is a powerful inhibitor of protein synthesis. Intracerebral injections of puromycin were made with the same procedure used with fluorescein.

Puromycin is used with caution. Its intracerebral injection in our albino mice causes toxic symptoms. There are often lethargy and loss of alertness followed by hyperexcitability, as well as loss of weight due to failure to eat and drink normally. If sufficient time is not given for recovery, there is the possibility that apparent loss of memory may be due to illness with an attendant impairment of motivation and performance. We delay tests for memory until weight is recovered and behavior is normal, usually 3 to 4 days after treatment. In addition, there is the possibility that an antibiotic may interfere with several cellular functions and so give a misleading answer to the question for which it was chosen. It may consequently be important to use several antibiotics before making firm interpretations of the effects of any one of them. This has proved to be the case with puromycin.

The effects on memory produced by puromycin 1 day or 11 to 60 days after training are given in Table 1. The table shows, after various types of

Table 1.
Effects of different sites of injection of puromycin on short- and longer-term memory. L, lost; I, impaired; R, retained; Days, days after learning. T, V, and F refer, respectively, to temporal, ventricular, and frontal injections, all given bilaterally. For the mice with loss of memory, the means and standard deviations for percentages of savings of trials and of errors were respectively 1 ± 3 and 2 ± 6; for those with impaired memory, 26 ± 29 and 39 ± 12; for those with retention of memory, 90 ± 14 and 90 ± 9. From Flexner, Flexner, and Stellar (2, 5).

Puromycin injections			No. of mice in which memory was		
Site	Days	Dose (mg)	L	I	R
SHORT-TERM MEMORY					
T + V + F	1	0.03–.06	7	0	0
T	1	.09	10	0	0
V	1	.09	0	0	5
F	1	.09	0	0	5
V + F	1	.09	0	1	2
LONGER-TERM MEMORY					
T + V + F	11–60	0.03	17	2	0
T	11–35	0.06–.09	0	0	7
V	12–38	.06–.09	0	0	3
F	16–27	.06–.09	0	0	3
V + F	28	.06–.09	0	2	2
V + T	28–43	0.09	1	1	2
T + F	28	.09	0	0	3

intracerebral injections, the number of mice in which memory was lost, impaired, or retained. The first series of experiments were made with mice trained to criterion and injected 1 day later with puromycin. After six injections (bilateral temporal, ventricular, and frontal), each of 30 to 60 micrograms of puromycin, retention tests showed that memory of the training experience had been lost completely and permanently (memory was absent when tested 3 months after puromycin). An effort was then made to localize this effect. Memory was also consistently lost with bitemporal injection of 90 micrograms of puromycin. By contrast bilateral frontal or ventricular or combined frontal plus ventricular injections were essentially without effect. The next series of experiments was made with mice injected with puromycin 11 to 60 days after training to criterion. In these mice only bilateral temporal plus ventricular plus frontal injections quite consistently destroyed memory. Bitemporal injections, which destroyed 1-day memory, were ineffective.

What do these results indicate about the parts of the brain concerned with recent (1-day-old) and longer-term (11- to 60-day-old) memory? Recent memory was lost when puromycin was given by temporal injections, involving, on the basis of the distribution of fluoresceine, the hippocampal area (hippocampus plus entorhinal cortex), while loss of longer-term memory required puromycin additionally in a substantial part of the neocortex. The conclusion from these observations that the hippocampal area is concerned with recent memory and an enlarged area of the neocortex with older memory is supported by the evidence that has come from neurosurgical and autopsy findings on man and from ablation experiments on animals (4).

As indicated by our method, how long does it require after learning for an enlarged area of the neocortex to participate in the effective memory trace? Bitemporal injections consistently destroyed memory 2 days after training (Table 2), but they were consistently without effect 6 days after training. Results were variable at 3, 4, and 5 days. Thus it appears that the enlarged locus of longer-term memory in the type of training experience we have used with mice becomes effective in from 3 to 6 days, depending upon the individual.

We have put these observations on recent and longer-term memory to an additional test by means of reversal training. A mouse was first trained, for example, to move from the stem of the Y into its left arm; then 3 weeks later it was retrained to move into the right arm. Puromycin was injected bitemporally 24 hours later. Would recent memory be destroyed by this treatment and longer-term memory be preserved? Shock was omitted in the retention trials 3 days after injection of puromycin since there was, within the design of the test, no right or wrong response. As shown in Table 3, when they were tested for memory, the first choice of all mice was consistent with the first learning experience, as were the large majority of subsequent choices. Untreated mice, in contrast to the experimental group, made choices consistent with their recent or reversal training. The results fit our evidence for the difference in the parts of the brain concerned with recent and longer-term memory.

We had chosen to use puromycin to test the possibility that continuing protein synthesis is essential for the maintenance of memory. We were en-

Table 2.

Effect of bilateral temporal injections of puromycin on memory of increasing age. Each injection contained 0.09 milligram of puromycin. For the seven mice with loss of memory, the means and standard deviations for percentages of savings of trials and of errors were respectively 1 ± 4 and 0 ± 0; for the seven mice with retention of memory. 85 ± 19 and 93 ± 7. In one mouse with impaired memory the percentages of savings for trials and errors were respectively 38 and 20; for the other, 39 and 55. From Flexner, Flexner, and Stellar (2).

Injections: days after learning	No. of mice in which memory was		
	Lost	Impaired	Retained
2	3	0	0
3	4	0	1
4	0	1	1
5	0	1	2
6	0	0	3

Table 3.

Differential effect of bilateral temporal injections of puromycin on recent and longer-term memory. Each injection had a volume of 0.012 milliliter and contained 0.06 or 0.09 milligram (mouse 49) of puromycin. Choices of the arm of the Y-maze by an animal after injection were scored as 1 if consistent with initial learning, and as 2 if consistent with reversal learning. Trials were continued irregularly beyond the ten originally planned. From Flexner, Flexner and Stellar (2). Learning was always to criterion, and reversal learning occurred 3 weeks after initial learning.

Mouse	Initial learning (No. trials)	Reversal learning (No. trials)	Choice of arm of Y-maze
		EXPERIMENTAL ANIMALS	
26A	13	22	1, 1, 1, 1, 1, 1, 1, 1, 1, 1, 1, 1, 1, 1, 1, 1
24A	7	10	1, 1, 2, 1, 1, 1, 1, 2, 1, 1, 1, 1, 1, 1, 1, 1, 1, 1, 1, 1, 2, 1, 1, 1
25A	8	10	1, 1, 1, 1, 2, 1, 1, 1, 1, 2, 1, 2, 2, 1, 2
22A	9	8	1, 2, 2, 1, 1, 2, 1, 2, 1, 2, 1, 1, 1, 1, 1, 1, 1, 1, 1, 1, 1
23A	13	4	1, 1, 1, 1, 1, 1, 1, 1, 1, 1, 1, 1, 1
49	22	9	1, 1, 2, 2, 1, 1, 1, 2, 1, 1, 1, 1, 2, 1, 1, 1, 1, 1, 1, 1, 1, 1, 1
27A	12	5	1, 1, 1, 1, 1, 1, 1, 1, 1, 2, 1
		CONTROL ANIMALS	
58A	10	14	2, 2, 2, 2, 2, 2, 2, 2, 2, 2, 2, 2, 2, 2, 2
60A	10	12	2, 2, 2, 2, 2, 2, 2, 2, 2, 2, 2

couraged in this view by the destructive effects of puromycin on memory. As has been mentioned, however, our results might have been due to some side effect not related to protein synthesis and it was consequently essential to test our tentative interpretation in other ways. We have done this by correlating the effects on memory and cerebral protein synthesis of consistently destructive and of smaller intracerebral doses of puromycin, of puromycin subcutaneously injected, of several substances related to puromycin, and of other antibiotics which are known to be inhibitors of protein synthesis (5).

Figure 2 gives the percentage of inhibition of protein synthesis in six areas of the brain as a function of time after bitemporal injections of 90 micrograms of puromycin, a treatment which uniformly leads to loss of recent memory. The figure shows that puromycin, unlike fluorescein, spreads widely from the site of the injection to other parts of the brain, but inhibition is most drastic in the hippocampus and temporal cortex (including entorhinal cortex). Inhibition in both of these areas with one exception was maintained at a level in excess of about 80 percent from the first to the tenth hour after the injection. On the supposition that destruction of memory by puromycin is related to its effect on protein synthesis, we tentatively concluded that to produce consistent loss of recent memory in our experimental situation, protein synthesis must be inhibited in the hippocampus and temporal cortex for about 9 hours at a level exceeding 80 percent.

Inhibition of protein synthesis in six areas of the brain was also measured after six injections (bilateral, temporal, ventricular, and frontal) each

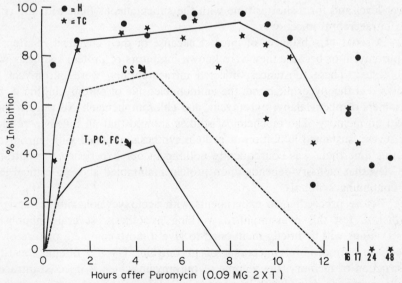

FIGURE 2. Changes with time in the inhibition of incorporation of radiovaline into protein of the hippocampus (H), temporal cortex (TC), corpus striatum (CS), thalamus (T), parietal cortex (PC), and frontal cortex (FC) after bitemporal injections each with 90 micrograms of puromycin in 12 microliters. (*From Flexner, Flexner, Roberts, and de la Haba* (5).)

of 30 micrograms of puromycin. This dose leads to loss of longer-term (greater than 5-day-old) memory. The inhibitory effects of these combined injections on protein synthesis is most pronounced in the hippocampus and temporal cortex. In these two areas inhibition exceeded 80 percent from at the most 1.7 hours to more than 11 hours after the injection. Inhibition in the frontal cortex was somewhat less over this period with a minimum of about 70 percent. The parietal cortex, thalamus, and corpus striatum showed with time a greater decrement, reaching 35 to 50 percent inhibition 11.7 hours after the injection. Again on the supposition that destruction of memory by puromycin is related to its effect on protein synthesis, we tentatively concluded that longer-term memory is destroyed by injections which inhibit protein synthesis in the hippocampus and temporal cortex by at least 80 percent for 10 hours, and in a substantial part of the remaining neocortex to a minimum of 70 percent for the same period of time.

The relationship between puromycin's effect on memory and on protein synthesis was studied further by injecting graded amounts of the antibiotic into the mouse brain. The amounts were smaller than required to consistently destroy memory. As the amount of puromycin was reduced it became progressively less effective in destroying memory; there was a similar trend in its effect on the degree and duration of inhibition of protein synthesis.

In studying the effects of subcutaneous injections of puromycin we used the highest amount of the antibiotic which could be tolerated. We could not detect any interference with memory in these experiments. Again, biochemical measurements showed that protein synthesis was inhibited at a substantially lower level and for a shorter time with the subcutaneous than with the effective intracerebral injections.

A series of substances of interest because of their chemical relationship to puromycin or because they were known inhibitors of protein synthesis were also tested. These substances, injected intracerebrally, were puromycin hydrolyzed at the glycosidic bond, the aminonucleoside of puromycin, the D- and L-isomers of phenylalanyl puromycin, and chloramphenicol. All were without effect on memory. The biochemical studies showed that all failed to produce the severe, sustained inhibition of protein synthesis obtained with puromycin. At this time there was consequently nothing in our experience to contradict the view that memory depends upon protein maintained above a critical level by continuing synthesis.

Before proceeding to experiments with acetoxycycloheximide, designed further to test this oversimplified working hypothesis, several unpublished observations will be briefly mentioned to give a more complete picture of the effects of intracerebral injections of puromycin. (i) To obtain consistent destruction of memory, the volume of puromycin which is injected intracerebrally must be increased with increased skull size. Our routine procedure is designed for mice that weigh 28 to 32 grams. In addition, injections must promptly follow one another. With bitemporal injections, for example, irregularities of response occur if the injections are made more than 5 minutes apart. (ii) In mice trained to criterion, both recent and longer-term memory are maintained for 10 to 20 hours after injection of puromycin, then they disappear permanently (the longest time at which memory has been tested after injection of puromycin is 3 months; at this time, memory was absent). (iii) If mice are run through the maze a sufficient number of times after reaching criterion (that is, over-trained), puromycin, as we inject it, has no effect on memory. About 60 trials beyond criterion on the average are needed to give this protection against puromycin. (iv) Dorsal hippocampal lesions and ventricular dilatation, varying from slight to moderately severe, may be found after injections of puromycin. Damage to other parts of the brain, including the entorhinal cortex, has not been seen except in areas of the neocortex surrounding the needle tracks. Under our conditions the effects of puromycin on memory are unrelated to the degree of severity of the hippocampal lesions. Indeed, ventricular injections cause damage to the hippocampus in the same way as temporal injections, but they have no effect on memory. (v) After treatment with puromycin, all mice are capable of relearning the maze, are capable of reversal learning, and retain memory of their last training indefinitely. Some reach criterion on second learning in practically the same number of trials with the same number of errors as on first learning; in others, second learning is substantially more difficult than first learning. No correlation has been found between this difference on second learning and the degree of hippocampal damage. (vi) Mice which had their memory destroyed by puromycin were retrained. In most instances the standard treatment with puromycin then failed to destroy memory and in addition had relatively little effect on protein synthesis. We have shown with tritiated puromycin that the antibiotic is lost more rapidly from the brain after the second injections, probably because of vascular changes which persist after the first injections. A similar resistance to puromycin often develops after any procedure in which the skull is entered.

Effects of Acetoxycycloheximide

The antibiotic acetoxycycloheximide became available to us at about the time we had completed these experiments with puromycin. It is a powerful inhibitor of protein synthesis and, importantly for us, suppresses protein synthesis by a mechanism different from that of puromycin. Puromycin produces its effect by being incorporated into the carboxyl ends of growing polypeptide chains and causing their premature release from ribosomes (6). Acetoxycycloheximide, by contrast, inhibits the transfer of amino acids from s-RNA to polypeptide (6). Thus, unlike puromycin, the heximide suppresses the formation of peptide bonds. Could we destroy memory with the heximide and, as with puromycin, correlate this effect with severe inhibition of protein synthesis? If this proved to be the case, our tentative view that memory depends upon the continuing synthesis of protein would receive strong support.

Figure 3 shows the drastic and sustained effect of bitemporal injections of the heximide, up to 10 hours after treatment, on rate of protein synthesis in the hippocampus, an effect at least equal to that produced by puromycin (Fig. 2). Unlike puromycin, however, the most severe inhibitory effect of bitemporal injections of the heximide is not limited to the hippocampus and temporal cortex. Suppression of protein synthesis in the other six areas of the brain which were studied over the first 10 hours after the injections was as severe as in the hippocampus. Acetoxycycloheximide provided just the agent which we needed to test our working hypothesis.

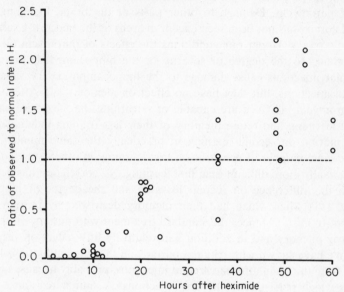

FIGURE 3. Rate of protein synthesis in the hippocampus after bitemporal injections of 60 micrograms of acetoxycycloheximide. Values below the dotted line show inhibition; values above, increase of rate over normal level. (*From Flexner and Flexner* (7), *and Flexner, Flexner, and Roberts* (8).)

Table 4 gives the results of the behavioral studies with acetoxycycloheximide. They, like the biochemical results, were unequivocal. Memory was not affected by the heximide in spite of its profound suppression of protein synthesis. Thus it was clear that the simplified version of our working hypothesis was inadequate to explain the destruction of memory by puromycin.

What explanation might be given for the differences between puromycin and acetoxycycloheximide in their effects on memory? One possibility is that the heximide also inhibits the degradation of protein; as a result continued synthesis would not be required to maintain the quantity above a critical level necessary for the expression of memory. That peptide bond formation occurs at a normal rate with puromycin but is suppressed by the heximide suggests two other possibilities. With puromycin it was possible that small, abnormal peptides are synthesized which are toxic and which somehow destroy memory. The second possibility rests upon the assumption, to be stated fully later, that

Table 4.

Lack of effect of acetoxycycloheximide (A) and of a mixture of it and puromycin (P) on recent (1 day) and longer-term (12 to 35 days) memory. T, V, and F refer, respectively, to temporal, ventricular, and frontal injections, all given bilaterally. For the 30 mice with retention of memory, the means and standard deviations for percentages of savings of trials and errors were, respectively, 90 ± 15 and 92 ± 10; for the three mice with impaired memory, the corresponding means were 45 and 68. From Flexner and Flexner (7).

Substance	Injection site	Dose (µg)	Days after learning	No. of mice in which memory was		
				Lost	Im-paired	Re-tained
A	T	60	1	0	1	8
A	T	120	1	0	1	3
A	T + V + F	15–30	1	0	0	2
A	T + V + F	15–30	12–35	0	0	5
A + P	T	120 A + 120 P	1	0	1	6
A + P	T + V + F	8 or 15 A + 30 P	14	0	0	6

memory depends in part upon the preservation of certain species of messenger RNA (mRNA) which are produced by a learning experience. It is also assumed that puromycin destroys memory because this essential mRNA decays without replacement, while with heximide memory is maintained because essential mRNA is preserved. In support of this possibility it has been found that mRNA is degraded at a normal rate in the presence of puromycin and that puromycin inhibits the synthesis of RNA (9). By contrast, the rate of decay of mRNA is decreased with suppression of peptide bond formation as occurs with acetoxycycloheximide (9).

If either of these latter explanations were valid, it could be predicted that puromycin would have no effect on memory in the presence of an agent which adequately suppresses the formation of peptide bonds. This prediction was tested (7) by using intracerebral injections of puromycin in mixture with acetoxycycloheximide, as well as with cycloheximide or chloramphenicol, which also interfere with transfer of amino acids to protein. All of these antibiotics protected memory against puromycin (Table 4).

Our attempts to demonstrate the presence of small, abnormal polypeptides was based on identification of the puromycin which they would be expected to contain in terminal position. Tritiated puromycin was injected intracerebrally. We were unable to demonstrate radioactivity in protein precipitates prepared from appropriate areas of the brain (5). Chromatographs of the supernatant fluid had significant radioactivity only in the spot occupied by free puromycin. However, marked effects on memory have been reported after the injection of small quantities of peptide (10). Accordingly, we do not consider that our failure to find an accumulation of abnormal peptides is conclusive evidence that they are not involved in the loss of memory. This possibility remains open.

Self-Inducing System

Understanding of an experimental test which we have made of the alternate possibility involving mRNA depends upon a more complete presentation of our working hypothesis than has thus far been given. We assume that an established memory of long duration depends, not on the continued presence of any protein or nucleic acid molecules, but on the establishment of a self-sustaining system for their synthesis. Such a system can occur whenever some of the products of a gene's expression act as inducers (or derepressors) of that gene. If the gene is repressed, inducers are not synthesized and the gene stays repressed. On the other hand, if the gene is induced for a sufficient time, inducers will accumulate above a critical level and the gene will stay induced, if, however, the synthetic processes are inhibited for a sufficient time, the level of inducers will fall below the critical level and the gene will revert to its repressed state. (A more quantitative description of the self-inducing system is given in 11.)

The processes involved in the establishment of a long-term memory can be described in terms of the self-inducing system. We assume that the initial learning experience triggers the synthesis of one or more species of mRNA. This mRNA alters the synthetic rate of one or more proteins which are essential for the expression of memory. These proteins are thought to modify the characteristics of synapses concerned in a learning process so that the passage of impulses between nerve cells is facilitated. In turn, the proteins or their products act as inducers of their related mRNA; in this way the concentration of the inducer proteins is maintained. In this view, expression of memory depends upon changes in proteins, changes which are initiated and sustained by qualitative and quantitative changes in mRNA produced by a learning experience. Loss of this mRNA would lead to loss of essential protein with consequent permanent loss of memory. In the presence of an inhibitor of protein synthesis, the concentration of essential protein could fall to levels too low for expression of memory, but loss of memory would be temporary if mRNA were conserved to direct the synthesis of protein when the inhibitor had disappeared (7).

Such a loss and recovery of memory has been observed in the behavior of mice at various times after training conducted (i) during or (ii) immediately before the severe suppression of protein synthesis which follows treatment with acetoxycycloheximide. Both sets of experiments showed an initial period in which memory was retained, an intermediate period in which memory was temporarily lost, and a final period during which expression of memory returned (8).

The duration of the initial period during which memory is retained in spite of severe inhibition of protein synthesis seems to vary with the conditions of learning and the inhibiting agent. Barondes and Cohen (12) observed that when mice are trained to a Y-maze in the presence of puromycin, they retain their memory of the maze at a high level for less than 45 minutes. In our mice trained immediately before treatment with acetoxycycloheximide, the initial period lasted for more than 14 hours. Memory of training in the presence of the heximide appeared to persist for between 3 to 5 hours, though the reliability of the upper limit is questionable because of the relatively poor condition of the mice at this time. In any event, there is a period in which memory is retained in spite of drastic inhibition of protein synthesis throughout the brain. Similar observations have been made on goldfish by Davis and Agranoff (12). Memory during the initial period may be based on changes in concentrations of ions or small molecules or in the configuration or location of preexisting macromolecules.

The intermediate period is characterized by failure of the mice to perform the training procedure. Our observations seem to indicate that the temporary loss of memory is not due to a general, nonspecific failure of performance or recall. Memory of training immediately before injection of heximide was expressed during a period when memory of training after injection of heximide could not be demonstrated. Furthermore, relearning occurred in both groups at the time when mice with loss of memory were given retention tests; this relearning indicated again an adequate capacity for performance. During the intermediate period memory appears to reside in a form which cannot be expressed until protein synthesis has been restored.

The final period is characterized by the return of memory to a condition where it can control performance. In essentially all mice in both experimental situations memory returned at a high level 58 to 96 hours after training. This period is at least 20 hours after protein synthesis was found to have returned to normal or higher than normal rates (Fig. 3).

Clearly only a beginning has been made in testing the hypothesis based on a self-sustaining system. The hypothesis is consistent with the results of Hydén and collaborators (12) who demonstrated an increase in nuclear RNA following training. It is also consistent with the recent finding by Zemp *et al.* (12) that rate of synthesis of nuclear RNA is increased in a learning situation. There is, however, as yet no completely convincing demonstration that changes in RNA and protein are fundamental to memory.

Conclusion

It is apparent that antibiotics are useful in differentiating different stages in the formation of memory. Puromycin gave the first indication that very early memory can be established and survive, for a short period at least, in spite of inhibition of protein synthesis (12). Injection of actinomycin D indicates that RNA synthesis is not essential during this early stage (13). The duration of this early period seems to vary with the inhibiting agent; with puromycin memory was notably degraded in less than an hour, but with actinomycin D or with acetoxycycloheximide it persisted for several hours or more.

The fixation or consolidation of memory involves whatever processes give permanence to memory. These processes are disrupted when electro-convulsive shock is administered shortly after a learning experience, presumably because of the interference with organized patterns of neuronal electrical activity. Memory acquired in the presence of antibiotics appears to proceed to a stage beyond that based purely on electrical activity because the memory persists beyond the period usually reported as sensitive to electroconvulsive shock. Further work should show whether this stage is truly insensitive to electroconvulsive shock. Memory acquired in the presence of puromycin does not seem to achieve any durable consolidation. In contrast, memory acquired in the presence of or immediately before injection of acetoxycycloheximide does appear to initiate the later stages of consolidation, as permanent memory reappears some days after the initial stages have become ineffective in controlling performance.

Finally, puromycin has provided evidence of the enlarged area of the neocortex which participates as memory matures. Puromycin also indicates the time required for this maturation process.

Since antibiotics have also been useful in studying learning and memory in goldfish (*14*), this approach seems to have general applicability in defining various stages in the process of memory formation.

The initial purpose of these investigations was to determine the molecular basis of the "memory trace." This goal still remains distant, although there are some indications that protein synthesizing systems are involved. This objective, though of enormous interest, is to be regarded as only a necessary first step. Whether new proteins or some other molecules cause the changes in synapses thought to underlie memory, this knowledge of itself will contribute only a beginning to our understanding of the events which account for the functioning of the brain. A determination of the composition of computer components would provide very little information toward unraveling their function.

As the experiments proceeded, however, information of a more general nature was being obtained. The identification of different stages of consolidation shows how injections of antibiotics can supplement electroconvulsive shock as a way of disrupting the establishment of memory and how it can supplement ablation in destroying memory already laid down in a permanent mode. Applied to larger animals the localization of various regions sensitive or insensitive to the action of the drugs should become more definitive. We hope that such experiments will contribute increasingly to the general problem of [understanding] brain function.

References and Notes

1. J. L. McGaugh, *Science* **153,** 1351 (1966); W. Halstead, in *Cerebral Mechanisms in Behavior,* L. A. Jeffress, Ed. (Wiley, New York, 1951), p. 244.
2. J. B. Flexner, L. B. Flexner, E. Stellar, *Science* **141,** 57 (1963).
3. M. B. Yarmolinsky and G. de la Haba, *Proc. Nat. Acad. Sci. U.S.* **45,** 1721 (1959).

4. B. Milner and W. Penfield, *Trans. Amer. Neurol. Ass.* **80,** 42 (1955); W. B. Scoville and B. Milner, *J. Neurol. Neurosurg. Psychiat.* **20,** 11 (1957); L. S. Stepien, J. P. Cordeau, T. Rasmussen, *Brain* **83,** 470 (1960).

5. J. B. Flexner, L. B. Flexner, E. Stellar, G. de la Haba, R. B. Roberts, *J. Neurochem.* **9,** 595 (1962); L. B. Flexner, J. B. Flexner, R. B. Roberts, G. de la Haba, *Proc. Nat. Acad. Sci. U.S.* **52,** 1165 (1964); L. B. Flexner, *et al. Neurochem.* **12,** 535 (1965); L. B. Flexner, J. B. Flexner, E. Stellar, *Exp. Neurol.* **13,** 264 (1965).

6. D. W. Allen and P. C. Zamecnik, *Biochim. Biophys. Acta.* **55,** 865 (1962); D. Nathans, *Proc. Nat. Acad. Sci. U.S.* **51,** 585 (1964); M. R. Siegel and H. D. Sisler. *Nature* **200,** 675 (1963); H. L. Ennis and M. Lubin, *Science* **146,** 1474 (1964).

7. L. B. Flexner and J. B. Flexner, *Proc. Nat. Acad. Sci. U.S.* **55,** 369 (1966).

8. L. B. Flexner, J. B. Flexner, R. B. Roberts, *ibid.* **56,** 730 (1966).

9. S. Villa-Trevino, E. Farber, T. Staehelin, F. O. Wettstein, H. Noli, *J. Biol. Chem.* **239,** 3826 (1964); R. R. Wagner and A. S. Huang, *Proc. Nat. Acad. Sci. U.S.* **54,** 1112 (1965); A. R. Williamson and R. Schweet, *J. Mol. Biol.* **11,** 358 (1965).

10. B. Bohus and D. de Wied, *Science* **153,** 318 (1966).

11. R. B. Roberts and L. B. Flexner, *Amer. Sci.* **54,** 174 (1966).

12. S. H. Barondes and H. D. Cohen, *Science* **151,** 594 (1966); R. E. Davis and B. W. Agranoff, *Proc. Nat. Acad. Sci. U.S.* **55,** 555 (1966); J. W. Zemp, J. E. Wilson, K. Schlesinger, W. O. Boggan, E. Glassman, *ibid.,* p. 1423; H. Hydén and E. Egyházi, *ibid.* **52,** 1030 (1964); H. Hydén and P. W. Lange, *ibid.* **53,** 946 (1965).

13. H. D. Cohen and S. H. Barondes, *J. Neurochem.* **13,** 207 (1966).

14. B. W. Agranoff, R. E. Davis, J. J. Brink, *Brain Res.* **1,** 303 (1966).

15. A substantial part of our investigations presented here were made in collaboration with G. de la Haba and E. Stellar.

Effects of Chronic Reductions in Acetylcholinesterase Activity on Serial Problem-Solving Behavior

AMELIA BANKS AND ROGER W. RUSSELL

Reprinted from *Journal of Comparative and Physiological Psychology*, 1967, Vol. 64, No. 2, pp. 262–267. Copyright 1967 by the American Psychological Association.

The present experiment was designed to study effects upon serial problem-solving behavior of chronic reductions in acetylcholinesterase (AChE) activity. AChE controls the rapid hydrolysis or inactivation of the neurohumoral transmitter substance, acetylcholine (ACh), once ACh has been released from its bound state by stimulation of the nerve membrane; the hydrolysis is associated with restoration of sodium conductance in the neuron. Preliminary studies

(Russell, 1954, 1958) suggested that reduction in AChE activity affects certain aspects of behavior and not others. Further research (Russell, Watson, and Frankenhaeuser, 1961) provided evidence that the speed of acquisition of a conditioned avoidance response was not altered by reductions within the range of 0–76.5%, whereas extinction of the response was significantly slower below a "critical level" at about 40% of normal AChE activity. The present paper reports results of testing the hypothesis that chronic reductions in AChE activity below this level would also affect behavior in a situation requiring seriatim extinctions of a series of similar but distinctive responses and involving positive reinforcement, i.e., food for hungry animals, rather than avoidance of a noxious stimulus.

Method

The research design required six groups of Ss. The neutral solvent, Arachis oil, was administered to a normal control group. Four experimental groups each received different concentrations of the organophosphorus anticholinesterase, OO-diethyl-S-ethymercaptoethanol thiophosphate (Systox), in Arachis oil. A caloric control group, which received Arachis oil only and whose daily food supply was restricted to the amount eaten on the previous day by paired E4 Ss, was included to check on the possibility that administration of the drug might reduce food intake and thus affect food-hunger motivation. The experiment was conducted during two independent periods, each involving 24 Ss assigned randomly to four replications.

Reduction of AChE

The required doses of Systox were administered by oral intubation in concentrations given in Table 1. Following completion of the behavioral tests, AChE activity levels were determined by analyses of whole brain homogenates using the methods of Nachmansohn and Rothenberg (1945), with details by Aldridge (1950). It should be emphasized that the reductions in AChE activity were *chronic*, i.e., by daily administration of Systox, and not acute.

Subjects

Forty-eight 100-day-old, naive male white rats of Wistar stock were assigned at random to the six groups, except that, on the first day of the experiment, Ss of the E4 and caloric control groups were paired on the basis of body weight.

Apparatus

The apparatus employed in presenting the two sets of standardized problems was the "closed-field" situation described by Rabinovitch and Rosvold

(1951): Problems A to F in the preliminary adaptation and training phases and the more difficult Problems 1–12 in the problem-solving phase. The most direct path between start and goal boxes was described for each problem in terms of squares painted on the floor of the closed field; an error was recorded whenever *S* placed one of its forepaws in a square which was not in the direct path.

Procedure

PRELIMINARY ADAPTATION.   A food deprivation schedule was established by daily reductions in feeding time until, at the end of 1 wk., all *S*s had food available for 2 hr. daily. The *S* was presented with 40 gm. of powdered M.R.C. 41 diet (Bruce and Parkes, 1949) at the start of each feeding period; food residue was recorded after feeding. The only exception occurred in the case of the caloric control *S*s, which, from the end of the first week, were given an amount of food equal to that eaten on the preceding day by their paired *S*s in Group E4.

Daily administration of the drug or placebo also started at the end of the first week. Preliminary adaptation to the closed-field situation began 3 wk. later. The procedure described by Rabinovitch and Rosvold (1951) was followed throughout the experiment. Each daily session terminated when *S* was returned to its home cage where food was available for the remainder of the 2-hr. feeding period.

TRAINING.   Discrete trials were introduced the day after preliminary training ended. Time between *S*'s exit from the start box and entrance into the goal box was recorded for each trial, which ended with 15 sec. for eating in the goal box. Criterion for completion of training was 9 trials in 60 sec. or less on 2 successive days. The *S*s in the first experimental group all reached criterion within 27 days; those in the second group, in 32 days.

PROBLEM SOLVING.   When this phase began all experimental *S*s had been receiving daily doses of Systox for 6–8 wk. Check experiments (Russell et al., 1961) had shown that consistent levels of reduction in brain AChE are maintained for as long as 55 wk. if concentrations of Systox remain constant.

Problems 1–12 were set up, one on each of 12 successive days, and each *S* was given seven trials per problem. Errors were recorded. On the following 3 days each *S* was given five daily trials in a straightaway, time per trial being recorded.

DETERMINATION OF BRAIN AChE ACTIVITY LEVELS.   The *S*s were sacrificed on the following day. Whole brains were removed after sectioning immediately posterior to the cerebellum; the tissue was washed, weighed, and then stored in a bicarbonate buffer solution at 18° C. until determinations of AChE activity levels were made.

Results

AChE Activity Levels

Table 1 shows that the percentage reductions in brain AChE activity levels increased systematically in magnitude from the control group to the group administered the highest dose of Systox. In only one instance was there any overlap between groups, i.e., one S in Group E3 fell within the range of Group E4. A Kruskal-Wallis one-way analysis of variance by ranks gave the very high H value of 33.01 ($p < .001$). Within-group variabilities of AChE levels showed a consistent decrease with reduction in AChE activity. Comparisons between the normal control and each of the other groups, using unbiased estimates of population variances, gave F ratios all of which were significant ($p < .01$) except for the normal control and caloric control groups.

Table 1.

Brain cholinesterase activity levels.

Group	Systox concentration[a]	Cholinesterase activity[b]		% reduction in activity[c]	normal % activity[d]
		M	Variability		
Normal control	0.00	194.46	23.54	0.0	100
E1	0.25	113.89	13.09	41.4	59
E2	0.50	80.23	5.24	58.7	41
E3	0.75	58.19	6.37	70.1	30
E4	1.00	48.08	3.30	75.3	25
Caloric control	0.00	186.79	18.52	3.94	96

[a] Concentration in mg/ml of Arachis oil.
[b] Microliters of CO_2 per minute per gram of tissue.
[c] Based upon the control group as zero reduction.
[d] Based upon the control group as 100%.

In light of the study of Krech, Rosenzweig, and Bennett (1964), which produced evidence that cortical and subcortical AChE activity may be affected by prior experience, it should be emphasized that AChE determinations in the present experiment were made after Ss had completed the various behavioral tests. Since all Ss, except for the caloric control group, received identical behavioral treatments, possible effects of prior experience were constant factors in comparisons between the normal control and experimental groups.

Effects upon Problem Solving

RELATION BETWEEN ERRORS AND AChE ACTIVITY.   If reduction of AChE activity is associated with slower rates of extinction (Russell et al.,

1961), it would be predicted that Ss with greater reductions in AChE activity would experience greater difficulty in shifting from problem to problem and, therefore, would obtain larger total error scores. The data in Table 2 appear to show a consistent trend in this direction. A Kruskal-Wallis one-way analysis of variance by ranks using individual scores for all Ss in the five groups results in an H value of 12.51 ($p < .02$). Furthermore, application of Jonckheere's (1954) distribution-free k-sample test against ordered alternatives indicated that the predicted trend toward increasing total errors with increasing reduction in AChE activity was significant ($p = .01$). The relation is shown graphically in Figure 1.

CRITICAL AChE LEVEL.   Although this trend was statistically significant, examination of Table 2 and Figure 1 shows that the relation was not a simple linear one. Total errors were less at 59% than at 100% AChE activity and increased rapidly at the 41, 30, and 25% levels. The difference between the 59 and 100% levels was not significant. Between 40 and 60%

Table 2.
Total errors in problem solving.

Group	% AChE activity	Total errors		
		Mdn	M	Variability
Normal control	100	167.5	177.9	35.62
E1	59	160.0	153.6	30.20
E2	41	182.0	196.0	66.84
E3	30	185.0	205.9	50.51
E4	25	242.0	228.3	86.34

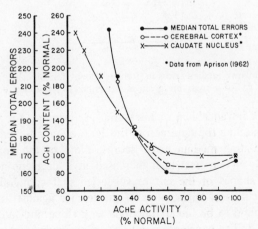

FIGURE 1. Changes in problem solving and in AChE content as functions of AChE activity.

of normal AChE activity there occurred a critical level at which the inverse
relation between errors and AChE activity originated.

    CUMULATIVE ERRORS.   The manner in which this relation developed
during the problem-solving period is shown in Figure 2, in which cumulative
median errors of the various groups are plotted for each of the 12 problems.
Each of the plots can best be described by a simple linear function; the fits
in Figure 2 were computed by the method of least squares, the slope and
intercept constants being given in Table 3. A Kruskal-Wallis analysis of
variance for group differences in errors on Problem 1 resulted in an H value
of 4.72, which is not significant. As the problem-solving period progressed,
there began to emerge consistent differences between the groups in the rates
at which errors accumulated, differences on Problem 12 being significant
($H = 12.06, p < .02$). As Figure 2 and Table 3 show, the rank order of the
different rates was lowest for 59% AChE activity and progressively greater
at the 100, 41, 30, and 25% levels, respectively. This rank order corresponds
to that of the total errors measure.

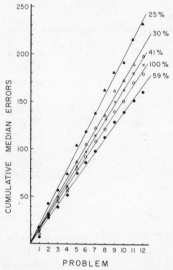

FIGURE 2. Cumulative median errors in problem solving for the control and experimental
groups. (Levels of AChE activity are given in percentages of the control group.)

    Analysis of intraproblem or intraserial performance for each group was
carried out by pooling the data across the 12 problems for each of the seven
trials and calculating median error scores. Plots of the cumulative scores
showed a family of curves which increased at a decelerating rate as trials
increased. The shapes of the curves suggested that cumulative errors were
logarithmic functions of trials; plots of the former against logs of the latter
were, indeed, found to be linear functions with slope and intercept constants
shown in Table 3. The constants point to two particular features of the intra-

problem performance: the rates at which errors accumulated increased sys-tematically as AChE activity levels decreased, and the number of errors on the first trial, as indicated by the intercept constants, was less for each of the experimental groups than for the normal control group. A Kruskal-Wallis analysis of variance for group differences in errors on Trial 1 results in an H value of 14.10 ($p < .01$). Related to both these features is the fact that the normal control group committed a considerably higher proportion of its total errors during Trial 1 than did the experimental groups: 46% vs. 28, 27, 31, and 31%, respectively, as level of AChE activity decreased.

Table 3.
Cumulative median errors.

Group	% AChE activity	Constants	
		Slope	Intercept
INTERPROBLEM CONSTANTS			
Normal control	100	14.89	2.75
E1	59	13.96	−1.12
E2	41	16.20	0.53
E3	30	17.52	−3.68
E4	25	19.55	0.26
INTRAPROBLEM CONSTANTS			
Normal control	100	115.07	72.98
E1	59	139.37	30.19
E2	41	150.27	44.92
E3	30	169.30	53.21
E4	25	214.37	44.69

INTRAGROUP VARIABILITY.   Intragroup variability in performance also appeared to increase as AChE activity decreased. Tests of differences between the normal control group and each experimental group using the F ratio based upon unbiased estimates of population variance established that the only sig-nificant comparison was between variances of the normal control and E4 groups ($p < .05$).

Effects upon Motivation

There was evidence that the experimental treatments produced no sig-nificant effects upon food-hunger motivation, which otherwise might have affected the problem-solving behavior. There were no significant differences in body weight between the groups at the start of the experiment, and there-after the general trend was toward steadily increasing body weight for all groups during the experimental period. Clearly Ss were not debilitated by the doses of Systox administered. Food intake, a measure of consummatory or goal response, did not differ significantly between groups at the predrug stage, and there continued to be great stability in all groups during the entire period of the experiment. Measures of the speed, i.e., reciprocal of time, of each S's instrumental approach response to food in the straightaway trials of Phase 3 also showed no significant differences between groups.

The caloric control group had been added to the research design to provide a means for comparing problem-solving behavior of Ss paired for amount of food intake but differing in AChE activity levels, had administration of Systox affected food intake. It was fortunate that this control was not needed, for Ss in this special group developed certain behavior patterns in the problem-solving situation which were qualitatively different from the behavior of the other groups. The differences were clear even during preliminary adaptation, when caloric control Ss were comparatively hyperexcitable, frequently had long delays in leaving the start box, often failed to eat in the goal box, and repeatedly gnawed on the apparatus despite free access to food. Similar responses have been observed in our laboratory during studies of the behavior of caloric control Ss in an avoidance-avoidance conflict situation (Khairy, Russell, and Yudkin, 1957). Because of the qualitative differences in their behavior, the caloric control Ss cannot be compared in a meaningful way with other groups in the study.

Discussion

The empirical finding of a significant relation between increasing total error scores and decreasing levels of AChE activity below a critical level within the range of 40–60% of normal is consistent with results from other investigations (Glow and Rose, 1965, 1966 *; Russell, 1958; Russell et al., 1961) which have focused attention upon the conditions of extinction as those sensitive to changes in this enzyme. Taken together, the results extend the generality of the relation beyond any particular behavior pattern generated under any particular set of experimental conditions: (a) The relation has been demonstrated when the behavior patterns measured involved extinction of a variety of different operant responses. The present experiment adds to the list problem-solving behavior which required seriatim extinctions of response patterns as S was presented with a series of similar but distinctive problems. (b) It has been shown to occur whether the behavior observed was under control of negative or positive reinforcement, as was the case in the present study. (c) It has been reported under conditions in which AChE activity was reduced by anticholinesterases with different chemical structures: OO-diethyl-S-ethyl-mercapto-ethanol thiophosphate and diisopropylfluorophosphate (DFP).

* We are indebted to P. H. Glow at the University of Adelaide, Australia, for permitting us to see, in advance of publication, reports which discuss the experiments in detail.

These anticholinesterases produce irreversible inhibition of AChE activity, recovery from which is presumably dependent upon de novo synthesis of the enzyme.

The results provide new information about relations between AChE activity and behavior in which seriatim extinctions of response patterns play a prominent role. The analysis showed that no significant differences existed between the control and experimental groups at the beginning of the problem-solving series; thereafter, errors accumulated at different rates for the various groups, resulting in highly significant differences in their performance by the end of the series. The analysis also showed that the experimental manipulation of AChE activity did not affect such characteristics of motor output as speed of locomotion or such measures of motivation as body weight and the consummatory response of food intake. These facts suggest the hypotheses that (*a*) altering AChE activity may affect sensory input, thus interfering with the encoding of information relevant to the change in environmental conditions, i.e., the presence of a new problem, or (*b*) altering AChE activity may affect the way in which such information is put to use once it is encoded. The data on intraproblem performance do not provide a basis for supporting one of these hypotheses in preference to the other. The fact that the control group made more errors than the experimental groups on Trial 1 could be interpreted as resulting from a broader input of information which could then be used to eliminate errors at a faster rate during subsequent trials. On the other hand, the systematic increase in rates at which errors for the various groups accumulated over the seven trials could be interpreted as due solely to effects of differences in AChE activity on the use of information, sensory input being similar in all groups.

The occurrence, in the present experiment, of a "critical level" between 40% and 60% of normal AChE activity has analogies with results of other investigations in which neurochemical and electrophysiological, rather than behavioral, variables have been measured. The relation between AChE activity and free ACh content in the cerebral cortex and caudate nucleus of rabbit brain following injection of DFP into the right common carotid artery has been described by Aprison (1962). The nature of the relation is shown in Figure 1. In the curves for both brain areas a critical level appears, indicating, as Aprison states, "the loss of physiological control of the enzyme for its substrate [1962, p. 139]." The critical level occurred between 40% and 60% of normal AChE activity; below this level free ACh content increased rapidly. Using the anticholinesterase DFP and recording electrophysiological activity in the nerve, Wilson and Cohen (1953) have reported that "There apparently is a critical enzyme activity in the neighborhood of 25% of the total activity below which conduction fails . . . [pp. 151–152]." Plots of their data show a sharp drop in percentage conductance beginning at about 40% of normal AChE activity. Such similarities as these suggest that the behavioral effects observed in the present experiment may be related to the ACh system through accumulation of ACh and its subsequent effects upon nerve conduction.

In attempting to define the relation between changes in AChE activity and changes in behavior more precisely, the question arises as to whether the critical locus of the former is peripheral or central. Although not stated specifically, discussion by Russell et al. (1961) of their results implied that resistance to extinction was due to reduction in brain AChE activity. Glow and Rose (1966) have, quite rightly, challenged this interpretation since in the earlier, as in the present, investigation the anticholinesterase affected biochemical events in both central and peripheral tissue. The present results make it possible only to report that there were no gross signs of peripheral sensory involvement and that there were no significant differences between the control and experimental groups in speed of locomotion or in consummatory responses on the peripheral motor side. Glow and Rose (1965, 1966) have examined the question of central vs. peripheral effects more specifically by comparing measures of behavior following reduction of whole-body AChE activity with measures following "selective reductions in central ChE" and have concluded that "a strong peripheral component is involved in the central organization of behavioural extinction [Glow and Rose, 1965, p. 477]." In the present experiment, reduction of AChE activity might have interfered with or retarded the input of information relevant to changes in the problem situation. Obviously such a hypothesis must be specifically tested. Further checks on the conclusions reached by Glow and Rose are also desirable, since, despite its ingenuity, their procedure provided partial and not complete peripheral "protection" for AChE.

References

Aldridge, W. N. Some properties of specific cholinesterase with particular reference to the mechanism of inhibition by Diethyl-p-Nitrophenyl thiophosphate (E605) and analogues. *Biochem. J.*, 1950, **46**, 451–460.

Aprison, M. H. On a proposed theory of the mechanism of action of serotonin in brain. *Recent Adv. biol. Psychiat.*, 1962, **4**, 133–146.

Bruce, H. M., and Parkes, A. S. Feeding and breeding of laboratory animals. IX. A complete cube diet for mice and rats. *J. Hyg., Cambridge,* 1949, **47**, 202–208.

Glow, P. H., and Rose, S. Effects of reduced acetylcholinesterase levels on extinction of a conditioned response. *Nature,* 1965, **206**, 475–477.

Glow, P. H., and Rose, S. Cholinesterase levels and operant extinction. *J. comp. physiol. Psychol.*, 1966, **61**, 165–172.

Jonckheere, A. R. A distribution-free k-sample test against ordered alternatives. *Biometrika,* 1954, **41**, 133–145.

Khairy, M., Russell, R. W., and Yudkin, J. Some effects of thiamine deficiency and reduced caloric intake on avoidance training and on reactions to conflict. *Quart. J. exp. Psychol.*, 1957, **9**, 190–205.

Krech, D., Rosenzweig, M. R., and Bennett, E. L. Chemical and anatomical plasticity of brain. *Science,* 1964, **146**, 610–619.

Nachmansohn, D., and Rothenberg, M. A. Studies on cholinesterase. I. On the specificity of the enzyme in nerve tissue. *J. biol. Chem.*, 1945, **158**, 653–666.

Rabinovitch, M. S., and Rosvold, H. E. A closed field intelligence test for rats. *Canad. J. Psychol.*, 1951, **5**, 122–128.

Russell, R. W. Effects of reduced brain cholinesterase on behavior. *Bull. Brit. Psychol. Soc.*, 1954, **23**, 6.

Russell, R. W. Effects of "biochemical lesions" on behavior. *Acta Psychol.*, 1958, **14**, 281–294.

Russell, R. W., Watson, R. H. J., and Frankenhaeuser, M. Effects of chronic reductions in brain cholinesterase activity on acquisition and extinction of a conditioned avoidance response. *Scand. J. Psychol.*, 1961, **2**, 21–29.

Wilson, I. B., and Cohen, M. The essentiality of acetylcholinesterase in conduction. *Biochem. biophys. Acta*, 1953, **11**, 147–156.

The Cholinergic Synapse and the Site of Memory

J. ANTHONY DEUTSCH

Reprinted from *Science*, Nov. 19, 1971, Vol. 174, pp. 788–794. Copyright 1971 by the American Association for the Advancement of Science.

That learning and memory are due to some form of change of synaptic conductance is a very old idea, having been suggested by Tanzi in 1893 (*1*). It is a simple idea and in many ways an obvious one. However, the evidence that learning is due to changes at the synapse has been meager (*2*). Although changes occur at a spinal synapse as a result of stimulation, there is no evidence that the changes are those utilized in the nervous system for information storage. To use an analogy, if we pass large amounts of current across resistors in a computer, temporary increases in temperature and perhaps even permanent increases in resistance occur. However, such an experiment shows only that the computer could store information by using "post-stimulation" alterations in its resistors, but it does not show that this is the actual way in which the computer stores information. Sharpless (*3*) has pointed out that learning is not due to simple use of stimulation of a pathway. He therefore questions whether the phenomena studied by Eccles (*2*) have anything to do with learning as observed in the intact organism. Nevertheless, this does not mean that learning is not due to synaptic changes of some sort. It means only that a different experimental test of the possibility must be devised.

In designing our experimental approach to this problem, clues from human clinical evidence were used. After an individual receives blows to the head, as might be sustained in accidents, he cannot recall events that occurred closest in time prior to the accident (retrograde amnesia). Such patches of amnesia may cover days or even weeks. The lost memories tend to return, with those most distant in time from the accident becoming available first (4). In the Korsakoff syndrome (5), retrograde amnesia may gradually increase until it covers a span of many years. An elderly patient may end up remembering only his youth, whereas there is no useful memory of the more recent intervening years. From such evidence concerning human retrograde amnesia we may conclude that the changes in the substrate of memory take a relatively long time and are measurable in hours, days, and even months. If we suppose from this that the substrate of memory is synaptic and that it is slowly changing, then it may be possible to follow such synaptic changes by pharmacological methods. If the same dose of a synaptically acting drug has different effects on remembering that depend on the age of the memory (and this can be shown for a number of synaptically acting drugs), then we may assume that there has been a synaptic alteration as a function of time after learning, and we may infer that such a synaptic change underlies memory.

Pharmacological Tools to Investigate Hypothesis

Pharmacological agents are available that can either increase or decrease the effectiveness of neural transmitters (6). For instance, anticholinesterase and anticholinergic drugs affect transmission at synapses which utilize acetylcholine as the transmitter. During normal transmission, acetylcholine is rapidly destroyed by the enzyme cholinesterase. Anticholinesterase drugs, such as physostigmine and diisopropyl fluorophosphate (DFP), inactivate cholinesterase. Therefore they indirectly prevent the destruction of acetylcholine. Because submaximum doses of these drugs inactivate not all but only a part of the cholinesterase present, they slow down but do not stop the destruction of acetylcholine. The overall effect at such submaximum levels of anticholinesterase is to increase by some constant the lifetime of any acetylcholine emitted into the synapse, which increases the concentrations of acetylcholine in the synapse which result from a given rate of emission. Within certain limits the greater this concentration the greater is the efficiency of transmission, that is, the conduction across the synapse. Above that limit, which is set by the sensitivity of the postsynaptic membrane, any further increase in acetylcholine concentration produces a synaptic block (6, 7). Thus, the application of a given dosage of anticholinesterase will (by protecting acetylcholine from destruction) have different effects on the efficiency of synaptic conduction that depend on the rate of acetylcholine emission during transmission and on the sensitivity of the postsynaptic membrane. When emission of acetylcholine is small, or when the sensitivity of the postsynaptic membrane is low, an application of anticholinesterase will render transmission more efficient, a property used to good effect in the treatment of myasthenia gravis. In the treatment of this disorder, anticholinesterase is used to raise the effective concentration of acetylcholine at the neuromuscular junction, which reduces apparent muscular weakness. On the other hand, the same dose of anticholinesterase that caused muscular contraction in the myasthenic patient produces paralysis in a man with normal function of the neuromuscular junction.

Over a period of time if there are changes after learning in the amounts of acetylcholine emitted at the modified synapse, then such a synapse should show either facilitation or block, depending on just when, after learning takes place, we inject the same dose of anticholinesterase. A similar argument with regard to the action of anticholinesterase can be applied if we assume that, instead of a presynaptic increment in transmitter, it is the postsynaptic membrane that becomes more sensitive to transmitter as a function of time after learning. But the use of an anticholinesterase does not allow us to decide which of these alternative arguments actually holds for the learning situation. I describe below how the use of other types of drugs, such as the cholinomimetics, allows us to surmise that postsynaptic sensitization is the more likely mechanism.

Memory Block and Facilitation with Anticholinesterase

The first two experiments (*8, 9*) show that facilitation or block of a memory can be obtained with the same dose of anticholinesterase simply as a function of time of injection after original learning, as might be expected if synaptic change formed the substrate of memory. In the first experiment, rats were trained on a simple task (*10*). Then anticholinesterase was injected intracerebrally at intervals after initial training, the time being varied from one group of subjects to another. After they were injected, all rats, irrespective of the group to which they were assigned, were tested again 24 hours after injection. Thus, the time between training and injection was varied, whereas the time between injection and retest was kept constant. Any difference between groups was therefore due to the time between initial training and injection.

Rats were placed on an electrified grid in a Y-maze. One arm of the Y was illuminated but not electrified, and its position was changed at random from trial to trial. The rats learned to run into the illuminated arm. The criterion of learning was met when they had chosen this arm ten trials in succession, whereupon training was concluded.

Then, at various times after training, the rats were injected intracerebrally with DFP dissolved in peanut oil (*11*). This dose did not increase the number of trials to criterion in a naive group of rats, and the result showed that learning capacity during training was not affected by the drug in the amounts used. At 24 hours after injection, the rats were retrained to the same criterion of ten correct trials in succession. The number of trials to criterion in this retraining session represented the measure of retention.

The first group was injected 30 minutes after training. Its retention was significantly worse than that of a control group injected only with peanut oil (*12*). By contrast, a group injected with DFP 3 days after training showed the same amount of retention as did the control group. Thus, up to this point it seems that the longer the item is stored, the less susceptible is memory to DFP.

In fact, a subsidiary experiment (13) has established that injections of DFP on habits 1 and 2 days old have no effect, which shows that the initial stage of vulnerability lasts less than 1 day. Beyond 3 days, however, the situation seems to reverse itself; the memory is more susceptible to DFP the older it is because a group injected with DFP 5 days after training showed only slight recollection at retest, and a further group injected 14 days after training showed complete amnesia. The score of the group trained 14 days before injection was the same as the score of the previously mentioned naive group that had not been trained before but had simply been injected with DFP 24 hours prior to testing. The amnesia of the DFP group trained 14 days before injection was not due to normal forgetting, because other controls showed almost perfect retention over a 15-day span. Using the same escape habit, Hamburg (14) obtained similar results with intraperitoneal injections of the anticholinesterase physostigmine. Biederman (15) confirmed the shape of the amnesic function with physostigmine in an operant situation. He used a latency measure of forgetting and a bar-press response.

To make sure that we were not observing some periodicity due to fear or emotionality interacting with the drug, we conducted an experiment with an appetitive rather than an escape task. The rats were taught to run to a reward of sugar water, the position of which always coincided with the illuminated arm of a Y-maze (16). These results and the results from the preceding experiments show a similar pattern of amnesia as a function of time of learning before injection (Fig. 1). It is, therefore, most likely that we are in fact study-

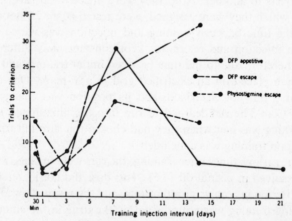

FIGURE 1. The effect of anticholinesterase injection on memories of different ages (from (8, 14, 16)). Trials to criterion during retest are plotted against the time that elapsed between retest and original learning; the larger the number of trials to criterion, the greater the amnesia. The time between injection and retest was constant. The differences past the 7-day point probably represent differing rates of forgetting in the three situations.

ing memory. The divergences in the curves after 7 days are probably due to differences in rates of forgetting among the three groups.

In this first set of experiments that dealt with the effects of the anticholinesterases DFP and physostigmine on habits that are normally well retained, the effects of these drugs were to decrease the retention of a habit depending on its age. Thus, one of the predicted effects of an anticholinesterase was verified. However, the other predicted effect, facilitation, was not shown. The reason for this is that the habit that was acquired was so well retained without treatment over 14 days that one could not, on methodological grounds, show any improvement of retention subsequent to injection of the drug. It may be the case that habits that were trained 1, 2, and 3 days prior to injection and retest were facilitated instead of merely being unaffected, but the design of the experiment would not allow us to detect this because there is an effective ceiling on performance. Therefore, an attempt was made to obtain facilitation where it was methodologically possible to detect it, namely, where retention of the habit by a control group was imperfect. For example, it was found that 29 days after learning, the escape habit described above was almost forgotten by a group of animals injected with peanut oil only, 24 hours before. On the basis of this observation, we devised a second kind of experiment.

Rats were divided into four groups. The first two groups were trained 14 days before injection, the second two groups, 28 days before injection. One 28-day group and one 14-day group were injected with the same dose of DFP, and the other 28-day group and the other 14-day group were injected with the same volume of pure peanut oil. The experimental procedure and dosage were exactly the same as previously described.

On retest, poor retention was exhibited by the 14-day group injected with DFP and by the 28-day group injected with peanut oil. By contrast, the 28-day group injected with DFP and the 14-day group injected with peanut oil exhibited good retention. The results of anticholinesterase injection show a large and clear facilitation of an otherwise almost-forgotten habit that was 28 days old, whereas they confirm the obliteration of an otherwise well-remembered habit that was 14 days old, as already demonstrated in the previous experiments (Fig. 2A). The same facilitation of a forgotten habit was shown by

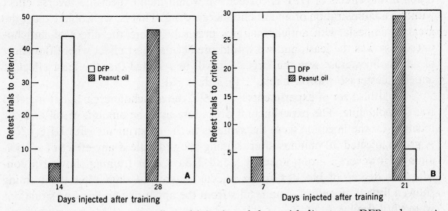

FIGURE 2. (*A* and *B*). The effect of injection of the anticholinesterase DFP and peanut oil on habits that were well retained or almost forgotten. Trials to criterion are plotted against time between retest and original training. When controls remember well, DFP-injected animals forget. When controls forget, DFP-injected animals remember well (*after* (9, 16)).

Wiener and Deutsch (*16*) using an appetitive habit and by Squire (*17*) using mice injected with physostigmine. Biederman (*18*) showed an improvement in memory in pigeons when physostigmine is injected 28 days after a line-tilt discrimination was partly learned. A well-learned color discrimination acquired by the same subjects showed no such improvement under the same conditions. Thus, these results also lend strong support to the notion that forgetting is due to a reversal of the change in synaptic conductance that underlies learning (Fig. 2*B*). It must be emphasized, however, that both the block and facilitation of a memory are temporary and wear off as the injected drug wears off.

Memory Block with Anticholinergics

We have shown that the anticholinesterases DFP and physostigmine have effects on memories that differ with the age of the memories. Although their actions on memory are consistent with, and plausibly interpreted by their anticholinesterase action, some other property besides their indirect action on acetylcholine could in some unknown manner produce the same results. Therefore, we conducted an independent check on the hypothesis that the effects observed might be due to an effect on acetylcholine by using an anticholinergic drug. An anticholinergic such as atropine or scopolamine, reduces the effective action of a given concentration of acetylcholine at the synapse without actually changing the concentration itself. It does this apparently by occupying some of the receptor sites on the potsynaptic membrane without producing depolarization. It thus prevents acetylcholine from reaching such receptor sites, which attenuates the effectiveness of this transmitter. We would therefore expect an anticholinergic to block conduction at a synapse where the postsynaptic membrane is relatively insensitive, whereas it would simply diminish conduction at synapses where the postsynaptic membrane is highly sensitive. If the interpretation of the effects of DFP is correct, we would then expect the reverse effect with the administration of an anticholinergic drug. That is, we would expect the greatest amnesia with anticholinergics precisely where the effect of anticholinesterase was the least; and we would predict the least effect where the effect of anticholinesterase was the largest. It will be recalled that the least effect of anticholinesterase was on habits 1 to 3 days old.

In a third set of experiments (*16, 19*), the anticholinergic agent injected was scopolamine. The experimental procedure and the amount of oil and the location for the injection were the same as in the experiments with DFP (*20*). A group injected 30 minutes after training showed little if any effect of scopolamine. However, a group injected 1 and 3 days after training showed a considerable degree of block. Groups injected 7 and 14 days after the training showed little if any effect. The results from the appetitive and escape situations were very similar.

As far as the experimental methodology allows us to discern, the anticholinergic effect is the mirror image of the anticholinesterase effect (Fig. 3); there is an increase of sensitivity between 30 minutes and 1 to 3 days which is fol-

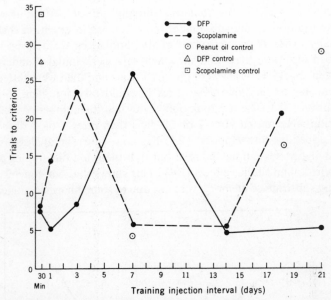

FIGURE 3. The effects of the injection of the anticholinergic scopolamine compared with that of the anticholinesterase DFP and the control of peanut oil on the retention of an appetitive task at various times after original learning. The time between injection and retest was constant. Also indicated is the number of trials to criterion when rats were injected with scopolamine (scopolamine control) or DFP (DFP control) before original learning to give an estimate of actual amount of amnesia produced (*from* (16)).

lowed by a decrease of sensitivity. This observation further confirms the notion that there are two phases present in memory storage. Finally, it is of interest that amnesia can result in man from anticholinergic therapy (*21*).

Memory Fluctuation Without Drugs

The above experiments support the idea that at the time of learning some unknown event stimulates a particular group of synapses to alter their state and to increase their conductivity. At this point two questions may be asked. Why does such an increase in synaptic conductivity not manifest itself with the passage of time when no drugs are injected, and why has it not been noted that habits are better remembered a week after initial learning than, say, 3 days after such learning? There are various possible answers. One is that the phenomena we have described are some artifact of drug injection. Another is that animal training has, in general, stretched over days in other studies and has blurred in time the initiation of a memory. In addition, and partly as a consequence of the foregoing, it is difficult to find studies on retention where the age of the habit, measured in days, has been used as an independent variable.

The question then arises as to whether or not we should have seen such an improvement in recall in our control groups. This would have been unlikely because our animals were trained to the very high criterion of ten out of ten trials correct. Given a score that was initially almost perfect, it was nearly impossible to observe any subsequent improvement in retention that might in fact actually exist. To rid ourselves of this limitation, we devised a study in which no drugs were used and in which rats were initially undertrained to escape from shock. The rats were given 15 trials and then were tested on some subsequent day to see how many trials it would take for them to reach our strict criterion (22). The rats took only about half the number of trials to reach the criterion when tested after 7 or 10 days than after 1 or 3 days (Fig. 4). Using an appetitive task Huppert (23) has now shown an analogous improvement. Finally, McGaugh has pointed out that there are old studies on animals that purport to find similar effects (24). This shows that our conclusions about the varying substrate of memory were not due to some pharmacological artifact.

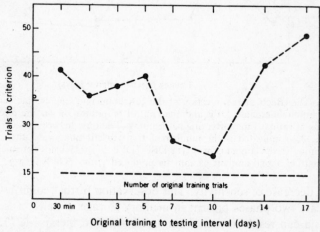

FIGURE 4. The effects of delay between original partial training (15 trials) and subsequent training to criterion. Plotted are trials to criterion in subsequent training against time since original partial training. Control (○) indicates the number of trials to criterion taken by a group that received its training all in one session.

Gradation of Memory Change

We may now ask whether the inferred modification of a synapse represents an all-or-none process or a graded process. In other words, can a synapse be modified only once during learning or does a repetition of the same learning task after some learning has already occurred further increase conductance at a single synapse? If we postulate an all-or-none process, then how according to such a model can we explain empirical increases in "habit strength" with increased training? Possibly they are due to a progressive involvement of fresh synapses and a spread involving more parallel connections in the nervous system. In support of a graded process, we may hypothesize that successive learning trials modify the same synapses in a cumulative way by producing an increase either in the rate at which conductance increases or in the upper limit of such conductance, or both.

There are tests of these two alternatives. If, with increased training a synapse becomes more conductive, then a habit should become increasingly more vulnerable to anticholinesterase with increased training. Furthermore, the memory of the same habit should be facilitated when its level of training is very low. In other words, we should be able to perform the same manipulations of memory by varying the level of training as we were already able to perform when we varied the time after training.

If, on the other hand, increases in training simply involve a larger number of synapses but no increase in transmission at any one synapse, then increases in training should not lead to an increased vulnerability of a habit to anticholinesterase. Rather, the opposite should be the case. As the number of synapses recruited is increased, some of the additional synapses will, by chance variation, be less sensitive to a given level of anticholinesterase. Thus, a larger number of synapses should be left functional after anitcholinesterase injection when we test an overtrained habit. Three experiments (*25–27*) show a large and unequivocal effect. Poorly learned habits are enormously facilitated, and well-learned habits are blocked (Fig. 5). This supports the hypothesis that a

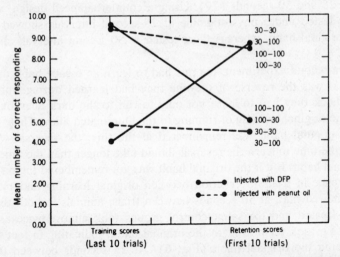

FIGURE 5. The effects of injection of DFP on the retention of well-learned and poorly learned habits. The mean number of correct responses of the last 10 of 30 trials for the two groups is shown on the left. One group had to learn to run to the alley illuminated by a normal 120-volt bulb with 30 volts across it to make it look dim; the other had to learn the same task except that the 120-volt bulb had 100 volts across it to make it look much brighter. As can be seen from the last ten trials, the dim light offered to the 30-volt group posed a difficult task that produced little learning by the end of the 30 trials. The group learning by the brighter cue (100 volt) displayed excellent acquisition. Because of the different rates of acquisition of the 100-volt and 30-volt habits, half of each group was shifted to retest on the other brightness and half was retrained on the same brightness (30–30, 100–100 retested on the same brightness; 30–100 trained on 30, retested on 100; 100–30 trained on 100, retested on 30). The scores of animals trained on the same brightness are combined. Half of the animals were injected with DFP, the other half with peanut oil. There is little change in the scores of the peanut oil–treated animals. However, there is a complete reversal of the animals injected with the drug, showing block of the well-learned habit and facilitation of the poorly learned habit.

set of synapses underlying a single habit remains restricted, and each synapse within such a set simply increases in conductance as learning proceeds.

Interval During Retest and Memory Block

The results presented so far have been interpreted in terms of the action of drugs on synapses that alter their conductance as a function of the time after training and of the amount of training. We can use our model to generate a somewhat different kind of prediction. An anticholinesterase in submaximum concentrations simply slows down the rate of destruction of acetylcholine. Because we have hypothesized that amnesia is due to a block resulting from an acetylcholine excess, we should predict no amnesia if we spaced our trials so that all or most of the acetylcholine emitted on the previous trial is destroyed by the time the next trial comes along. Bacq and Brown (28) showed that (with an intermediate dose of anticholinesterase) block at a synapse occurred only when the intervals between successive stimuli were shortened. Accordingly, an experiment was performed where we varied the interval during retest between 25 and 50 seconds (29). Using a counterbalanced design, we found that rats tested under physostigmine at 25-second intervals showed amnesia for the original habit, whereas those tested at 50-second intervals showed no amnesia.

In a second experiment, the rats had to learn an escape habit during the retest that was the reverse of the one they had learned during training. To escape shock they had to learn not only to run to the dark alley but also to inhibit the original learning of running to the illuminated alley. Thus, provided that the original habit was remembered at the time the reversal was being learned, the time to learn the reversal should take longer than the time to learn the original habit. But if the original habit was not remembered there should be no difference in trials to criterion between original learning and retest. The results showed that, at 50 seconds between trials, animals in both the physostigmine-treated and the saline-control groups took almost twice as long to reverse as it took them to learn the original habit, indicating in fact that they remembered the original habit (Fig. 6). At 25 seconds between trials, the animals treated with physostigmine learned the reversal as quickly as the original habit, whereas again the control animals took much longer. This second experiment shows that the amnesia of the 25-second group injected with physostigmine in the first experiment is not due to either disorientation or incapacity to perform or learn, but to an amnesia. We might explain the high relearning scores of the same habit of the rats at 25-second intervals under physostigmine by saying that the rats were somehow incapacitated by the physostigmine if they had to run at 25-second intervals. However, it is difficult to see how such incapacitation could produce abnormally low learning scores of the reversal habit. This dependence of the amnesia on the precise interval between trials during retest should of course not be seen with anticholinergics or cholinomimetics but only with anticholinesterases. This further prediction from the hypothesis should be tested.

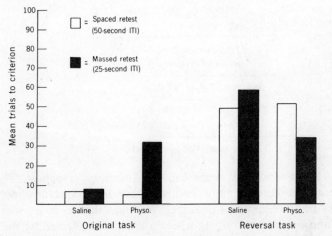

FIGURE 6. The effect of massing and spacing trials during retest on amnesia induced by anticholinesterase. On the left, retest consisted of relearning original habit (run to light, avoid dark). On the right, retest consisted of unlearning original habit. On retest, the animal had to learn to run to dark and avoid light (reversal). *ITI*, intertrial interval; *Physo.*, physostigmine.

Postsynaptic Change More Likely

So far, then, it seems that the drugs we are using to block or facilitate memory have their effect on synaptic conductance. However, what is it that changes when synaptic conductance alters? As was mentioned previously, the two main hypotheses are (i) that the amount of transmitter emitted at the presynaptic ending increases or (ii) that the postsynaptic ending increases in its sensitivity to transmitter. To test this idea, carbachol (carbamoylcholine chloride) was injected before retest. This drug is a cholinomimetic. It acts on the postsynaptic membrane much like acetylcholine. However, it is not susceptible to destruction by the enzyme acetylcholinesterase. Therefore, by injecting this drug, we can test the sensitivity of the postsynaptic membrane. It seems that habits learned 7 days before injection and retest are blocked by a dose of this cholinomimetic that leaves a habit learned 3 days before unaffected (Table 1). This would indicate that it is probably the postsynaptic membrane that has increased its sensitivity and so increased synaptic conductance.

One of the questions that often arises is why it is that we do not block all cholinergic synaptic activity with the drugs we use. As was seen above, rats learn appetitive tasks at a normal rate under doses of drug that under some circumstances produce complete amnesia. There is very little in the overt behavior of the rat to indicate that it has been drugged. The doses of drugs used produce no apparent malaise or incoordination. The dose we use only

Table 1.

The effect of carbachol injection on recall of habits that were 3 and 7 days old. Criterion was seven correct trials in succession. Numbers in parentheses indicate number of rats tested.

Treatment	Median number of trials to criterion	
	3 days	7 days
Carbachol	6.0 (15)	20 (15)*
Saline	4.0 (8)	0 (7)

* $P < .01$ compared with saline, Mann-Whitney U test.

seems to affect what one might call the "memory" synapses. Therefore, it would seem that these are more sensitive to our drugs. Such an abnormal sensitivity may be more apparent than real. We know that there are some levels of training and times after training where a habit is unaffected by the dosage of drug we use, and this shows that memory synapses are not always affected. It seems that the memory synapses have a much larger range of postsynaptic sensitivity, whereas normal synapses are in the middle of the sensitivity range of the memory synapse. In other words, sensitivity of the memory synapse must range from extreme insensitivity to transmitter to extreme sensitivity in order to manifest those changes in conductance that we have demonstrated. It will therefore be much more susceptible to anticholinergic agents when conductance is low and to anticholinesterases and cholinomimetics when conductance is high. In the middle of the range, sensitivity to all agents will resemble that of a normal synapse, and only grossly toxic doses will affect memory. This, of course, will have to be further tested. So far, the experiments implicate the cholinergic system in memory. It is, of course, possible that other systems, such as the adrenergic, may have a similar function, and this, too, we hope to test.

Analysis of Extinction Through Selective Amnesia

When an animal is rewarded for performing a habit, such a habit will be learned or acquired. However, when the habit is no longer rewarded, the animal will cease to perform the habit. Another kind of learning takes place, and this is called extinction. If initial learning consists of the formation of some synaptic (or other) connection, does extinction consist of the weakening or uncoupling of this connection? Or is it the formation of some other connection that then works to oppose the effects of the first (learning) connection? If extinction consists of weakening the connection set up in original learning, then an extinguished habit should be similar to a forgotten habit pharmacologically. We have already shown that a habit that is almost forgotten is facilitated by anticholinesterase. We would, then, on the "weakening" hypothesis of extinction, expect an injection of an anticholinesterase to produce less amnesia of an extinguished habit than of the same unextinguished habit.

If, on the other hand, during extinction there is another habit acquired that inhibits the expression of the original habit, another pattern of results should be discernible after injection with an anticholinesterase. If original learning occurs 7 days before anticholinesterase injection and retest, there should be amnesia for the original habit. If extinction of the habit is given close in time to its acquisition, there should be amnesia for both the original learning and extinction. If, on the other hand, original learning is 7 days before injection and retest, and the extinction is 3 days before injection and retest, then the original habit should be lost but the extinction habit should be retained. (As we noted above, 3-day habits are unaffected by our dose of anticholinesterase.) When extinction was given to rats close in time to the original training, both the original training and extinction were blocked by physostigmine (*30*). These rats took the same number of trials to relearn as control animals, which were trained, not extinguished, and then injected with physostigmine. However, when extinction was placed 3 days before injection and retest, it took the rats approximately twice as many trials to learn as control animals, showing that extinction has been retained whereas the original habit was blocked (Fig. 7). This supports the idea that extinction is the learning of a separate habit that opposes the performance of the initially rewarded habit.

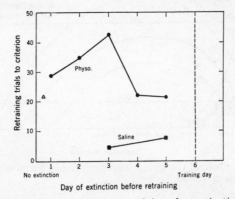

FIGURE 7. The effect of physostigmine on retraining after extinction. The time between original learning and retraining is the same for all groups. When time of extinction is close to original learning, there is amnesia but no difference from the group receiving no extinction. At extinction 3 days before learning, the number of trials to relearn is almost double. *Saline*, scores of controls injected with saline; *Physo.*, scores of animals injected with physostigmine.

It has also been suggested (*31*) that different systems, such as excitatory or inhibitory systems, are subserved by different transmitters. Habits acquired during extinction have been viewed as inhibitory. However, the last experiment we have outlined also shows that extinction placed close to original learning is equally as vulnerable to anticholinesterase as original learning. Habits can probably not be classified into synaptically inhibitory and excitatory on the basis of behavioral excitation or inhibition. However, as all habits compete for behavioral expression, there must be excitation and reciprocal inhibition connected with all habits.

Conclusions

A simple hypothesis can explain the results obtained to date if we disregard those results when we wait 30 minutes after original learning to inject. The hypothesis is that, as a result of learning, the postsynaptic endings at a specific set of synapses become more sensitive to transmitter. This sensitivity increases with time after initial learning and then declines. The rate at which such sensitivity increases depends on the amount of initial learning. If the curve of transmission plotted againt time is displaced upward with anticholinesterases then the very low portions will show facilitation, and the high portions will cause block (Fig. 8). The middle portion will appear unaffected (unless special experimental tests are made). If the curve of transmission is displaced down with anticholinergics, then the middle portion will appear unaffected and only the very early or late components will show block.

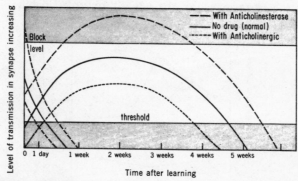

FIGURE 8. The hypothesized changes in "memory" synapses with time after training and with pharmacological intervention.

The results are evidence that synaptic conductance is altered as a result of learning. So far it seems (i) that cholinergic synapses are modified as a result of learning and that it probably is the postsynaptic membrane that becomes increasingly more sensitive to acetylcholine with time after learning, up to a certain point. (ii) After this point, sensitivity declines, leading to the phenomenon of forgetting. (iii) There is also good evidence that there is an initial phase of declining sensitivity to cholinesterase or increasing sensitivity to anticholinergics. This could reflect the existence of a parallel set of synapses with fast decay that serve as a short-term store. (iv) Increasing the amount of learning leads to an increase in conductance in each of a set of synapses without an increase in their number. (v) Both original learning and extinction are subserved by cholinergic synapses.

References and Notes

1. E. Tanzi, *Riv. Sper. Freniat.* **19**, 149 (1893).
2. Eccles has attempted to supply such evidence by studying the effect of stimulation on transmission across a synapse at the spinal level. After repetitive stimulation, a stimulus produces a larger effect at the synapse than before stimulation. J. C. Eccles, in *Brain Mechanisms and Learning* (Thomas, Springfield, Ill., 1961), pp. 335–352; *The Physiology of Synapses* (Academic Press, New York, 1964). W. A. Spencer and R. Wigdor [*Physiologist* **8**, 278 (1965)] and F. B. Beswick and R. T. W. L. Conroy [*J. Physiol. London* **180**, 134 (1965)] have also shown such an effect. On the other hand, J. C. Fentress and R. Doty [*Fed. Proc.* **25**, 573 (1965)] have reported a depression of responsiveness at a synapse after stimulation.
3. S. K. Sharpless, *Annu. Rev. Physiol.* **26**, 357 (1964).
4. W. R. Russell and P. W. Nathan, *Brain* **69**, 280 (1946).
5. G. A. Talland, *Deranged Memory* (Academic Press, New York, 1965).
6. L. S. Goodman and A. Gilman, *The Pharmacological Basis of Therapeutics* (Macmillan, New York, 1965).
7. W. Feldberg and A. Vartiainen, *J. Physiol. London* **83**, 103 (1934); R. L. Volle and G. B. Koelle, *J. Pharmacol. Exp. Ther.* **133**, 223 (1961).
8. J. A. Deutsch, M. D. Hamburg, H. Dahl, *Science* **151**, 221 (1966).
9. J. A. Deutsch and S. F. Leibowitz, *ibid.* **153**, 1917 (1966).
10. The rats were Sprague-Dawley males approximately 350 grams at the start of the experiment.
11. The animals were placed in a stereotaxic instrument under Nembutal anesthesia. They were intracerebrally injected in two bilateral loci that were symmetrically placed. The placements were: anterior 3, lateral 3, vertical +2 and anterior 3, lateral 4.75, vertical −2, according to the atlas of DeGroot [J. DeGroot, *Verh. Kon. Ned. Akad. Wettensch. Afdel-Natuurk.* Sect. II, **52** (1957)] Peanut oil (0.01 milliliter) containing 0.1 percent of DFP was injected in each locus.
12. Except as otherwise stated, the results quoted are significant beyond the 1 percent level. The tests used were the *t*-test, Mann-Whitney U test, and analysis of variance.
13. J. A. Deutsch and J. Stone, in preparation.
14. M. D. Hamburg, *Science* **156**, 973 (1967).
15. G. B. Biederman, *Quart. J. Exp. Psychol.* **22**, 384 (1970).
16. N. I. Wiener and J. A. Deutsch, *J. Comp. Physiol. Psychol.* **66**, 613 (1968).
17. L. R. Squire, *Psychon. Sci.* **19** (1), **49** (1970).
18. G. B. Biederman, *ibid.*, in press.
19. J. A. Deutsch and K. Rocklin, *Nature* **216**, 89 (1967). See also A. Pazzagli and G. Pepeu, *Int. J. Neuropharmacol.* **4**, 291 (1964).
20. Deutsch and Rocklin (*19*) used an injection of scopolamine at the same loci as in (*11*). Peanut oil (0.01 milliliter) containing 0.58 percent of scopolamine was injected in each placement. Wiener and Deutsch (*16*) used only the first locus, but doubled the amount injected at that site (both of scopolamine and DFP).
21. W. C. Cutting, *Handbook of Pharmacology; The Actions and Uses of Drugs* (Appleton-Century-Crofts, New York, 1964).

22. F. A. Huppert and J. A. Deutsch, *Quart. J. Exp. Psychol.* **21,** 267 (1969).
23. F. A. Huppert, personal communication.
24. A. C. Anderson, *J. Comp. Psychol.* **30,** 399 (1940); M. E. Bunch and W. K. Magdsick, *ibid.* **16,** 385 (1933); M. E. Bunch and E. S. Lang, *ibid.* **27,** 449 (1939); H. B. Hubert, *Behavior Monogr.* **2,** No. 6 (1915).
25. J. A. Deutsch and S. F. Leibowitz, *Science* **153,** 1017 (1966).
26. J. A. Deutsch and H. Lutzky, *Nature* **213,** 742 (1967).
27. S. F. Leibowitz, J. A. Deutsch, E. E. Coons, in preparation.
28. Z. M. Bacq and G. C. Brown, *J. Physiol. London* **89,** 45 (1937).
29. J. A. Deutsch and K. Rocklin, in preparation.
30. J. A. Deutsch and N. I. Wiener, *J. Comp. Physiol. Psychol.* **69,** 179 (1969).
31. P. L. Carlton, in *Reinforcement and Behavior,* J. T. Tapp, Ed. (Academic Press, New York, 1969), pp. 286–327.

Time-Dependent Processes in Memory Storage

JAMES L. McGAUGH

Reprinted from *Science*, 1966, Vol. 153, pp. 1351–1358. Copyright 1966 by the American Association for the Advancement of Science.

The ability of animals to record experiences and to modify their behavior according to the nature of the experiences clearly ranks as one of the most important as well as one of the most exciting phenomena of biology. In the last decade, and particularly during the last few years, interest in the nature of the processes underlying learning and memory has surged dramatically. To a considerable degree research into the physiological bases of memory has consisted of attempts to find evidence of some permanent change in neural functioning produced by experience.

Although there is increasing evidence that experiences do in fact produce relatively long-lasting neural changes (*1*), clear evidence of specific changes produced by specific experiences has so far eluded even the most imaginative researchers. The problem of the basis or bases of memory would be much easier to solve if neural functioning and behavior were less plastic than they have been found to be. It has been known for many years that learning does not consist simply of acquiring tendencies to make specific responses in the presence of particular stimuli. Most animals can readily demonstrate retention of an experience by performing in a variety of ways in the presence of complex and varied stimulation (*2, 3*). "Fixation of memory" is clearly *not* synonymous with fixation of behavior. As far as behavior is concerned, memory is not only the capacity to repeat, it is the capacity to vary. This simple fact of behavior has for many years provided serious difficulties for theoretical speculations concerning the nature of the processes underlying memory.

A complete theory of memory must not only encompass this embarrassing fact but also handle the complicated problem of memory trace consolidation. It is becoming increasingly clear, on the basis of recent research findings, that the memory trace of an experience is not laid down in any lasting way either during or immediately after the experience. Rather, it appears that short-term processes provide a temporary basis for recall of experiences and that the consolidation of long-term traces involves processes occurring over relatively long intervals of time. It seems likely that an understanding of memory trace consolidation processes will provide important clues to the nature of long-term storage and retrieval processes. For these reasons the problem of memory trace consolidation is currently the focus of research in numerous laboratories. In this article I review some of the findings of recent studies concerned with this problem. In the first sections I review evidence that memory trace consolidation can be influenced—either impaired or enhanced—by a variety of treatments. In the final section I discuss some recent behavioral evidence concerning time-dependent effects in memory storage.

Experimental Analysis of Retrograde Amnesia

The most extensive evidence concerning memory consolidation has come from studies of experimentally induced amnesia. It has been known for many years that human patients who have suffered head injuries tend to have difficulty recalling events that occurred shortly before the inquiry even though older memories may be completely intact (4). This selective loss for recent memory, termed "retrograde amnesia," has also been observed in patients given electroshock treatments (5). Systematic experimental studies of retrograde amnesia in infrahuman species were initiated almost 20 years ago, but the theoretical and methodological questions raised by the initial experiments are currently active issues. In the first of such experiments (6), animals were given an electroconvulsive shock (ECS) after each trial in a learning task. Animals given electroshock immediately after each training trial showed little evidence of learning. In general, learning rate increased directly with increases in the interval between learning trial and treatment. Since electroshock produces—at least momentarily—profound electrophysiological disturbances in the brain, these experiments, as well as numerous similar ones (7), provided strong evidence for the general hypothesis that memory trace consolidation processes are time-dependent. However, the experiments did not completely rule out the possibility that the results were due to some other effect or effects of electroshock. For example, it was suggested that punishment, rather than amnesia, might be the basis of the retrograde effect of electroshock treatments (8). That is, since electroshock was administered immediately after each training trial, it seemed at least possible that the animals were merely learning to avoid making the responses that were followed by the electroshock treatment. According to this view, the failure of animals to perform under such conditions is not due to a memory loss.

Recent evidence does not support this alternative view of the basis of electroshock effects. In one experiment in our laboratory, for example (9), rats were placed on a small platform and were given a mild shock to the feet as they stepped from the platform onto the floor. Half the animals were given electroshock within a few seconds. On a retention test given the next day, the rats given only the foot shock tended to remain on the platform—that is, they appeared to remember the shock—while those given electroshock after the foot shock gave no evidence of remembering either the foot shock or the electroshock. They readily stepped off the platform. In subsequent experiments my associates and I, as well as other investigators, have made extensive use of one-trial inhibitory learning tasks (or so-called "passive avoidance") in studies of memory consolidation.

In other experiments we have found that electroshock treatments are aversive if they are given repeatedly. Rats can learn to avoid making responses that are repeatedly followed by electroshock, and they can learn to avoid going to a place in a maze where they have received several electroshock treatments (10). However, in all of our experiments, aversive or punishing effects were observed only after *several* electroshock treatments had been administered, while retrograde amnesia was readily obtained with a single treatment. Thus, the amnesic effects of a single electroshock treatment cannot be interpreted in terms of punishing effects. Other investigators have shown that the amnesic effect of a single treatment is independent of the place (the training apparatus, home cage, and so on) in which the treatment is given (11, 12). It seems clear then that electroshock treatments can produce retrograde amnesia, and it seems highly likely that the amnesia is produced directly by the electroshock stimulation. Recent results support this view. The convulsion usually produced by electroshock stimulation seems to be unnecessary for the occurrence of amnesia. In an experiment in our laboratory (13), mice were placed one at a time on a small platform attached to the side of a box and were allowed to enter the box through a small hole. Each mouse received a foot shock as it entered. The mice were then given light ether anesthesia, electroshock, or electroshock stimulation delivered while the animals were anesthetized with ether. The ether anesthesia prevented the electroshock convulsions. On a retention test trial the following day, animals in groups given, 25 seconds after the foot shock, either a typical electroshock treatment or electroshock stimulation while anesthetized, showed little evidence of remembering the shock. For both of these groups, the percentage of mice remaining (for over 10 seconds) on the platform on the retention trial was significantly lower than the percentage for the other groups. In this experiment the ether anesthesia produced no amnesia.

The findings of the experiment just discussed also indicated that the electroshock stimulation did not significantly affect performance when it was administered 1 hour after the training trial. In other research we have found that the magnitude of the retrograde amnesic effects of electroshock depends upon the duration of the electroshock stimulation. The intensity of the current seems not to be important so long as it is sufficient to elicit convulsions in unanesthetized animals. The standard duration in most experiments, including the one just described, is 200 milliseconds. With the 200-millisecond treatment, we have generally obtained a relatively steep gradient with relatively little amnesia when electroshock is administered more than 30 minutes after training. Some investigators have reported even steeper gradients of retrograde amnesia with little or no amnesia when more than a minute elapses between the training trial and the electroshock treatment (*12, 14*). In recent experiments (Fig. 1) we have produced retrograde amnesia in mice with intervals

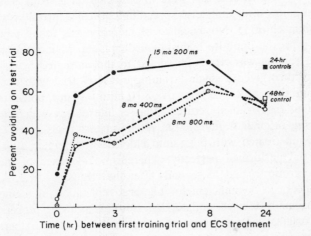

FIGURE 1. The effect of duration of electroshock stimulation on retrograde amnesia. With durations of 400 or 800 milliseconds, amnesia is observed when electroshock is administered as long as 3 hours after a single training trial on an inhibitory avoidance learning task. The 24-hour and 48-hour controls did not receive electroshock. (*McGaugh and Alpern* (34).)

between training and treatment as great as 3 hours when the duration of the electroshock stimulation was increased to 400 or 800 milliseconds (*15*). These results suggest that it should be profitable to study the differential effects of electroshock stimulation of differing duration on brain electrophysiological activity. We have just started to work on this problem, and initial findings indicate that different durations of electroshock stimulation have markedly different effects on electrophysiological activity of the brains of mice.

In a general way, the findings of studies of the effects of electroshock stimulation are highly similar to results obtained with other treatments which have been found to produce retrograde amnesia. A number of investigators have reported that deep anesthesia can produce retrograde amnesia. The duration of the temporal gradient has been found to differ considerably with different treatments. When a relatively simple learning task is used, deep ether anesthesia produces amnesic effects only if the ether is administered within a few seconds of the task, while with pentobarbital, significant effects are found with intervals between training and treatment of as much as 10 minutes (16). With a highly complex task (successive discrimination learning), we have found evidence of amnesic effects of barbiturates even when the drug (pentobarbital sodium or Brevital sodium) was administered several hours after training (17).

Investigators in several laboratories have reported that retrograde amnesia can be produced by inducing "spreading depression." Topical application of potassium chloride (18) to the cerebral cortex produces a depression of electrical activity which spreads across the cortex of the treated hemisphere and results in a temporary inhibition of functioning of the affected cortex. In a study by Ray and Emley, rats were first trained on a visual discrimination task a few minutes after unilateral spreading cortical depression was induced with potassium chloride. No evidence of memory was found when the rats were tested with the opposite hemisphere depressed. Memory storage during the original training was clearly restricted to the untreated hemisphere. The animals were then given a single "training-transfer" trial with neither cortex depressed, and then, either 15 seconds or 10 minutes later, potassium chloride was applied to the "trained" cortex (that is, the cortex which was not depressed during original training). On retention test trials given 30 minutes later, the group treated with potassium chloride 10 minutes after the single "transfer" trial performed perfectly, whereas no evidence of memory was found in the group treated 15 seconds after the "transfer" trial. A single experience appears to be sufficient for bilateral replication of memory storage processes originally located unilaterally. But this transfer process, like that involved in original learning, appears to be time-dependent. Albert (19) has reported that even greater amnesic effects are found when potassium chloride is applied to the "naive" or "receiving" cortex within 2 hours after a single "transfer" trial with neither cortex depressed. These findings suggest that the time required for initial transfer of a replicated trace from one hemisphere to another is considerably shorter than that required for the complete fixation of the replicated trace in the previously "naive" hemisphere. Of further interest is the finding that the magnitude of the amnesic effect found with potassium chloride treatments is a function of the duration of the treatment. With long (up to 30 minutes) potassium chloride treatments, the degree of retrograde amnesia obtained is roughly comparable to that we have found with 800-millisecond electroshock stimulation.

Other recent research findings indicate that memory consolidation in mice and goldfish is impaired by intracranial injections of the protein synthesis inhibitor, puromycin (20, 21). Agranoff *et al.* (21) have reported that puromycin injected prior to training does not impair acquisition of an avoidance response but does impair retention of the response, as observed when animals are tested several days later without further drug treatments. Retention is also impaired if the compound is injected after training, but only if the injections are given within an hour of training. Thus, puromycin seems to act selectively on memory consolidation. With either pre- or post-training injections, the degree of impairment of retention increases directly with increases in the dose of puromycin injected. This finding is interesting in view of evidence that the duration of protein synthesis inhibition varies directly with the dose of puromycin. As Agranoff and his associates point out, the behavioral and biochemical findings are not completely consistent. For example, a dose of 90 milligrams of puromycin injected prior to training does not impair memory consolidation 1 hour after the injection even though evidence indicates that this dose of puromycin inhibits protein synthesis for at least 2 hours following administration. Also, under some conditions, the amnesic effects of electroshock appear to be greater than those of puromycin.

Although it seems clear, on the basis of this evidence, that memory consolidation is impaired by puromycin, it has not yet been demonstrated either that the impairment of memory consolidation is due solely to impairment of protein synthesis or that inhibition of protein synthesis is essential for impairment of memory consolidation. It is highly likely that protein synthesis is in some way involved in long-term memory consolidation.

These recent findings of experimental studies of retrograde amnesia provide very strong evidence that long-term memory trace consolidation processes are time-dependent. The findings have not as yet, however, provided an understanding of the nature of the processes involved in the consolidation of durable memory traces. In particular, it is not known whether the effects of the various treatments discussed above have a common physiological basis or whether the common effect—retrograde amnesia—is produced by a number of different mechanisms. The problem is amenable to analysis, however, and the results of research currently in progress in several laboratories will in all probability help to clarify these issues.

Drug Facilitation of Learning and Memory

There is little doubt that memory storage can be impaired. There is also accumulating evidence that memory storage can be facilitated. Several years ago Lewis Petrinovich and I initiated a series of studies of the effects of central-nervous-system stimulants on learning. We were guided initially by a "discovery" of Lashley's early report that maze learning in rats was facilitated by administration of low doses of strychnine sulfate (22). In several experiments we, as well as others, have obtained additional evidence that strychnine facilitates learning (23). Petrinovich and I found, for example, that injection of low doses of strychnine sulfate prior to training trials enhanced rats' learning of an alley maze. Subsequently we found that strychnine injections facilitated learning of other tasks, including discrimination learning. The results of one experiment are shown in Figure 2. Rats were injected with strychnine sulfate a few minutes before they were given massed training trials on a visual

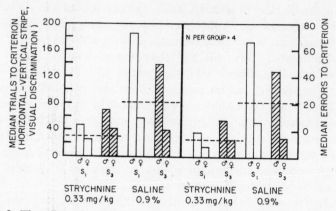

FIGURE 2. The effect of strychnine sulfate on simultaneous discrimination learning in two strains of rats. The animals were injected prior to massed training trials. Horizontal dashed lines indicate overall medians for strychnine-injected and control (saline-injected) animals. (*Based on findings of McGaugh and Thomson* (35).)

discrimination problem, with foot-shock motivation. As may be seen, the strychnine-injected animals learned to meet a criterion with fewer trials and errors than the controls did. These results, as well as those of other studies, suggest that strychnine may facilitate processes underlying learning of the task. Other interpretations of the results of these experiments, including interpretations stressing possible motivational effects of the drug, could not be readily excluded, however.

Recent experimental findings have provided strong evidence that central-nervous-system stimulants can facilitate learning by enhancing memory consolidation. In several experiments we, and subsequently others (24, 25), have found that the learning of a variety of tasks in rats and mice is facilitated by injection of strychnine shortly *after* training trials. No facilitation is obtained, however, if the strychnine is administered more than 30 minutes after the training is terminated. In most of these experiments, retention tests were given at least 23 hours after the injections; the animals were never tested while drugged. Consequently the posttrial injection studies are difficult to interpret in terms of motivational or perceptual effects. Similar facilitating effects of posttrial administration of drugs have been obtained with a number of central-nervous-system stimulants. Figure 3 shows the results of a study of the effect of posttrial injections of picrotoxin on maze learning. Rats in this experiment were given either saline or one of several doses of picrotoxin immediately after each daily trial in a complex maze. In both strains tested, but particularly in the S_3 strain, errors decreased with increases in the dose of picrotoxin. Recently Hunt and Krivanek (24) reported that rats' learning of a variety of tasks is facilitated by either pre- or posttrial injections of Metrazol (pentylenetetrazol). We have confirmed this finding in several experiments. Figure 4 shows the results of one of our experiments. Mice of two strains were injected with either saline or one of three doses of Metrazol immediately after

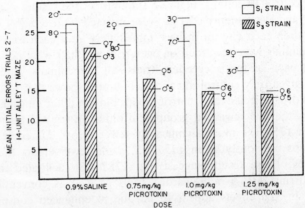

FIGURE 3. The effect of picrotoxin on maze learning in two strains of rats. The rats were injected immediately after each daily trial. Horizontal lines indicate means for males and females in each group; numbers indicate number of animals in each subgroup. (*Based on findings of Breen and McGaugh* (36).)

each daily trial in a Lashley III alley maze. As Figure 4 shows, facilitation was found with both strains, but the most effective dose was found to differ for animals of the two strains. In most, but not all, of our experiments with central-nervous-system stimulants, we have found significant strain differences in dose-response effects.

In several experiments we studied the effect of the synthetic strychnine-like compound 5,7-diphenyl-1,3-diazaadamantan-6-ol (1757 I.S.) on learning and memory storage. Clearly facilitating effects have been found with both

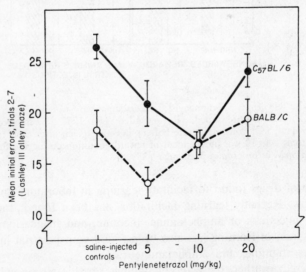

FIGURE 4. The effect of Metrazol (pentylenetetrazol) on maze learning in two strains of mice. The mice were given an injection after each daily trial. Vertical lines indicate standard error of ± 1. (*McGaugh* (37).)

pretrial and posttrial injections. Figure 5 summarizes the results of one experiment. Food- and water-deprived rats were injected with either 1757 I.S. or a control solution each day for 5 days immediately after each trial in a maze. Half of the animals were rewarded on each trial and half were not. Following the fifth and each of five succeeding trials, all the animals were rewarded and all were given only control injections. Figure 5 shows that results for the nonrewarded drug-injected and control groups did not differ on trials 2 through 5. Results for the two rewarded groups did differ on trials 2 through 5: the animals given 1757 I.S. made significantly fewer errors. On trials 6 through 10 both groups previously given 1757 I.S. made fewer errors than the two control groups. These results suggest that 1757 I.S. facilitated the "latent" learning occurring during nonrewarded trials as well as conventional maze learning. Again, the effects appear to be due to enhanced consolidation of memory.

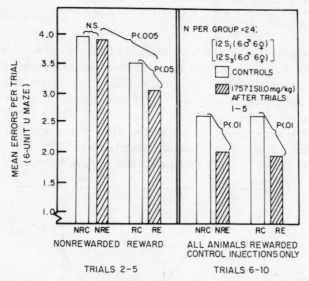

FIGURE 5. The effect of 5,7-diphenyl-1,3-diazaadamantan-6-ol (1757 I.S.) on maze learning in rats. (NR) Nonrewarded; (R) rewarded; (E) 1757 I.S. injected after each daily trial for 5 days; (C) control (citrate buffer) injection given after each trial. Facilitation found on trials 6 to 10 was independent of reward condition during the first five trials. (*Based on data of Westbrook and McGaugh* (38).)

The list of drugs found to facilitate learning in laboratory animals continues to grow. Recently learning facilitation has been found, for example, with pretrial injections of amphetamine, nicotine, and magnesium pemoline (26). Facilitation of learning has also been found with posttrial injections of caffeine, physostigmine, and amphetamine (27).

Considered together, these recent findings provide strong evidence that learning can be facilitated by drugs and that drugs can affect learning in several ways. Some of the drugs studied seem to improve performance by enhancing attentional or short-term memory processes, or both. Posttrial injections of nicotine, for example, seem not to affect learning (28). Other drugs seem to enhance posttrial memory storage processes. An understanding of the nature of these drugs' effects on central-nervous-system processes could provide important clues to memory storage. However, each drug has diverse and complex effects on central-nervous-system activity. It may be that the various drugs do not have a common mechanism of action and that they affect memory storage in different ways. At a more general level it would be of interest to know whether the drugs which enhance memory when administered after training can either prevent or attenuate retrograde amnesia produced by electroshock treatments. Such evidence would strengthen the interpretation that the drugs enhance memory consolidation. In a number of unpublished studies (29), rats have been injected with central-nervous-system stimulants prior to training and given an electroshock several minutes after training. In general the results of retention tests given later suggest that the drugs attenuate but do not prevent electroshock-induced retrograde amnesia; however, the findings have not been consistent, and more research on this problem is needed. The fact that most of the drugs investigated potentiate the convulsive effects of electroshock makes the results of this type of experiment difficult to interpret. The hypothesis that the drugs facilitate memory by enhancing consolidation does not necessarily imply that the drugs should prevent retrograde amnesia. It may be, for example, that the drugs increase the duration of consolidation processes without increasing the rate at which consolidation occurs. According to this interpretation, it might be possible to prevent posttrial facilitating effects of central-nervous-system stimulants on learning by administering electroshock to animals at just the time after training at which it produces little or no amnesia in control animals. This possibility has not yet been investigated.

Time and Repetition Effects in Memory Storage

Overall, the evidence from studies of the effects on memory of electroshock and drugs clearly indicates that memory trace consolidation involves processes which are time-dependent. There is also a considerable amount of purely behavioral evidence that memory storage is time-dependent (30). Recently Alpern and I conducted a series of behavioral studies of retention in mice to see if retention at various intervals following one or more training trials varies systematically with the time between training and retention testing. To investigate this problem, we first gave mice a single training trial on the inhibitory avoidance task described above (see 13) and a retention test either 5 seconds, 30 seconds, 2 minutes, 1 hour, or 24 hours later. As may be seen in Figure 6 (middle curve), for intervals up to 2 minutes, retention increased as the time between the training trial and the retention trial was increased. No significant retention was found for the 5-second and 30-second intervals. Over the intervals tested, retention does appear to be time-dependent. These results caused us to wonder whether the rate of increase in retention within a 2-minute period was completely time-dependent or whether the retention could be improved by giving the mice additional training trials during the 2-minute interval. To answer this question, we gave mice massed training trials on the step-through task for 2 minutes. As Figure 6 shows, the performance of these animals (top dashed curve) on the last training trial (that is, at 2 minutes) was superior to that of animals given a single trial. Improvement in performance over the 2-minute period appears to be both time- and event-dependent. Other results shown in Figure 6 indicate that the

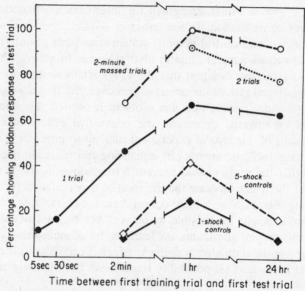

FIGURE 6. Retention of inhibitory avoidance (step-through task) (see *13*) as a function of time and number of training trials given during the first 2 minutes of training. Retention (that is, percentage of mice showing avoidance response on retention test) after a single trial increases with increase in the interval between the training and test trials (middle curve). Retention is enhanced by repetition of trials. The two lower curves show that the retention performance is not due to a nonspecific effect of foot shock: animals in the groups represented by the lower curves were given foot shocks in a different apparatus and then tested on the step-through apparatus at one of the times indicated. (*McGaugh and Alpern* (*15*).)

performance, on delayed retention tests, of mice given either two trials (the second trial 2 minutes after the first—dotted curve) or massed training trials for 2 minutes (top curve) was also superior to the performance of those given only one trial (middle curve). To provide a control for possible nonspecific effects of the foot-shock punishment, control mice were given foot shock in a different apparatus and then tested on the step-through apparatus. Although there were some increases in latency found with this procedure (Fig. 6, bottom curves), it is clear that the latencies of the trained animals were not due simply to the fact that they had received foot shock.

Retention in this task increases with both time and number of trials. But do the increases in retention directly reflect memory consolidation processes? In an attempt to answer this question we gave mice a single electroshock treatment (8 milliamperes, 800 milliseconds) either 2 minutes or 1 hour after the first trial on the step-through apparatus. Different groups were given either one trial, two trials, or massed training trials during the first 2 minutes. All the animals were given a single retention test the next day. For purposes of comparison, other groups were given a single trial followed by an electroshock treatment 5 seconds or 24 hours later. As Figure 7 shows (solid curve), the

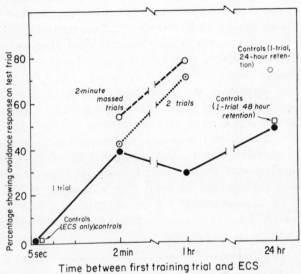

FIGURE 7. The effect of electroshock (8 milliamperes, 800 milliseconds) on retention of an inhibitory avoidance response. The lower curve shows that the effect of electroshock decreased as the time between a single training trial and the electroshock treatment was increased (this is also shown in Figure 1). The two upper curves show that the effect of electroshock given 1 hour after training was attenuated by increasing the number of training trials during the first 2 minutes of training. The retention trials were given 24 hours after training for all groups except for the 48-hour controls. As may be seen, the performance (50 percent) of this control group was poorer than that (63 percent) of the 24-hour-retention group shown in Figure 6. Thus for all groups given electroshock, with the exception of the 24-hour group, performance on the 24-hour retention test was lower than that of controls on the 24-hour retention test (see Figure 6). The controls were given electroshock only and received no foot shock. (*McGaugh and Alpern* (34).)

group given electroshock 5 seconds after the trial showed no retention, and the group shocked 24 hours after the trial showed no impairment of retention (relative to retention for a control group which received a single training trial followed by a single retention trial after 48 hours). The effect of the number of training trials varied with the time of administration of electroshock. When electroshock was administered 2 minutes after the first training trial, retention 24 hours later did not vary significantly with the number of training trials. The number of training trials did affect retention, however, when electroshock was given 1 hour after training. The retention of animals given two or more training trials was significantly better than that of animals given in single trial.

A comparison of the results of Figure 6 with those of Figure 7 shows that increases in retention found with increases in time do not depend solely upon consolidation processes as indexed by electroshock effects. For all intervals up to 1 hour that were investigated, the performance of animals *tested* at the end of the interval in question was superior to that of comparably trained animals given an electroshock at the end of that interval and a retention test the following day. This effect is seen most clearly in the one-trial groups. When tested at 1 hour after training (Fig. 6), 68 percent of the animals in the one-trial group remained on the platform. When animals were given electroshock 1 hour after training and a single retention trial the next day, only 28 percent remained on the platform. During the first few hours after training, memory seems to be based, at least in part, on processes other than those involved in long-term storage.

In another experiment we studied the effect on memory storage of a single additional training trial given 1 hour after previous single and multiple trials. As Figure 8 shows, when only one original training trial was given, a single additional trial given 1 hour later significantly increased avoidance in tests made the next day. Electroshock attenuated the effect of the additional trial. If the animals were given an electroshock immediately after the additional trial, their performance 24 hours later was similar to that of animals given neither an additional trial nor an electroshock. Each training trial, whether given early or later in training, initiates memory storage processes that are time-dependent.

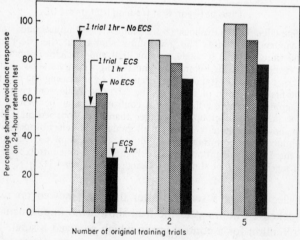

FIGURE 8. The effect of an additional training trial 1 hour after the original training trial or trials (given during the first 2 minutes of training) on 24-hour retention of an inhibitory avoidance response. In groups given a single original training trial, a single repetition significantly enhanced retention. A single electroshock administered after the additional trial attenuated the effect of the trial on subsequent retention. The effects of the additional training trial as well as the effects of electroshock decreased as the number of original training trials was increased. (*McGaugh and Alpern* (34).)

Conclusions

These observations indicate that the long-lasting trace of an experience is not completely fixed, consolidated, or coded at the time of the experience. Consolidation requires time, and under at least some circumstances the processes of consolidation appear to be susceptible to a variety of influences—both facilitating and impairing—for several hours after the experience. There must be, it seems, more than one kind of memory trace process (31). If permanent memory traces consolidate slowly over time, then other processes must provide a temporary basis for memory while consolidation is occurring. The evidence clearly indicates that trial-to-trial improvement, or learning, in animals cannot be based completely on permanent memory storage. Amnesia can be produced by electroshock and drugs even if the animals are given the treatment long after they have demonstrated "learning" of the task.

Of particular interest is the finding that retention of the inhibitory avoidance response increases with time. In a sense this should be expected, for it has long been known (and ignored) that, within limits, learning is facilitated by increasing the interval between repeated trials (7, 30). Our result may be the simplest case of such an effect. Since the improvement in retention with time seemed not to be due solely to consolidation (as indicated by electroshock effects), it would seem that the "distribution of practice" effect, as it is typically designated, may be due in part to a time-dependent *temporary* memory storage process. In our work with animals we have found no analog of human immediate memory such as that required for repeating digits (or finishing sentences). Animals tested immediately on the task described above after a trial typically showed no evidence of memory. It could be that the poor performance is due to excessive fright, but the "distribution of practice effect" is also typically observed in learning experiments in which food reward is used rather than shock avoidance. Since the retention tasks require the animals to change their behavior in some way, it could well be that the growth of retention over the first few minutes after a trial is due to time-dependent processes involved in the organization of processes necessary for changing behavior, in addition to those involved in temporary storage and retrieval. It is worth pointing out that there is evidence of an analogous process in human memory (32).

A complex picture of memory storage is emerging. There may be three memory trace systems: one for immediate memory (and not studied in our laboratory); one for short-term memory which develops within a few seconds or minutes and lasts for several hours; and one which consolidates slowly and is relatively permanent. The nature of the durability of the long-term memory trace (that is, the nature and basis of forgetting) is a separate but important issue. There is increasing evidence and speculation (20, 21, 33) that memory storage requires a "tri-trace" system, and our findings are at least consistent with such a view.

If there are, as seems possible, at least three kinds of traces involved in memory storage, how are they related? Is permanent memory produced by activity of temporary traces (*31*), or are the trace systems relatively independent? Although available findings do not provide an answer to this question, there does seem to be increasing evidence that the systems are independent. Acquisition can occur, as we have seen, without permanent consolidation, and both short-term and long-term memory increase with time. All this evidence suggests (but obviously does not prove) that *each* experience triggers activity in *each* memory system. Each repeated training trial may, according to this view, potentiate short-term processes underlying acquisition while simultaneously enhancing independent underlying long-term consolidation. Obviously, acceptance of these conclusions will require additional research.

If this view is substantially correct, it seems clear that any search for *the* engram or *the* basis of memory is not going to be successful. Recognition of the possibility that several independent processes may be involved at different stages of memory may help to organize the search. A careful examination of the time course of retention and memory trace consolidation, as well as examination of the bases of the effects of memory-impairing and memory-facilitating treatments, may help to guide the search. It is clear that a complete theory of memory storage must eventually provide an understanding of time-dependent processes in memory.

In 1930 Lashley wrote (*2*), "The facts of both psychology and neurology show a degree of plasticity, of organization, and of adaptation and behavior which is far beyond any present possibility of explanation." Although this conclusion is still valid, the current surge of interest in memory storage offers hope that this conclusion may soon need to be modified.

References and Notes

1. E. L. Bennett, M. C. Diamond, D. Krech, M. R. Rosenzweig, *Science* **146,** 610 (1964).
2. K. S. Lashley, in *The Neuropsychology of Lashley,* F. A. Beach, D. O. Hebb, C. T. Morgan, H. W. Nissen, Eds. (McGraw-Hill, New York, 1960).
3. E. C. Tolman, *Purposive Behavior in Animals and Men* (Century, New York, 1932).
4. W. R. Russell, *Brain, Memory, Learning* (Clarendon, Oxford, 1959).
5. W. Meyer-Gross, *Lancet* **1943-II,** 603 (1943).
6. C. P. Duncan, *J. Comp. Physiol. Psychol.* **42,** 32 (1949); R. W. Gerard, *Science* **122,** 225 (1955).
7. For reviews of these experiments, see S. E. Glickman, *Psychol. Bull.* **58,** 218 (1961); A. J. Deutsch, *Ann. Rev. Physiol.* **24,** 259 (1962); J. L. McGaugh and L. Petrinovich, *Psychol. Rev.* **7,** 382 (1966).
8. M. H. Friedman, *J. Abnormal Soc. Psychol.* **48,** 555 (1953); E. E. Coons and N. E. Miller, *J. Comp. Physiol. Psychol.* **53,** 524 (1960); D. J. Lewis and H. E. Adams, *Science* **141,** 516 (1963).
9. M. C. Madsen and J. L. McGaugh, *J. Comp. Physiol. Psychol.* **54,** 522 (1961).
10. W. J. Hudspeth, J. L. McGaugh, C. W. Thompson, *ibid.* **57,** 61 (1964); J. L. McGaugh and M. C. Madsen, *Science* **144,** 182 (1964).

11. D. J. Leonard and A. Zavala, *Science* **146,** 1073 (1964).
12. D. Quartermain, R. M. Paolino, N. E. Miller, *ibid.* **149,** 1116 (1965).
13. J. L. McGaugh and H. P. Alpern, *ibid.* **152,** 665 (1966).
14. S. L. Chorover, *J. Comp. Physiol. Psychol.* **59,** 73 (1965).
15. J. L. McGaugh and H. Alpern, unpublished findings.
16. C. S. Pearlman, S. K. Sharpless, M. E. Jarvik, *J. Comp. Physiol. Psychol.* **54,** 109 (1961); for a review of these findings see J. L. McGaugh and L. Petrinovich, *Intern. Rev. Neurobiol.* **8,** 139 (1965).
17. J. L. McGaugh, unpublished findings.
18. O. S. Ray and G. Emley, *Science* **144,** 76 (1964); C. Pearlman and M. E. Jarvik, *Federation Proc.* **20,** 340 (1961); J. Bureš and O. Burešová, *J. Comp. Physiol. Psychol.* **56,** 268 (1963).
19. D. J. Albert, *Neuropsychologia* **1,** 49 (1966).
20. J. B. Flexner, L. B. Flexner, E. Stellar, *Science* **141,** 57 (1963); S. H. Barondes and H. D. Cohen, *ibid.* **151,** 594 (1966).
21. B. W. Agranoff, R. E. Davis, J. J. Brink, *Proc. Nat. Acad. Sci. U.S.* **54,** 788 (1965); R. E. Davis and B. W. Agranoff, *ibid.* **55,** 555 (1966).
22. K. S. Lashley, *Psychobiology* **1,** 141 (1917).
23. J. L. McGaugh and L. Petrinovich, *Intern. Rev. Neurobiol.* **8,** 139 (1965); J. L. McGaugh, in *The Anatomy of Memory,* D. P. Kimble, Ed. (Science and Behavior Books, Palo Alto, 1965).
24. E. B. Hunt and J. Krivanek, *Psychopharmacologia* **9,** 1 (1966); J. Krivanek and E. B. Hunt, *ibid.,* in press.
25. W. H. Calhoun, *Psychol. Rep.,* in press; W. J. Hudspeth, *Science* **145,** 1331 (1964); S. Irwin and A. Benuazizi, *ibid.* **152,** 100 (1966).
26. R. Rensch and H. Rahmann, *Arch. Ges. Physiol.* **271,** 693 (1960); D. Bovet, G. Biganmi, F. Robustelli, *Compt. Rend.* **276,** 778 (1963); A. J. Glasky and L. N. Simon, *Science* **151,** 702 (1966); N. Plotnikoff, *ibid.* **151,** 703 (1966).
27. W. Paré, *J. Comp. Physiol. Psychol.* **54,** 506 (1961); L. O. Stratton and L. Petrinovich, *Psychopharmacologia* **5,** 47 (1963); B. A. Doty and L. A. Doty, *ibid.* **9,** 234 (1966).
28. D. Bovet, personal communication.
29. J. L. McGaugh, unpublished findings; A. Weissman, unpublished paper, 1965.
30. N. L. Munn, *Handbook of Psychobiological Research on the Rat* (Houghton Mifflin, Boston, 1950).
31. D. O. Hebb, *The Organization of Behavior* (Wiley, New York, 1949).
32. J. Crawford and E. B. Hunt, in press.
33. E. A. Feigenbaum, Monograph P-1817, Rand Corp., Santa Monica, Calif. (1959); J. A. Deutsch and M. D. Hamburg, *Science* **151,** 221 (1966).
34. J. L. McGaugh and H. Alpern, unpublished recent data.
35. J. L. McGaugh and C. W. Thomson, *Psychopharmacologia* **3,** 166 (1962).
36. R. A. Breen and J. L. McGaugh, *J. Comp. Physiol. Psychol.* **54,** 498 (1961).
37. J. L. McGaugh, unpublished recent data.
38. W. H. Westbrook and J. L. McGaugh, *Psychopharmacologia* **5,** 440 (1964).
39. The research from my laboratory reported here was supported by research grants MY 3541, MH 07015, MH 10261, and MH 12526 from the National Institutes of Health, U.S. Public Health Service, Bethesda, Md. I thank W. Sparks for his assistance in conducting some of the experiments and Professors David Krech and Norman Weinberger for their comments on a preliminary draft of this article.

Study Question for Part III

On the basis of what you have read in this section, it does not appear that a single biochemical substrate or process can account for information storage and retrieval. Given the various kinds of evidence presented in the readings, try to develop a model of memory storage that would take into account each of the findings presented in this chapter. In outline, or diagrammatic form, present the steps necessary to encode the "engram" and describe how you think the trace can be activated when needed.

33-202